Mind, Brain, and Function

MIND, BRAIN, AND FUNCTION

Essays in the Philosophy of Mind

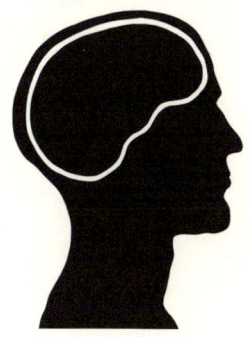

Edited by
J. I. Biro and Robert W. Shahan

University of Oklahoma Press : Norman

Library of Congress Cataloging in Publication Data
Main entry under title:

Mind, brain, and function.

   Papers reprinted from the Spring, 1981, issue of Philosophical topics.
   Includes bibliographical references and index.
   1. Psychology—Philosophy—Addresses, essays, lectures. 2. Functionalism (Psychology)—Addresses, essays, lectures. I. Biro, J. I. (John Ivan), 1940– . II. Shahan, Robert W., 1935– . III. Philosophical topics.
BF38.M56   153'.01   81-40296
                                                                  AACR2

Copyright © 1982 by the University of Oklahoma Press, Norman, Publishing Division of the University. Manufactured in the U.S.A. First edition.

Contents

Preface ... 7

1. *Psychological Laws*
   William G. Lycan ... 9
2. *Dennett on Intentional Systems*
   Stephen P. Stich ... 39
3. *Making Sense of Ourselves*
   Daniel C. Dennett ... 63
4. *What Can Be Learned from* Brainstorms?
   Robert Cummins ... 83
5. *Some Varieties of Functionalism*
   Sydney Shoemaker ... 93
6. *Functionalism, Qualia, and Intentionality*
   Paul M. Churchland and Patricia Smith Churchland ... 121
7. *Functionalism, Psychology, and the Philosophy of Mind*
   K. V. Wilkes ... 147
8. *A Note on Functionalism and Function*
   Colin McGinn ... 169
9. *Internal Representation: Prologue to a Theory of Intentionality*
   Robert C. Richardson ... 171
10. *Analog and Analog*
    John Haugeland ... 213

Notes on Contributors ... 227

Index ... 229

Preface

The papers in this volume are reprinted from the Spring 1981 issue of *Philosophical Topics*, successor to *The Southwestern Journal of Philosophy*. The editors decided to devote the inaugural issue of the new journal to the topic of functionalism and the philosophy of mind in the belief that some of the most interesting and challenging work in philosophy today is being done in that area. It is the same belief that prompts our desire to make these papers more widely available in book form.

While many of the problems discussed by the contributors are recognizably the same as, or are at least very closely related to, those that have occupied philosophers of mind in the past, their treatment here is in important respects new and different. A number of recent developments in both philosophy and the cognitive sciences have led to a reformulation of old problems and in some cases to the resurrection of problems thought long dead and buried. In psychology, theories about mental states and processes have once again become respectable. Cognitive psychologists once again take seriously the idea of explaining various abilities people have (perceiving, problem-solving, speaking and understanding speech, etc.) by postulating internal processes occurring in them, processes specified in terms of their role in subserving such abilities and in causing the behavior that manifests them.

These psychological processes are to be distinguished from the neuro-physiological processes occurring in people whenever they exercise these abilities. However, we are learning fast about the latter, too; and their relation to the processes psychologists posit and study is an increasingly pressing question, with implications for the autonomy of psychology as a science.

The astonishing march of computer science and artificial-intelligence research has helped to develop a powerful model for psychology. Speaking very roughly, this model involves seeing psychological processes as computations (mostly unconscious, of course) by a subject over various internal representations he has as a result of interacting with the world in which he lives. These computations lead to the generation of other representations, which in turn cause him to behave in the ways he does in his dealings with the world. The formal, or functional, properties of these computations, in virtue of which they have the causal roles they do, are one of the things that a science of the mental, and thus a psychology that aspires to be that, must, on this view, study.

At the same time, and partly in response to these developments in the cognitive sciences, some recent orthodoxies of the philosophy of mind have come to be largely abandoned. The strictures of some so-called ordinary-language philosophers against "meaningless" mentalistic talk in describing and explaining behavior (strictures that earlier culminated in such doctrines as logical behaviorism) no longer intimidate most philosophers of mind into eschewing talk of internal representations and of internal processes involving them. (These internal representations may seem more than a little like the *ideas* of an earlier era and thus, not surprisingly, give rise to many of the same problems: Are they necessarily linguistic in character? How are they related to world? To what extent do they act as a veil between the mind and the world? On which side of the veil should our explanations of a subject's behavior focus? etc.)

Philosophers of mind espousing this new outlook take seriously the experiments pursued by cognitive scientists; indeed, they take seriously the possibility that empirical theories based on such experiments exhaust whatever might be legitimately regarded as the philosophy of mind. Their interest lies in clarifying and facing the conceptual issues arising in the course of developing such empirical theories. In this way, at least part and perhaps all of what was traditionally thought of as the philosophy of mind is supplanted by the philosophy of psychology, in something like the way some think of the philosophy of science as replacing at least parts of traditional metaphysics.

At the same time, practicing cognitive psychologists are becoming more aware of the conceptual questions raised by their inquiries, so that they find it increasingly difficult to maintain their usual practice of keeping philosophical questions at arm's length. These include such time-honored questions as the relation of the mental and the physical, discussions of which have been in the past often dismissed by scientists as philosophers' nonsense. Now no responsible cognitive scientist can pretend that his own theorizing does not lead inexorably to such questions.

We thus hope that the essays included here will be of interest to all those concerned with the challenge of understanding the mind, from whatever direction they approach it.

Psychological Laws[†]

WILLIAM G. LYCAN
The Ohio State University

What is a psychological law? Narrowly and familiarly understood, I suppose, a "psychological law" would be a lawlike universal statement which correlates some psychological state or event in an organism with things that can happen to the organism, with behavior on the organism's part, or with other psychological states or events. But on a broader and probably more useful understanding of the term, a "psychological law" may be taken to be a law *of psychology* considered as a technical discipline, as a self-conscious science. Thus, such a law may be expected to incorporate unfamiliar jargon of any of a number of kinds, either in alluding to theoretical entities newly introduced or in its description of the otherwise ordinary mental and physical phenomena which are its topic.

What would a psychological law look like, in this sense of "psychological law"? Obviously that would depend on one's psychological theory or theories—particularly on their vocabularies and on their projected, potential or fancied axiomatizations. Somewhat less obviously, it would depend on one's philosophical theory of mind, so far as this can be distinguished from one's psychological theory. Brentano's or Meinong's purported psychological laws would be written in a language quite different (both lexically and syntactically) from Hobbes'—or from W. V. Quine's.

[†] Earlier versions of this paper have been presented under various titles at the Fourteenth Annual University of Cincinnati Philosophy Colloquium, the University of Auckland, Victoria University of Wellington, the University of Adelaide, the University of Melbourne, and the Twentieth Annual Oberlin Colloquium in Philosophy (with acute comments by David Sanford). I am indebted to many, many people for helpful criticism, but in particular I must mention David Armstrong, William Bechtel, John Biro, Ned Block, Dan Dennett, Michael Devitt, Ray Elugardo, Gilbert Harman, Ausonio Marras, Robert Richardson, David Sanford, Elliot Sober, Stephen Stich, Rick Suiter, Jan Szrednicki, and David Williams.

I

For some years the going philosophical theory of mind was the Identity Theory as defended by U. T. Place and J. J. C. Smart. As Smart developed it, the Identity Theory identified psychological or mental state- and event-*types* with neurophysiological state- and event-types, a main motivation for this identification being to explain supposed type-type correlations between the mental and the neurophysiological.[1] It was said that such correlations had already been noted in laboratory experiments on humans, and it seemed reasonable to expect that further testing would establish beyond scientific doubt that the correlations were lawlike and not merely accidental. Since the Identity Theory, if true, is itself lawlike (on the assumption that any true metaphysical theory is lawlike) and since it entails or predicts the existence of our lawlike type-type correlations, it explains them, and moreover explains them in the neatest possible manner. (What better way to explain a lawlike correlation between A's and B's than by supposing, in the absence of significant evidence to the contrary, that in fact A's *are* just B's?[2]) Thus, some of the Identity Theorist's psychological laws would correlate events described in mental terms with events described neurophysiologically; others presumably would detail neurphysiological interchanges that involved those physical states and events which are also mental. Psycho–physical laws, codifying lawlike correlations between mental events and neurophysiological events, are therefore bound up with the Type–Type Identity Theory in two ways: their existence is entailed by the Theory, and their existence, allegedly established on independent empirical grounds, is strong evidence for the Theory.

In a series of papers,[3] Donald Davidson has attacked the Type–Type Identity Theory at just this point, on the basis of what he calls "the Principle of the Anomalism of the Mental" (*PAM*):

> . . . there are no strict deterministic laws on the basis of which mental events can be predicted and explained. ["ME," p. 81]

I quote some related passages:

> (A) . . . the mental is nomologically irreducible; there may be *true* general statements relating the mental and the physical, statements that have the logical form of a law; but they are not *lawlike* (in a strong sense yet to be described). ["ME," p. 90]
>
> (B) The generalizations that embody such practical wisdom [concerning actual *de facto* mental–physical correlations] are

assumed to be only roughly true, or they are explicitly stated in probabilistic terms, or they are insulated from counterexample by generous escape clauses. ["ME," p. 93]

(C) Mental events *as a class* cannot be explained by physical science. ["ME," p. 100; italics mine]

(D) . . . what emerge are not the strict quantitative laws embedded in sophisticated theory that we confidently expect in physics, but irreducibly statistical correlations that resist, and resist in principle, improvement without limit . . . . This does not mean there are any events that are in themselves undetermined or unpredictable; it is only events *as described in [mental] vocabulary* . . . that resist incorporation into a closed deterministic system. These same events, described in appropriate physical terms, may be as amenable to prediction and explanation as any. ["PP," pp. 42–43]

Davidson's skepticism concerning psychological laws spreads, naturally enough, to psychological explanation, and by that route to psychology itself considered as a scientific discipline. In some (none too exact) sense, Davidson holds that because psychology cannot yield genuine laws and does not treat of genuine natural kinds, psychological "explanation" is not genuine explanation in the sense of revealing underlying realities in nature, but is rather a kind of interpretive—and in part evaluative—scheme that *we* impose on certain beings for our own purposes of dealing with those things. Hence his title, "Psychology *as* Philosophy."

In this paper I shall set out Davidson's view, pinpoint what I think is his key skeptical argument, and then sketch a format for psychological theory that I believe both resists his skepticism and promises considerable illumination for an ontology of the mental. After applying this format very briefly to the notion of *believing*, in particular, I shall try to exhibit the way in which belief states are real entities to be found in nature, while accounting backhandedly for the lure of skeptical Davidsonian intuitions.[4]

A few more introductory words about the passages I have quoted above: First, notice that the claim Davidson makes in passage (A), which is what he attempts to defend in section II of "ME," is not precisely the same as the *PAM*. The claim that there are no psycho–physical laws does not entail that mental events (*qua* mental) cannot be explained or predicted at all, since such events might be explained or predicted (*qua* mental) on the basis of *purely* psychological laws (laws involving only mental predicates) which

11

might themselves be strict and deterministic. Davidson says ("ME," p. 81) that the denial of the existence of psycho–physical laws, together with some "reasonable assumptions," yields the *PAM*, but he does not say what "reasonable assumptions" he has in mind. Possibly he believes that (due to his "Principle of Causal Interaction") some of the things we will have to explain about mental events are their causal interactions with physical events; a set of purely psychological laws could not accomplish this. In any case, Davidson thinks there cannot be any purely psychological laws either; hence the *PAM*.

Passage (B) gives us some idea of what he requires of a genuinely lawlike statement. A law must be precise, must admit no exceptions, must have no escape clauses or *ceteris paribus* provisos, must not be probabilistic, and (he adds in "MM," p. 713) must be *supported* by its instances.[5] Passages (C) and (D) remind us that, since for Davidson laws and explanations are linguistic items, viz., sentences, an event is *explained* only under some description, and what explains it under one description may not explain it under another. When Davidson speaks of "mental events as a class," he means mental events *qua* mental, i.e., under a mental description.[6]

II

Davidson goes on to defend the Token–Token Identity thesis, that is, the claim that every mental event–*token* is identical with some physical event–token. This claim is entailed by the Type–Type Identity Theory but does not entail it; and Davidson denies the Type–Type Theory on the basis of the *PAM*. Thus, Davidson's theory of mind, which he calls "anomalous monism" (*AM*), asserts token–token identity between mental events and physical events but at the same time denies type–type identity between mental events and physical or any other sort of events; this is what is distinctive about the view.

There are several grounds for initial dissatisfaction with *AM*. First, as a metaphysical theory, *AM* is exasperatingly coy. It amounts to monism *simpliciter*; it denies that a person has two different sorts of event–properties one of which is spiritual or immaterial, but refuses to say anything more about the nature of mental entities except perhaps that there is no more to say. If *AM* is true, then whatever we do eventually find out about the physiological basis of human desire, say (if there *is* anything even statistically approaching a single sort of physiological basis), will plainly not be generalizable to desire in other species. It has been argued by many that this in itself is all to the good; but *AM* also implies that there are *no* laws, even purely psychological ones, on the basis of which we might extrapolate facts about our own and our experimental subjects' desires to the desires of others. *AM* thus frustrates psychology by blocking significant generalization at every turn. It will also forestall some obvious shortcuts in research programs.

Davidson has two possible replies to this. First, he may say that if *AM* is metaphysically laconic, at least that makes it more likely to be true. To be precise, what is cautious is the specifically metaphysical part of *AM* (the Token–Token Identity thesis), and that, Davidson might point out, is a virtue, not a flaw. The *PAM*, of course, is not cautious at all, since normally we are inclined to suppose that there *are* lawlike psycho–physical correlations (even Descartes granted this, at least to a limited extent). As for my whining about lack of generalizability and the frustration of research programs, Davidson may respond, that is just too bad. If there are no correlations, there are no correlations, and if the *PAM* has been sufficiently well defended on independent grounds, then we should just conclude that psychology is a much more elusive and less rigorous discipline than in our youthful optimism we had hoped it was.

I do not think we can let it go at that. A second objection to *AM* will bring out the reason why. As I have observed elsewhere,[7] philosophers who have offered noneliminative theories of mind have generally been taken to be offering theories of the *nature* of mental entities, or programs for such theories. We expect such philosophers to tell us, to the best of their technical abilities, what it is to have a belief, what it is to have a desire, what it is to be afraid, and so on—we expect the philosophers, in short, to show us the metaphysical/scientific essences of the various mental events, states, and processes. My objection to *AM* is that it cannot do this.

Of course, Davidson's claim seems to be precisely that there *is no* scientific essence of belief, of desire, or of fear, assuming that it takes genuine laws to make a scientific essence. Belief and the rest simply do not have (single) scientific natures. So Davidson need not be impressed with my second objection either. On this desolate understanding of *AM*, what Davidson seems to be saying amounts to the thesis that there is no single such state as belief (desire, fear, etc.)—that what we happen to group together under a well-worn common term, do not in fact have anything nonaccidentally in common and do not form a natural class of kind.[8]

Nice as scientific natures and essences are, we must remind ourselves (following Wittgenstein) that ordinary physical objects sometimes do not have them either. Tables and chairs do not figure in strict deterministic laws *qua* furniture; and, since very likely tables are related to each other only by family resemblance, there is probably no metaphysical or scientific essence of tablehood. Now why, Davidson might reasonably ask, should we blanch at the thought that "desire" and "thought" and "belief" might be family–resemblance notions as well?[9] It is possible that our use of the word 'desire' or 'want,' for example, is governed only by loosely overlapping criteria involving distal stimuli, verbal utterances, apparently goal–directed behavior, phenomenal urges of certain sorts, related emotional reactions, and perhaps even more scientific considerations such as physio–chemical reations to drugs and the like. We have been troubled by the thought that desire as a type might disappear entirely if *AM* is true, but *AM* evidently need not be taken to have such a serious consequence; for ordinary family–resemblance concepts, it seems, are "anomalous" in Davidson's sense as well, and they do not "disappear entirely" as types. Mental categories are no worse off than many of the gross physical–object types that even philosophers take for granted.

I believe that this final response sounds as plausible as it does only because of a common confusion concerning the notion of a mental state–type. The important thing to notice is that the type "desire" is a *genus*, an umbrella category which serves only to subsume all the many and richly varied *specific* types of desire that there are. (This point is often overlooked in discussions of mind–body gerrymandering.) We may agree that it is presumptuous to suppose that "desire" and "belief" are crisp natural kinds; in fact, it seems overwhelmingly probable that these generic categories *are* merely loose family–resemblance collections (though I would insist that only a well–developed future psychology could establish that claim decisively). But it is far less plausible to contend that specific types, such as "having an urgent desire (of such-and-such a phenomenological description) for a cool, frosty beer" or "believing strongly that it is snowing outside University Hall this afternoon," are loosely family–resemblance notions rather than natural kinds.

Remember, too, that psychological laws concerning desires and beliefs will probably not be statable entirely in laymen's language. We may expect that no common–sense psychological generalization stated in ordinary English will be strict and lawlike. Genuine psychological laws, as I said in beginning this paper, would incorporate futuristic technical jargon as well as mention of familiar mental items. So our inability to think of any plausible *examples* of psychological laws off the tops of our heads (or off the tops of current psychological theories) is no evidence against the existence of such laws.

Finally, we have at least one powerful motive for hoping that the mental is not anomalous, which distinguishes its case from that of tables and chairs: while no one has ever formulated a scientific theory of furniture *qua* furniture (so far as I know), psychologists have thought and worked under the assumption that a genuinely scientific psychology is possible, occasionally with encouraging results. More to the point, we have considerable use for as scientific a psychology as we can get our hands on, since as intelligent human beings we set great store by the understanding and prediction of behavior. This dims the appeal of *AM* somewhat even in *AM*'s family–resemblance version, and encourages us to keep looking for something better, bearing in mind that some of our mental concepts may have to be cleaned up and regimented in bracing but harmless ways.[10]

III

Perhaps, it might be thought, Davidson does not really mean to insist that desire has no scientific nature or essence. In "ME" he concentrates on defending claim (A), and obtains the *PAM* primarily by inferring it from (A); so possibly the main point is just that desire has no *physical* (and in particular no neurophysiological) nature or essence. This less startling claim, though still incompatible with the Type–Type Identity Theory, is nowadays almost universally granted; Putnam and others years ago exposed the chauvinistic presumptuousness of extrapolating observed human psycho–physiological correlations outside the human species.[11] And even within the class of humans, Smart's vaunted type–type correlations have not materialized on any large scale.[12] Rather, it is generally thought that to be a mental entity of some particular kind (say, to be a belief or a thought or an intention or a desire) is to play a certain functional role in mediating between the stimuli which impinge on one's owner and the owner's resulting behavior; mental state– and event–types are correlated or identified with roles of this sort, rather than with whatever various physiological states or events happen to play these roles in various humans and nonhumans from occasion to occasion. Thus, according to such a view, mental entities have no physical essences, but they do have *functional* essences. And distinctive sorts of psychological laws would fall out of such a view—not psycho-physical laws, but psycho-functional laws.

For the sake of discussion, let us consider what I have argued elsewhere[13] is the most promising current theory of this kind: *homuncular* functionalism. The homuncular functionalist[14] sees a human being or other sentient creature as an integrated collection of component subsystems or agencies which communicate with each other and cooperate to produce their host creature's overall behavioral responses to stimuli. A psychologist who adopts the homuncular format and applies it to humans will describe a person by means of a flow-chart that portrays the person's immediately subpersonal agencies and their various routes of communicative access to each other.[15] Each of these agencies, represented by a "black box" on the original flow-chart, will in turn be described by a flow-chart which breaks *it* down into further, more specialized sub-subsystems which corporately produce *its* behavior, and so on; and each of the subsystems, sub-subsystems and sub- . . . subsystems will be characterized in terms of its job or function within the corporate hierarchy: thus, the psychologist will posit an executive unit, a speech center, a buffer memory, a perceptual analyzer, a goal-setter and the like at the immediately subpersonal level, and will employ presumably more specialized jargon characterizing those agencies' own components in turn, talking of triggers, receptors, filters, damping mechanisms, inhibitors, pathways, stores, etc. (Eventually, if the psychologist intrepidly continues his exploratory descent through the subject's institutional architecture, he will find himself using neuroanatomical terms, which at their own level are job-descriptive too.[16]) In the end, the psychologist will be able to explain the subject's behavioral capacities by reference to the joint capacities of the subsystems that mediate them, and if a deeper account is desired, he will explain the capacities of the subsystems in terms of the joint capacities of their own respective components, and so on down; though at some point the psychologist would have to turn biologist, then chemist, and finally physicist in order to bring this explanatory process to completion.

I believe the homuncular model has great advantages to offer both psychology and metaphysics, but this is not the place to detail them; here I merely want to use the model to rehabilitate the notion of a psychological law in response to skeptical Davidsonian arguments concerning the propositional attitudes. I shall begin by proposing, as I have proposed before, to identify the attitudes (and all other mental states) with occurrences of institutionally characterized states in their owners' various subpersonal and sub– . . . subpersonal agencies at various levels of corporate abstraction. I mean this proposal as a reductive type–identification of mental states with functionally characterized states. Thus, a typical homunctionalist explication would take the form, "To be in mental state S is for one's ϕ–er to be in functional state S(ϕ)."

As is well known, functional or job–descriptive types are irreducible to more concrete types such as physical types; a valve–lifter or an adding machine or even a typewriter can be made of any of a number of different kinds of material. Notice that this irreducibility affords homunctionalism an important advantage as a philosophical theory of mind. As Davidson says, our mental concepts as a family do seem to comprise a "seamless whole," quite disjoint from the family of physiological concepts and from that of physical concepts; and despite the naturalistic temper of the past two decades, the actual *prospects* for reducing the mental directly to the physical have never really seemed very bright. This is what we would expect if homunctionalism is correct. The apparent seamlessness of the mental realm is the genuine irreducibility of homuncular types to any more concrete types, I maintain, and the difficulty of *detailing* a reduction of the mental even to the homuncular is due to our ignorance of the organizational plan of the human corporation itself at a sufficiently low level of abstraction. Thus, homunctionalism has the virtue of helping to explain (in part) why there is a mind-body problem in the first place.

What kinds of psychological laws fall out of a homunctionalist theory of the mental? Presumably those laws (perhaps involving determinate and precise transition probabilities) which can be read off a flow–chart of the homuncular type, along with (of course) the metaphysical laws which would follow from the identification of mental states with homuncular states itself. And so the homunctionalist may consistently agree with Davidson that mental entities have no physiological or other physical essences and that there are no (true) psycho–physical laws, but maintain that mental entities have functional essences and that there are true psychological laws, namely, psycho–functional ones of our homuncular sort. But before going on to assess this suggestion and seeing whether it successfully blocks Davidson's skepticism, let us apply our homunctionalist schema very briefly to a particular propositional attitude, belief, in order to infuse our picture of the mental with at least a little more detail.

Naturally, the information–storage paradigm insinuates itself, and it is the paradigm I would like to defend, despite the bad press it has recently received from several prominent philosophers of psychology.[17] At any rate, it is a good position from which to start, in order to see what can be accommodated within it and what modifications or departures might later be forced by encounters with less tractable phenomena. Even at the outset we would have to draw careful distinctions between many kinds, modes and levels of information and many kinds, modes and levels of storage. (We would arrive at these distinctions by drawing on our ordinary commonsensical concepts and refinements of them, by careful attention to people's introspective reports under usual and unusual circumstances, and by following the implications of technical findings in cognitive psychology and neuropsychology.) For example, beliefs of some kinds must be distinguished from memory traces, and the relation between belief and memory charted in detail (the same goes for beliefs and perceptual states).

A different kind of complexity will have to be introduced into an information–storage model if we are to account for the relative degrees of *firmness* of belief (from "tentative" to "rock–bottom"). Each of our posited information–bearing entities[18] will have to be assigned some quantitative measure of strength. Obviously, a simple numerical tag will not suffice, so long as it is unconnected to any of the believer's conative apparatus, because the strength of a belief surely is a relational property: a matter of the belief's use in inference, the way in which it is produced and sustained by its source of evidence, and its *de facto* authority in determining action. Some combinations of factors of this kind must be marshaled by an account of belief–strength.

What *kind* of homunctional state might a belief–state be? I take it to be obvious that beliefs have structures of some kind, both on intuitive and on theoretical grounds. Intuitively, because the belief that Donald is intelligent and the belief that Donald is a vegetarian share an element of some kind (either Donald himself or some mental representation of him), as do the belief that Donald is intelligent and the belief that Dan is intelligent; theoretically, because (seemingly) we must suppose Dan's belief that the liquid in front of him is beer and his desire to drink beer share a component if we are to explain their joint function in causing Dan to reach for the liquid in front of him. This leaves us with the question of what kind of structure to attribute to beliefs in our homunctional model.

I distinguish between *occurrent* beliefs, or judgments, and *implicit* beliefs, which are roughly dispositions to make judgments. For reasons which I have set out in other works,[19] I predict that our theory will want to characterize occurrent beliefs in semantical terms, construing them as being playbacks of internal representations patterned either after the sentences of the believer's native (natural) language or after the well-formed formulas of some logical theory. More accurately: To judge or believe occurrently that p is to harbor some internal representation which has semantical properties analogous to those of the sentence that replaces 'p'.[20] What makes such a state of affairs constitute a belief *that p* is the representation's distinctive semantical properties; what makes it a *belief* that p is the nature of the harboring, storage or playback—the representation's contribution to the believer's inner bureaucratic order of business. Of course, insofar as a "representation" of the sort I am invoking approximates a little sentence in the head, my paradigm drags with it the apparatus of a "language of thought," since any sentence is a sentence only relative to some language. However, I mean to rest no great philosophical weight on that apparatus. In particular, I would not suppose that there is any *single, unified* language in which all cognitive activity is carried out: just the opposite is suggested by the homuncular model, since distinct homuncular agencies which perform very different tasks will probably differ accordingly in their respective office jargons.

The little–sentence–in–the–head paradigm obviously needs a great deal of very careful spelling out, particularly in response to powerful objections that have been raised against it.[21] I am fairly confident that the objections can be met, but I cannot here defend the paradigm; I am only using it as an example of the form a homuncular theory of believing might take. Let us now return to the anomalism issue.

IV

The homunctionalist agrees with Davidson that mental entities have no physiological or other physical essences and that there are no (true) psycho–physical laws; but it is consistent with this to maintain that mental entities (our *specific* state– and event–types) have functional essences and that there are true psychological laws, namely, psycho–functional ones. Is this, as was suggested above, compatible with Davidson's preferred view of the psychological? And do beliefs or desires, after all, have something in common that makes them beliefs or desires, consistently with Davidson's strictures?

It seems that Davidson would not want to give in so easily, contrary to what I mendaciously proposed at the beginning of the foregoing section. If, in the very abstract sort of psychology we are considering, beliefs and other mental entities are to be defined in terms of their functional roles and/or their relations to each other, then these roles and relations must be presumed lawlike. This is tantamount to supposing that there are purely psychological laws, or psycho–functional laws, or both. On the basis of such laws, the occurrences of mental events could be predicted and explained; but this is exactly what the *PAM* rules out. Therefore, if the *PAM* is correct and if *the belief that p* has a distinctive essence, this essence cannot be a functional role any more than it can be a physical character.

This leaves Davidson with three options: (a) to capitulate, and concede that claim (A) is all he really meant, repudiating his inference from (A) to the full–fledged *PAM*; (b) to concede that psychological states and events have scientific essences even though those essences are neither physiological nor functional; or (c) to continue to insist on the *PAM* in its uncompromising form and to deny that psychological states and events form any natural kinds whatever. Option (a) is unattractive, since it renders Davidson's view almost entirely uncontroversial, thus robbing it of interest. It also would not serve Davidson's purpose of spearheading a positive argument in favor of the Token–Token Identity thesis. Option (b) would commit Davidson to seeking some new, so far unenvisioned sort of metaphysical nature for mental entities, presumably one which somehow failed to yield psychological laws concerning these entities; and his text betrays no inclination at all toward taking such a line. Therefore, if we are to understand Davidson as holding an interesting view that is anything like his text taken fairly literally, we must understand him as choosing option (C). And, as we have seen, (C) entails repudiating homunctionalism and almost any other current theory of the mental;[22] so Davidson's arguments for the *PAM* are carrying a heavy load, and demand close scrutiny.

His reasons for holding the *PAM* are obscure; they are the most elusive element in "ME," though they are clarified a bit in "PP" and in "MM." Davidson seems to be resting his case on a number of different general theses about language and translation, about grammatical properties of propositional–attitude expressions, about scientific theories *tout court*, about psychological methodology, and about the Belief–Desire–Perception Cycle. But he takes no pains to distinguish these theses, and in spots seems to assume that they are all equivalent or at least come to much the same thing. I shall catalogue them, and then focus on the few that seem to bear the most weight.

1. The Belief–Desire–Perception Cycle[23] and related points. This is the first consideration Davidson appeals to in "ME" (p. 91), though he says only that turning our attention to the Cycle will "sharpen our appreciation of" the alleged anomalism of the mental. He picks up this theme again in "PP" (pp. 43ff) and in "MM" (p. 721). He concludes,

> Beliefs and desires issue in behavior only as modified by further beliefs and desires, attitudes and attendings, without limit. Clearly this holism of the mental realm is a clue both to the autonomy and to the anomalous character of the mental. ["ME," p. 92]

2. The assumption of *rationality* in psychological explanation. Davidson gives at least four different arguments in support of this ("ME," pp. 96–98; "PP," pp. 45–51).

3. A rather subtle point about lawlikeness and confirmation, and the distinction between "homonomic" and "heteronomic" generalizations. Heteronomic generalizations are portrayed as a kind of hybrid, standing between genuinely lawlike generalizations on the one hand and totally unlawlike ones, such as "All emeralds are grue," on the other ("ME"," pp. 92–94; see also "MM," p. 713).

4. The claim that the required precision and correctibility are obtainable only within a "comprehensive closed system" ("ME," p. 94).

5. The need for synthetic *a priori* "constitutive elements" in a theory able to give rise to genuine laws. Davidson advances an analogy ("ME," p. 96) having to do with the measurement of length, which he intends as an illustration of his general point (a similar analogy is put forward on p. 49 of "PP"), and then argues on p. 98 that rationality (cf. 2 above) is a constitutive element in psychological explanation and prediction (see also "PP," pp. 47ff). Thus, this kind of consideration is intended to explain item 2, and probably item 1 as well. It seems to me that it may also explain 3.

6. The indeterminacy of translation, and its use against the possibility of alternative conceptual schemes. Davidson appeals to considerations concerning translation on p. 97 of "ME," on pp. 51–52 of "PP," and on p. 714 of "MM."[24] Indeterminacy is tied to the "holism" of the mental on p. 721 of "MM"; it also seems to be part of the explanation of item 2.

7. The intentionality of the mental and the intensionality of mental expressions. Davidson follows Quine in taking this consideration to be "of a piece with" 6. And, though Davidson does not mention the fact, Quine thinks that intentionality and

intensionality by themselves make the mental anomalous even if they are not simply the same thing as the indeterminacy of translation.

Davidson does not clearly distinguish 1 from 2, evidently thinking that 2 is just the same as 1 or trivially explains it. This is not quite right. Although it may be true that 2 explains 1 in some sense, the point about the Belief–Desire–Perception Cycle can be made without any reference to rationality; Davidson introduced it simply in terms of the failure of Analytical Behaviorism. Nor, so far as I can see, does item 1 *require* 2; superficially, at least, it seems that the Cycle would obtain whether or not psychologists were methodologically constrained in favor of ascribing rationality to their subjects. But I do not think the distinction between 1 and 2 is really crucial to a successful evaluation of Davidson's defense of the *PAM*. 1 is widely considered congenial, and Davidson defends 2 at some length; we can take him as offering both together in support of the *PAM*.

Four separate arguments are used to establish 2, though (again) Davidson himself does not clearly distinguish them ("ME," pp. 96–97; "ME," p. 97, and especially "PP," pp. 50–51; "ME," pp. 95–96, 98; and "PP," pp. 45–51). I shall not go through these arguments, since I think at least two of them are convincing and give us excellent reason to accept 2; so let us grant Davidson 2 and go on to ask whether 1 and 2 do militate strongly in favor of the *PAM*. Davidson writes:

> Any effort at increasing the accuracy and power of a theory of behaviour forces us to bring more and more of the whole system of the agent's beliefs and motives directly into account. But in inferring this system from the evidence, we necessarily impose conditions of coherence, rationality, and consistency. These conditions have no echo in physical theory, which is why we can look for no more than rough correlations between psychological and physical phenomena. ["PP," p. 43; see also "ME," p. 98]

This passage contains the most direct and explicit argument Davidson gives for the *PAM*, or rather, for the weaker claim (A) which suggests the *PAM* to him. Three obvious questions arise: (i) What exactly does Davidson mean by saying that the Cycle and the rationality assumption "have no echo in" physical theory? (ii) Why does it follow that there cannot be strict, lawlike psycho–physical generalizations? (iii) Even if the latter does follow, does the argument also prove that there cannot be laws of psychology at all? Let us take up (i) first.

One thing that Davidson does *not* mean is that the *seamlessness* of psychological theory is not a feature of physical theory. Just as psychology has its rationality assumption (accompanied by the Cycle) as a "constitutive element" or ideal, physical theory (as Davidson's measurement examples are designed to indicate) has constitutive ideals of its own, and the holism that comes with them. Where psychology assumes rationality, physics assumes the transitivity of length and other magnitudes. What Davidson seems to mean is rather that *rationality* in particular is not a constitutive ideal in physics and in fact does not figure in physical explanations of human movements at all. When we explain an action in everyday terms of beliefs, perceptions, motives, desires and reasons, we (must) assume rationality and a general stock of shared background beliefs. When we explain that same action physically, we make reference only to chemical, electrical, and mechanical goings–on. (Notice that the two explanations, both sentences, will refer to the action in question under respectively different descriptions, one in terms of something a *person did* and the other in terms of a more or less specific *motion* that *occurred* in an *object*. Davidson holds that if we are speaking properly, the former description will be a term of psychological theory, while the latter will be part of the vernacular of physics or biophysics.)

If this were all Davidson meant in saying that his first two considerations "have no echo in" physical theory, no one will quarrel with him. But now we must ask why this relatively unexciting fact should matter. In particular, why does it entail or suggest that there cannot be strict psycho–physical laws? Davidson maintains that the trouble with psycho–physical generalizations of this sort is that they involve some sort of linguistic incongruity, brought on by mixing *terms* that are not "made for each other." Elsewhere he hints that the point is instead epistemological ("There cannot be tight connections between the realms if each is to retain allegiance to its proper source of evidence" ("ME," p. 98)).[25] But more to the point (turning now to my third question above), Davidson's considerations certainly do not show that a psycho–*functional* vocabulary would not be "tightly closed," since according to homunctionalism, black boxes of a sufficiently high level of institutional abstraction are described in virtually psychological terms as things are now; so Davidson's argument fails against homunctionalism even if it succeeds against the Type–Type Identity Theory, and so fails to prove the *PAM* even if it proves (A).

Possibly Davidson's point is rather the epistemological one: given a neural process which in fact caused a certain bodily motion, we cannot show under a mental description of that process that it caused that motion (even when the latter is mentioned under an action–theoretic description) without the addition of a host of other assumptions about the agent's psychological capacities and states of mind. That observation by itself does not entail that we cannot show the mental causation to have occurred at all, but perhaps Davidson holds that the number of needed background assumptions is *indefinitely large* (note the phrase 'without limit' in our quoted passage (D)). This is an extremely interesting hypothesis, and if true it would be strong evidence for thinking that we could not formulate strict psycho–physical laws unless we were able to find some axiom schemata to bring indefinitely many assumptions under one rule, which is unlikely. It would also impugn homunctionalism as well as the Identity Theory, in the same way. If this is what Davidson intends, then we would have to add to his argument the premise that the Cycle is indefinitely large, and we would have to spell out the rationality assumption by saying that the number of different shared beliefs and inference–rules we must posit in psychological explanation is without limit.

How could Davidson motivate these strengthened theses? Perhaps by looking at some cases of mental ascription and some cases of motivational explanation, and showing in each case that we have to keep adding further psychological assumptions in order to approach (on the one hand) a sufficiency relation between mental ascription and behavioral–evidence–plus–other–mental–assumptions, and (on the other) a complete and law–like explanation of the subject's behavior. If Davidson could show that more and more assumptions had to be added successively in each case and that no end was in sight, this would be good evidence for thinking that the process would continue indefinitely—that there would *always* be counterexamples to any generalization connecting mental events and behavioral or other mental or physical events. (That he might support the *PAM* in this way is suggested by his remarks on pp. 44–45 of "PP.") But, pending his offering at least a rough algorithm for generating such counterexamples, I think we must regard his case based on the Belief–Desire–Perception Cycle as unproven.[26]

In his own anomalist writings,[27] D. C. Dennett has given the rationality assumption an argumentative twist that is somewhat different from Davidson's: When we ascribe beliefs or desires to people, we do so against the backdrop of a general assumption that the people's other mental states and conditions are rational to at least a minimal degree. But the concept of rationality is a *normative* concept; when we call a person's beliefs rational, we are *evaluating* both the person and the beliefs. If psychology essentially involves evaluation and (as Davidson agrees) cannot proceed a step without it, then is it not after all quite different from chemistry or physics?

It is hard to get clear as to exactly what is being claimed. Let us distinguish three possible theses that are suggested by Dennett's recent writings—though more may be lurking in the neighborhood:

(1) We are entitled to regard behavioral facts as evidence in favor of propositional–attitude ascriptions only in virtue of our making an assumption that is in part a normative assumption.

(2) When we ascribe a propositional attitude, say, a belief, to an organism, we commit ourselves *via* doxastic logic or the probability calculus or some other description of an *ideal* believer to a normative claim about what else the organism ought to believe.

(3) A belief–ascription is *itself* a normative remark concerning the organism to which the belief is ascribed.

I shall not go into these claims in any detail, but we would have to be shown an argument that derives the anomalism of the mental from any of them. (1) is an epistemological thesis, and so is not likely to entail a metaphysical one (see again note 26). (2) is so obvious that it would be very surprising to find out that it entailed so substantive a doctrine as the *PAM*. When I ascribe a *pain* to an organism, I commit myself *via* the hedonic calculus or the Categorical Imperative or some other description of an *ideal* agent to a normative claim about what we ought to do for that organism, but that fact does nothing to show that the pain is not a real, straightforward, factual inner state of the organism. (3), I suppose, has the best chance.

But (3) is the least plausible of the three claims. Belief–ascriptions do not at all seem to *be* normative remarks. When we impute a belief to someone we do not *thereby* praise the belief as being a reasonable one. (On countless occasions an amateur or professional psychologist has explained someone's behavior by ascribing to that person a belief or a desire or both that is admitted by everyone to be stupid, silly, irrational, perverse, sick, etc.) Besides, even if psychologists did routinely characterize the beliefs and desires they posit as being "reasonable" ones, I should think that "reasonableness" of this sort could very easily be naturalized in crypto–evolutionary terms; "reasonableness" would be cashed in terms of promoting fitness of one kind or another. Thus, propositional–attitude ascriptions would not be *irreducibly* normative. Finally, if the beliefs posited by psychologists are ideal beliefs in the sense of being the beliefs that the psychologist thinks the subject ought to have, how is it that they could help us predict the subject's actual behavior, given that the subject in fact does not live up to the ideal in question? It seems these normative "beliefs" would generate the wrong predictions.[28]

In a longer manuscript from which the present paper is drawn, I argue that Davidson's next three considerations—3, 4, and 5—are parasitic in that they simply stand or fall with the first two; I shall omit discussion of them here, and move directly to Davidson's appeal to the indeterminacy of translation.

V

As Quine understands it, the underdetermination of translators' "analytical" hypotheses by their observational evidence supports the *PAM* in a direct way that makes no mention of the Belief–Desire–Perception Cycle or the rationality assumption. Quine takes the underdetermination of analytical hypotheses, together with some further assumptions about scientific method and about the linguist's enterprise, to show that analytical hypotheses are *indeterminate*. Quine holds that analytical hypotheses are not true or false reports of any objective fact, but are "correct" or "incorrect" only relative to pre–chosen translation manuals which have been originally selected more or less arbitrarily on the basis of sheer convenience.

I cannot here go into Quine's reasons for holding this extremely strong position.[29] I want only to show its relevance to the *PAM* and the force it would have if true. The first important point to see is that the indeterminancy of translation would infect ascriptions of propositional attitudes to other persons (and ultimately to ourselves): When we say of a speaker of German that he believes it is snowing, we are in effect *translating* the words or other behavior he would use to express his belief into words of our own.[30] If translation is indeterminate, then our ascription of the belief *that it is snowing* to the German is indeterminate. The same would go for desires, fears, hopes, and so on. And to say that the ascription of beliefs and desires to the German is indeterminate is to say (on Quine's usage) that there is no fact of the matter concerning what particular mental states the German is in. So if there were strict laws correlating neural states with mental states, then there would be a fact of the matter concerning the German's beliefs and desires; it would be deductively determined by his actual neural states and the psycho–physical laws. Therefore, if translation is indeterminate, as Quine and others believe, there are no psycho–physical laws, and claim (A) is vindicated. And this time a similar argument could be wielded against psycho–functional laws and in favor of the full–fledged *PAM* as well, for there is presumably also a fact of the matter concerning what homunctional states the German is in.

I believe, then, that one who denies the *PAM* ought also to deny the indeterminacy doctrine in its Quinean form. The doctrine is unlikely to trouble the Identity Theorist in particular, since Quine's discussion of the mind–body problem in *Word and Object* appears to show that no reductive materialist of the standard sort may hold Quine's views on translation and reference anyway.[31] More importantly, on our Quinean interpretation, the argument from genuine indeterminacy of translation proves too much: the genuine indeterminacy of propositional–attitude ascriptions warrants the claim that there are no beliefs or desires in nature; to ascribe "beliefs" or "desires" to the German is to engage in a bit of useful but entirely subjective interpretation of the German's behavior–pattern. Therefore, a proponent of *AM*, who is committed to the claim that there are belief– and desire–tokens in nature, seemingly must deny the full–scale indeterminacy of propositional–attitude ascriptions anyway. A champion of indeterminacy who is also a materialist must be an *eliminative* materialist of some sort.[32]

Finally, what about intentionality and intensionality? Davidson has run together several distinct points here. First, there is that at which he hints on p. 97 of "ME" (particularly in note 15): Quine has claimed that intensional sentences are irreducible, in that they have no nonintensional equivalents. Quine also maintains, somewhat surprisingly, that the irreducibility of intensional sentences necessitates and is necessitated by the indeterminacy of translation.[33] If so, and if indeterminacy implies the *PAM* as I have argued it does, then the undisputed intensionality of our central mental ascriptions itself implies the *PAM*. Further, Quine holds independently that intensional expressions cannot be incorporated into serious science (see the last few chapters of *Word and Object*). The *PAM* follows directly, if we assume that we need intensional expressions in order to give mental descriptions of events.[34] But the first of these points has the same flaw as does the Quinean argument that I based on indeterminacy, that of proving too much; the second depends on Quine's weighty complex of views on referential opacity, physics, metaphysics, and "serious" science, and pending a final evaluation of that complex, there is no immediate reason for scrapping homunctionalism.

A second point subsumed under our final consideration is Brentano's, which Davidson follows Chisholm in conflating with the thesis of the intensionality or our paradigmatic mental verbs. According to Brentano, the distinguishing feature of mental states, events and processes is their "aboutness." This feature too has been taken to preclude the possibility of integrating psychology into physical science or indeed into serious science at all; if it does preclude these possibilities, then presumably it also rules out the existence of psychological laws. It has never been clear, though, that "content" or "aboutness" cannot be ascribed to entities that are in fact neural items, particularly when those neural entities are referred to under psychological descriptions. The vindication of such ascriptions has been a main motivation of Dennett's own work for years;[35] and I have already hinted in section III at the ability of a Sellarsian brain–writing theory of belief and other propositional attitudes to ride the coattails of the aboutness of sentences, especially when we modify Sellars' own account by telling a causal story about denotation.[36] Even if there cannot be laws correlating mental entities, their contents, and neural entities, it is still quite plausible to think that the contents and/or intentional objects of mental entities can be characterized in psycho–functional terms.

VI

The upshot of our discussion of Davidson's arguments is that the most convincing support for the *PAM* comes from the Belief–Desire–Perception Cycle, but that support is very weak, in view of the intervention of homunctionalism as an attractive program for an ontology of the psychological. So we have been given no particularly convincing reason to accept the *PAM* (and hence no convincing reason to accept *AM* as a theory of mind). But neither have we any very concrete reason, not counting hope, for supposing that the *PAM* is false. What is really at issue is the question of what philosophical reality it is that lies behind the admitted complexity of the conceptual interrelations between our various sorts of mental entities and the concomitant holism of the mental, as these are revealed by such considerations as those we have discussed. The homunctionalist welcomes the complexity as a rich source of data and directions for a homuncular model of the mind, and happily accommodates the holism in insisting (as any functionalist does) on the inescapably relational character of mental states and on the impossibility of there being individual mental state–tokens in isolation from mental state–tokens of other types. Further, as we have seen, the homunctionalist thinks he has an explanation of the apparent seamlessness of the mental and the felt lack of congruence between the family of mental concepts and the family of physicalistic concepts that occasions the mind–body problem in the first place. So the homunctionalist and Davidson agree on a great deal, *including* the nonexistence of laws ("genuine" or otherwise) relating the mental *qua* mental to the physiological, since the homunctionalist is not a species chauvinist. On what, then do they disagree?

There seems to be only one serious difference between them: the homunctionalist as I have understood him believes in the existence of psycho–functional laws, while Davidson does not. But now it is time to inquire more precisely into the notion of the "genuineness" or "strictness" of a law.

Functionalists in general have been silent on the question of whether they intend the laws of the psychology they envision to be "genuine," "strict," and deterministic laws. Naturally, the more ambitiously Davidson understands his idea of "genuineness," the more plausible his view will become and the more adherents even among functionalists it will attract—but at the price of loss of interest. There may well turn out to be no "strict and deterministic" laws in biology or in chemistry either; it is not obvious even that there are any absolutely deterministic laws in physics, for that matter.[37] (More about this shortly.) In general, I take no stand on the larger issue of determinism vs. indeterminism in any branch of science; my main concern is to block Davidson's (and more recently Putnam's) attempt to split off psychology from the "hard" sciences as being a quite different sort of enterprise, a poor relation or black sheep of some kind.

But there is a final concessive word to be said concerning the *genuineness* of psychological laws, and to a small extent it vindicates Davidson's skepticism on this score. I said in section III that the laws of a homunctionalist psychology would be those which can be read off a flow–chart of the type I have described. Thus, a homunctionalist law would take the form, "If an organism of type X receives an input of type Y while its ϕ–er is in state A and its ψ–er is in state B (etc.), then (it is probable to degree n that) the organism will spit out an output of type Z."

However, a "law" of this form would seem to be subject to falsification by *hardware malfunction*. And, given the prevalence of hardware malfunction at least among those of us living in dangerous times like these, we can be sure that such falsification will be ubiquitous. Does this not confirm Davidson's thesis that there are no genuine and *true* psychological laws?

An obvious reply is available: the notions of a thing's "having a φ–er which is in a state A" or "having a ψ–er which is in state B" are functional notions, defined in terms of their *satisfactory* domestic and foreign relations. A hardware breakdown does not falsify the laws which we read off our flow–charts; rather, it causes the organism formerly described by the flow–chart to cease to be (correctly) described by that flow–chart, i.e., to cease to realize the relevant program(s). This would mean that the organism no longer *has* a φ–er and a ψ–er, and so the organism is no longer of type X and cannot be a counterexample to our law.

Indeed, this reply is so obvious as to raise the suspicion that the law is unfalsifiable. And this suspicion is easily confirmed. For the law as we are now understanding it may be rewritten as follows: "If an organism receives an input of type Y, and if the organism has a φ–er and if the φ–er is in state A, and if the organism has an ψ–er and if the ψ–er is in state B (etc.), then (it is probable to degree n that) the organism will spit out an output of type Z." Now, the functional term 'φ–er' is *defined* by the set of conditionals codified in the relevant flow–chart; so any law of the foregoing form will be *tautologous*.[38] (Simplest example: "If an organism receives an input of type Y, and if the organism has a component such that if the organism receives an input of type Y it will spit out an output of type Z, then the organism will spit out an output of type Z.") But a tautology is a law of logic, not a "law" of psychology.

In his comments on an earlier version of this essay,[39] David Sanford pointed out that

> [a]lthough no malfunction can falsify a tautologous conditional, a malfunction does present the problem of locating which parts of the antecedent of the conditional are false . . . . something can malfunction without everything malfunctioning. The organism can still have a φ–er, indeed still have a φ–er in state A, if the malfunction is elsewhere. Flow charts invite us to locate malfunctions when they occur.

This is true, important, and crucial in particular to the sort of psycho–physiological research that inspires homunctionalism in the first place. But to take account of it would require giving up the simple method proposed by David Lewis (*op. cit.*) for defining mental and homuncular terms explicitly by way of Ramsey sentences, and I am not sure what to adopt in place of that method. Presumably what we need is some way of exploiting and making precise the notion of something's *approximately* realizing a particular homuncular flow–chart. No doubt there are various formal ways of trying to spell this out, but at present I see no chance of discovering strict, deterministic, *exceptionless and nontautologous* psychological laws; after all this effort and verbiage we may have to concede to Davidson that every psychological generalization must be qualified by *ceteris paribus* or other escape clauses. Indeed, we would have to be careful to see that such qualifications did not themselves render the generalizations tautologous; it seems to me that we could do this only by appealing to "normal functioning" or to some other background condition which smacks of norms, and what Davidson suspects is precisely that we must choose between the tautologous and the normative. This might even be why he (and Putnam) contend that psychology is not really a *science*.

Ausonio Marras has remarked that to put the problem in this way is to ratify the unwarranted assumption that all genuine explanation *is* explanation in terms of strictly exceptionless laws.[40] The type of explanation favored by the homunctionalist, vividly and compellingly described in the works of Fodor and Dennett, is not deductive–nomological explanation of that sort, but is *functional* explanation of the sort we give every day in biology, in experimental chemistry, in automotive mechanics, and in engineering generally. It is explanation of the behavior of a single organized system in terms of the joint workings of the system's components. Such explanation does not presuppose the existence of strictly exceptionless mechanical laws, precisely because of the nonnegligible likelihood of hardware breakdowns. Its rational structure is still very unclear and controversial. Yet there is no doubt of its value, of its epistemic genuineness, or of its status as *scientific* in any but a plainly neologistic sense of that word.

The following observation will reinforce the present point: Our difficulty is occasioned by the possibility of hardware breakdown. Now, hardware does not break down only in computers and in human bodies; it breaks down in other biological systems as well. Chemistry too is subject to "hardware" malfunction: laws of *chemistry* (pure chemistry, not physical chemistry) are falsified by disruptive subatomic events produced by radiation, and could be protected against such falsification only by the assumption (parallel to our "obvious" reply above) that an "atom" which has been split by radiation no longer counts (functions!) as an *atom*. This is intuitively right, though it raises the spectre of tautologousness just as the "obvious" reply did.[41] Further, quite commonly, satisfactory explanation of phenomena in one science will require descent to a more fundamental science one or even two levels down (hence "physical chemistry," "biophysics"), without damage to the status of the higher-level science as a *science*.

In short: If my "hardware malfunction" objection shows that the mental is anomalous in the sense Davidson intends, then it also shows that the biological and the chemical are anomalous too. And so Davidson should have entitled his article, "Psychology, *Biology and Chemistry* as Philosophy"; he fails to show that psychology is a nonscience in a way that makes it unlike a truly factual, decent, hardnosed discipline.

The final disposition or disposal of the issue of psycho–functional laws, it seems to me, rests with the future success of the homunctionalist (or some other functionalist) program. If functionalist philosophers and psychologists together manage to put forward a fairly detailed psychology that explains and predicts not only behavior but the esoteric and finely articulated phenomena that Dennett concerns himself with, then we will have excellent reason for thinking (a) that the Belief–Desire–Perception Cycle, though large, is finite and completable, (b) that intensionality and intentionality are compatible with a functionalist materialism, and (c) that translation is not indeterminate after all. Should it turn out that homunctionalism and other functionalist programs end in disappointment for more sweeping reasons, we will have to consider explaining this by concluding that *AM* is correct after all. As for present research, however, the homunctionalist ontology permits and contributes to an already ongoing program for psychology, while the defender of *AM* has no program but only the conviction that no truly scientific psychology is possible; and so, it seems to me, we have no choice but to pursue homunctionalism or some other functionalist ideal wherever it may lead us.

NOTES

1. Other materialists who have been called 'Identity Theorists' have not shared this motivation and have not necessarily believed that any such correlations existed; David Lewis is an obvious example ("Psychophysical and Theoretical Identifications," *Australasian Journal of Philosophy*, Vol. 50 (1972)). In this paper I shall reserve the term 'the Identity Theory' to refer to Smart's type–type view. (However, Smart has protested to me in correspondence that he never intended to posit as broad a type–type identification as I and others have attributed to him.)

2. Jaegwon Kim has attacked this reasoning in "On the Psycho–Physical Identity Theory," *American PhilosophicalQuarterly*, Vol. III (1966). (For an excellent discussion of issues concerning psycho–physical laws and psycho–physical causation, see Kim's "Causality, Identity, and Supervenience in the Mind–Body Problem," *Midwest Studies in Philosophy*, Vol. IV (University of Minnesota Press, 1979).) David Armstrong has also objected (in correspondence) that there cannot be explanations of this kind if laws are taken as relations between distinct universals (see Armstrong's *A Theory of Universals* (*Universals and Scientific Realism*, Vol. II), Cambridge University Press, 1978).

3. "Mental Events" (hereafter "ME"), in Foster and Swanson (eds), *Experience and Theory* (University of Massachusetts Press, 1970); "Psychology as Philosophy" (hereafter "PP"), in S. C. Brown (ed.), *Philosophy of Psychology* (Barnes and Noble, 1974); "The Material Mind" ("MM"), in Suppes et. al. (eds.), *Logic, Methodology and Philosophy of Science*, Vol. IV (North–Holland, 1973).

4. Of course, Davidson is not the only philosopher recently to challenge the possibility of a science of the mental. Related arguments have been put forward by D. C. Dennett in *Brainstorms* (Bradford Books, 1978) and elsewhere, by Jerry Fodor in his Introduction to *The Language of Thought* (Harvester Books, 1975), by Stephen Stich in "On the Ascription of Content" (to appear in a forthcoming collection edited by Andrew Woodfield), by Paul Churchland in "Is 'Thinker' a Natural Kind?" (Xerox), and others. Each of these works advances arguments that deserve separate and careful examination; I shall mention the most germane points below, as they arise. And some philosophers, such as W. V. Quine, Paul Feyerabend, and perhaps Hilary Putnam in *Meaning and the Moral Sciences* (Routledge and Kegan Paul, 1978) have made the stronger claim that mental state–tokens do not even exist *qua* real inner states of sentient beings.

5. There are, of course, laws of physics which are explicitly probablistic. But these laws are still "strict" and "deterministic" in Davidson's sense, because the probabilities themselves are absolutely precise and are determined without exception or escape clause by the containing physical theory. Notice that these strong constraints on what is to count as a "genuine" law entail that whenever there occurs an actual case of psycho–physical causation, that case falls under some "genuine" law in the mathematically strict sense. This claim is essential to Davidson's later defense of his own monism.

6. We could put the same point in Humean terms: A causal explanation of event–token E_2 requires some mention of a "constant conjunction" between event–token E_1's type and event–tokens of E_2's type. But what *is* E_1's particular type? Obviously E_1 is a member of any number of distinct classes, depending on which other event–tokens we choose to group it with. (We make such a choice routinely by referring to an event–token under one appropriate true description rather than another.) Thus, whether we have a correct causal explanation of E_1's resulting in E_2 depends on a choice of event–type for E_1 and for E_2, and this corresponds to the

choice of description that we must make in order to formulate our explanatory argument at all.

7. "Mental States and Putnam's Functionalist Hypothesis," *Australasian Journal of Philosophy*, Vol. 52 (1974).

8. This may be taken to suggest that in a way *AM* is an eliminative rather than a purely reductive view. One might fill out this suggestion by arguing, as I have heard some philosophers do, as follows: If *AM* is correct, then beliefs do not comprise a natural kind. But in the ultimate nature of reality, as displayed to us by the ideal future physics plus whatever, everything (every substance) falls under a natural kind. If beliefs to *not* comprise a natural kind, then our talk of them fails to correspond to anything in the ultimate nature of reality, and thus does not succeed in referring to anything real. Therefore, if *AM* is correct, beliefs are not real, i.e., are not found among the actual constituents of the universe; and thus in reality there are no beliefs—for them, eliminative materialism is correct.

This argument is fallacious in that it confuses types and tokens. Let us define a new class of items:

x is a schmental entity $=_{def}$ x is a dog or x is a pool table or x is a light bulb or x is the Eiffel Tower or x is the number 352 or x is Donald Davidson.

It seems clear that schmental entities do not form a natural kind. Certainly schmental entities (*qua* schmental) figure in no strict deterministic laws. If the foregoing argument is sound, we should be able to infer that schmental entities are not real and therefore that there are no schmental entities and that eliminative schmaterialism is correct. But these conclusions are false. There certainly are schmental entities; any dog, for example, is one, and Donald Davidson is one. Although I have not stated the argument precisely enough for us to pinpoint the fallacious step definitively, it seems to be marked by the "thus" in "and thus does not succeed in referring to anything real." *Individual* beliefs are found among the actual constituents of the universe.

Roy Edelstein has attacked this sort of argument more trenchantly in "The Diagonal Defense," unpublished.

9. Hilary Putnam has taken this line in *Meaning and the Moral Sciences*, op. cit.

10. Unlike David Lewis (op. cit.), and unlike Dennett (op. cit) and Stich (op. cit.) also, I am entirely willing to give up fairly large chunks of our commonsensical or platitudinous theory of belief or of desire (or of almost anything else) and decide that we were just wrong about a lot of things, without drawing the inference that we are no longer talking about *belief* or *desire*. To put the matter crudely, I incline away from Lewis' Carnapian and/or Rylean cluster theory of the reference of theoretical terms, and toward Putnam's causal–historical theory ("The Meaning of 'Meaning'," in *Minnesota Studies in the Philosophy of Science, Vol. VII* (University of Minnesota Press, 1975)). As in Putnam's examples of "water," "tiger," and so on, I think the ordinary word "belief" (*qua* theoretical term of folk psychology) points dimly toward a natural kind that we have not yet fully grasped and that only a mature psychology will reveal. I expect that "belief" will turn out to refer to some kind of information–bearing inner state of a sentient being (more on this below), but the kind of state it refers to may have only a few of the properties usually attributed to beliefs by common sense. Thus, I think our ordinary way of picking out "beliefs" and "desires" succeeds in picking out real entities in nature, but it may not succeed in picking out exactly the entities that common sense suggests that it does.

11. Putnam, "Psychological Predicates," in Capitan and Merrill (eds.), *Art, Mind, and Religion* (University of Pittsburgh Press, 1967). See also my "Mental States and Putnam's Functionalist Hypothesis," loc. cit.

12. See, e.g., L. Mucciolo, "The Identity Thesis and Neuropsychology," *Nous*, Vol. VIII (1974).

13. "Form, Function, and Feel," *Journal of Philosophy*, Vol. LXXVIII (1981).

14. The philosophical theory or picture of the psychological to which I am attaching this term is due to Jerry Fodor ("The Appeal to Tacit Knowledge in Psychological Explanation," *Journal of Philosophy*, Vol. LXV (1968)) and especially to D. C. Dennett (op. cit.), though it is suggested by certain research programs in cognitive psychology and in artificial intelligence; see also Robert Cummins' "Functional Analysis," *Journal of Philosophy*, Vol. LXXII (1975) and John Haugeland's "The Nature and Plausibility of Cognitivism," *Behavioral and Brain Sciences*, Vol. 2 (1978) for very useful discussion. In "Form, Function, and Feel," op. cit. I have tried to bring out the very considerable virtues of the view and to apply it to the task of accounting for "feels" or "qualia" within a materialist framework.

15. For more detailed illustration and commentary, see Dennett, op. cit., particularly Chs. 9 and 11, and my "Form, Function, and Feel," op. cit.

16. In "Form, Function, and Feel," op. cit., I argue that job–descriptive or teleological characterization reaches further down toward fundamental physical reality than is usually recognized, and that even the Identity Theorist is a functionalist—one who locates mental types at a very low level of institutional abstraction. Ned Block has urged against this that at least when one descends from the neuroanatomical level to the level of *chemistry*, no teleological element remains; but consider the etymologies of such chemical terms as 'hydrogen' and 'oxygen.'

17. Well-known partisans of the model include Wilfrid Sellars, Gilbert Harman, Jay Rosenberg, and Jerry Fodor. A classic opponent is Roderick Chisholm; some more recent critics are Dennett himself (*op. cit.*, particularly Chs. 2, 3 and 6; and elsewhere), Zeno Vendler (*Res Cogitans*, Cornell University Press, 1972), Arthur W. Collins ("Could Our Beliefs Be Mental Representations in Our Brains?" *Journal of Philosophy*, Vol. LXXVI (1979)), Paul Churchland (*Scientific Realism and the Plasticity of Mind* (Cambridge University Press, 1979)), and Patricia Smith Churchland ("Language, Thought, and Information Processing," *Nous*, Vol. XIV (1980)). I discuss some arguments pro and con in "Toward A Homuncular Theory of Believing," *Cognition and Brain Theory*, forthcoming.

18. I do not mean anything particularly technical by 'information' here, and I am certainly not presupposing any one mathematical representation of informational content. However, I mean 'information' less in the Shannon–Weaver sense than in Carnap's and Bar–Hillel's sense of "semantic" information.

19. "Form, Function, and Feel," and "Toward a Homuncular Theory of Believing."

20. This account of "belief that" derives (obviously) from the works of Wilfrid Sellars, such as *Science and Metaphysics* (Humanities Press, 1967), Ch. III, and "Reply to Quine," *Synthese*, Vol. XXVI (1973). See also Christopher S. Hill, "Toward a Theory of Meaning for Belief Sentences," *Philosophical Studies*, Vol. 30 (1976), Hartry Field, "Mental Representation," *Erkenntnis*, Vol. 13 (1978), and Jerry Fodor, "Propositional Attitudes," *Monist*, Vol. 61 (1978).

21. See again note 17 above. Besides the "external" difficulties raised in the works cited there, some internal problems are occasioned by the recent "methodological solipsist" literature; see Jerry Fodor, "Methodological Solipsism Considered as a Research Strategy in Cognitive Psychology," *Behavioral and Brain Sciences*, Vol. 3 (1980), Stephen Stich, "Paying the Price for Methodological Solipsism," *ibid.*, and Stich, "Autonomous Psychology and the Belief–Desire Thesis," *Monist*, Vol. 61 (1978).

22. David Lewis' view (op. cit.) is perhaps an exception, since Lewis defines mental expressions in terms of the platitudes and folk wisdom in which they figure.

23. See, e.g., Harman, *Thought* (Princeton University Press, 1973), Chapters 2 and 3.

24. To grasp his point fully one must be familiar with Quine's presentation of the indeterminacy doctrine in Chapter 2 of *Word and Object* (Massachusetts Institute of Technology Press, 1960), and perhaps with several more recent papers such as Wallace, "On the Frame of Reference," in Davidson and Harman (eds.), *Semantics of Natural Language* (Reidel, 1972); Rorty, "The World Well Lost," *Journal of Philosophy*, Vol. LXIX (1972); and Davidson, "On the Very Idea of a Conceptual Scheme," *Proceedings and Addresses of the American Philosophical Association*, Vol. 47 (1973–74). Davidson applies all this to the present issue on p. 97 of "ME," on pp. 51–52 of "PP," and on p. 714 of "MM."

25. Davidson holds that genuine laws can be stated only within some very tightly closed system of vocabulary. But what is to prevent the Identity Theorist from simply envisioning an eventually pooled psycho–physical vocabulary containing both mental and physical expressions, and predicting with some confidence that such a system can be made as strictly, precisely, and tightly closed as one likes? Obviously Davidson believes this to be impossible, but the fact that rationality assumptions are neither needed nor desired in physics does not show that it is. (However, for some fairly persuasive reasons, see Fodor's Introduction to *The Language of Thought*, op. cit.)

26. In his comments on my 1979 Oberlin Colloquium presentation, David Sanford reminded me of Davidson's remark that

> It is an error to compare a truism like 'If a man wants to eat an acorn omelette, then he generally will if the opportunity exists and no other desire overrides' with a law that says how fast a body will fall in a vacuum. It is an error, because in the latter case, but not the former, we can tell in advance whether the condition holds, and we know what allowance to make if it doesn't. What is needed in the case of action, if we are to predict on the basis of desires and beliefs, is a quantitative calculus that brings all relevant beliefs and desires into the picture. ["PP," p. 45]

Sanford adds,

> Before we can show that the desire, *qua* desire, caused the behavior, we must determine that no other desire overrides; yet this sort of condition is not appropriately mentioned in the formulation of a proper law because there is no independent way of telling when it obtains. [p. 12]

I grant that this difference between Davidson's truism and the law of falling bodies poses an epistemological problem for the homunctional psychologist. It seems that in order to be justified in attributing a desire to a subject, we must antecedently know something about that subject's desires or lack of them; the rationality assumption (or perhaps some other assumption that makes certain desires *a priori* likely or unlikely) is needed to block the regress. But there are two points to be made in mitigation of this: (i) Davidson's truism may be a "law" of *folk* psychology, but it is not the sort of lawlike statement one would find in a homunctionalist psychology. As I have said, homunctionalist laws will be highly technical and detailed generalizations of the sort that can be read off an immensely complex flow–chart of the sort I have described, and they will be couched in our characteristically job–descriptive sub–personal jargon. Granted, they will contain *ceteris paribus* clauses of a sort which I shall discuss in section VI below, but those clauses will be quite a different sort from those which infest folk-psychological truisms of the sort Davidson illustrates. So Davidson's illustration is not a counterexample to anything I maintain here. (ii) It is not clear why an *epistemic* defect in a putative law should make that law less of a law. I take it that a generalization might in fact be both true and lawlike, this being a metaphysical matter, and still pose nasty epistemological problems. Suppose homunctionalism is correct, or rather (not to beg the question), suppose that every human being is at least in part a homunctional system of the sort I have described. Then for all Davidson's arguments have shown, there will be homunctionalist laws governing the behavior of human beings *whether or not* we can ever devise a methodology sophisticated enough to enable us to discover those laws.

27. See *Brainstorms*, op. cit., pp. xvi–xvii, 28, and 105; also "Three Kinds of Intentional Psychology," forthcoming in a Thyssen Philosophy Group volume edited by R. A. Healey, and "True Believers: The Intentional Strategy and Why it Works," forthcoming in a volume of 1979 Herbert Spencer Lectures (Oxford University Press).

28. A naturalistic psychology of the kind I am envisaging has a hard time leaving room for the genuinely normative notions that are the subject–matter of logic and of the theory of epistemic justification generally. How does a naturalistic theorist, who holds that a complete causal description of the natural order is all there is for science or philosophy to offer, reconstruct the distinction between rational and irrational beliefs? Alternatively: What would a naturalist's philosophy of logic look like? This question has received little attention in the recent literature on philosophy of psychology, despite the gathering momentum of the "naturalization" of epistemology spearheaded by Armstrong and Goldman (see Armstrong, *Belief, Truth and Knowledge* (Cambridge University Press, 1973), and Goldman, "Discrimination and Perceptual Knowledge," *Journal of Philosophy*, Vol. LXXIII (1976), "The Internalist Conception of Justification," *Midwest Studies in Philosophy*, Vol. V (University of Minnesota Press, 1980), and elsewhere). Naturalistic epistemologists typically concentrate all their efforts on relatively immediate perceptual knowledge, where it *is* plausible to explicate justification and epistemic "obligation" in terms of causal sufficiencies obtaining within mechanisms. But as soon as we move any distance away from this epistemologically idiosyncratic kind of belief, the inferences that people ought to draw and the inferences that people do draw are going to diverge quite a bit, and no naturalistic causal-functional account of the latter is going to have much to say about the former. (However, see Elliot Sober's "The Evolution of Rationality," *Synthese*, vol. 46 (1981), and my "Epistemic Rectitude and the Canons of Theory–Preference" (ditto).)

29. I discuss these reasons in Ch. X of *Logical Form*, in preparation. See also Edwin Martin and D. W. Smith, "On the Nature and Relevance of Indeterminacy," *Foundations of Language*, Vol. 12 (1974).

30. This connection is nicely brought out by Harman in "An Introduction to 'Translation and Meaning': Chapter Two of *Word and Object*," in Davidson and Hintikka (eds.), *Words and Objections: Essays on the Work of W. V. Quine* (Reidel, 1969).

31. I have argued this in Lycan and Pappas, "Quine's Materialism," *Philosophia*, Vol. 6 (1976).

32. Or so I have contended in "Quine's Materialism," op. cit. Quine himself questions the tenability of the "reductive"/"eliminative" distinction in the first place; and he has explained his view of the mind–body problem somewhat differently in more recent works ("Mind and Verbal Dispositions," in Guttenplan (ed.), *Mind and Language* (Oxford University Press, 1975), and "Reply to Lycan and Pappas," *Philosophia*, Vol. 7 (1978)).

33. *Word and Object*, p. 221. I try to explain the connection further in *Logical Form*, op. cit.

34. Chisholm has defended this claim in a number of works and agrees that intensional expressions cannot be incorporated into physical science; but he argues, following Brentano, that this simply calls for a separate science of the mental. The possibility of such a science is ruled out by the *PAM*; Quine accordingly rejects that part of Chisholm's view.

35. See his *Content and Consciousness* (Routledge and Kegan Paul, 1969).

36. Admittedly, the causal account will run into trouble in the case of beliefs "about" fictional entities, but there are encouraging signs that this trouble can be overcome; see Devitt, *Designation*, Columbia University Press, forthcoming.

37. Elliot Sober has suggested in conversation that virtually any law of physics contains tacit *ceteris paribus* clauses due to such laws' usual implicit relativizations to "closed systems," "perfect vacuums," "frictionless surfaces," "black boxes," etc. This does not actually make such laws any the less lawlike; it makes their antecedents vacuous. I shall not suggest that the laws of a homunctionalist psychology in effect have vacuous antecedents in much the same way.

38. Grice touches on what I think may be the same point in "Method in Philosophical Psychology (From the Banal to the Bizarre)," *Proceedings and Addresses of the American Philosophical Association*, Vol. XLVIII (1974–75), p. 28.

39. 1979 Oberlin Colloquium, op. cit.

40. "Cognitivism and the Computational Approach," unpublished Xerox.

41. Elliot Sober observes (in correspondence) that although a chemist always has the *opportunity* of treating a chemical law as unfalsifiable, "a *good* chemist will not choose to do so." This brings us back to the problem of "locating the malfunctions when they occur."

Dennett on Intentional Systems

STEPHEN P. STICH
University of Maryland

During the last dozen years, Daniel Dennett has been elaborating an interconnected—and increasingly influential—set of views in the philosophy of mind, the philosophy of psychology, and those parts of moral philosophy that deal with the notions of freedom, responsibility and personhood. The central unifying theme running through Dennett's writings on each of these topics is his concept of an *intentional system*. He invokes the concept to "legitimize" mentalistic predicates (*Brainstorms*, p. xvii),[1] to explain the theoretical strategy of cognitive psychology and artificial intelligence, and, ultimately, to attempt a reconciliation between "our vision of ourselves as responsible, free, rational agents, and our vision of ourselves as complex parts of the physical world of science" (*BS*, p. x). My goal in this paper is to raise some doubts about the "intentional coin" (*BS*, p. xviii) with which Dennett proposes to purchase his moral and "mental treasures." Since I aim to offer a critique of Dennett's views, it is inevitable that much of what I say will be negative in tone. But this tone should not be misconstrued. It is my view that Dennett's theories are of great importance and will shape discussion in the philosophy of mind for decades to come. Moreover, I think that much of what Dennett says is close to being true. If we reconstruct his notion of an intentional system to eliminate its instrumentalism and its unfortunate infatuation with idealized rationality, we can use the result to give a better account of common–sense mentalistic notions, and also to give a clearer and more tenable account of the strategy of cognitive science. Toward the end of this paper I will sketch the outlines of such a "de–rationalized" cousin to Dennett's idea of an intentional system.

I

In explaining the idea of an intentional system, Dennett's recurrent illustration is the chess-playing computer. There are, he urges, three quite different stances we might "adopt in trying to predict and explain its behavior" (*BS* p. 237).

First there is the *design stance*. If one knows exactly how the computer's program has been designed . . . one can predict the computer's designed response to any move one makes. One's prediction will come true provided only that the computer performs as designed, that is, without breakdown. . . . The essential feature of the design stance is that we make predictions solely from knowledge or assumptions about the system's design, often without making any examination of the innards of the particular object.

Second, there is what we may call the *physical stance*. From this stance our predictions are based on the actual state of the particular system, and are worked out by applying whatever knowledge we have of the laws of nature. . . . One seldom adopts the physical stance in dealing with a computer just because the number of critical variables in the physical constitution of a computer would overwhelm the most prodigious human calculator. . . . Attempting to give a physical account or prediction of the chess playing computer would be a pointless and herculean labor, but it would work in principle. One could predict the response it would make in a chess game by tracing out the effects of the input energies all the way through the computer until once more type was pressed against paper and a response was printed.

There is a third stance one can adopt toward a system, and that is the *intentional stance*. This tends to be the most appropriate when the system one is dealing with is too complex to be dealt with effectively from the other stances. In the case of a chess playing computer one adopts this stance when one tries to predict its response to one's move by figuring out what a good or reasonable response would be, given the information the computer has about the situation. Here one assumes not just the absence of malfunction but the rationality of the design or programming as well.

Whenever one can successfully adopt the intentional stance toward an object, I call that object an *intentional* system. The success of the stance is of course a matter settled pragmatically, without reference to whether the object *really* has beliefs, intentions, and so forth; so whether or not any computer can be conscious, or have thoughts or desires, some computers undeniably *are* intentional systems, for they are systems whose behavior can be predicted, and most efficiently predicted, by adopting the intentional stance towards them. [*BS*, pp. 237–38; for a largely identical passage, cf. *BS*, pp. 4–7]

So *any* object will count as an intentional system if we can usefully predict its behavior by assuming that it will behave *rationally*. And what is it to behave rationally? Here, Dennett suggests, the full answer must ultimately be provided by a new sort of theory, *intentional–system theory*, which will provide us with a *normative* account of rationality. This new theory "is envisaged as a close kin of—and overlapping with—such already existing disciplines as epistemic logic, decision theory and game theory, which are all similarly abstract, normative and couched in intentional language" (*Three Kinds*, p. 19). Of course, we already have some "rough and ready principles" of rationality which we can and do press into service pending a more detailed normative theory:

(1) A system's beliefs are those it *ought to have*, given its perceptual capacities, its epistemic needs, and its biography. Thus in general, its beliefs are both true and relevant to its life. . . .

(2) A system's desires are those it ought to have, given its biological needs and the most practicable means of satisfying them. Thus [naturally evolved] intentional systems desire survival and procreation, and hence desire food, security, health, sex, wealth, power, influence, and so forth, and also whatever local arrangements tend (in their eyes—given their beliefs) to further these ends in appropriate measure. . . .

(3) A system's behavior will consist of those acts that *it would be rational* for an agent with those beliefs and desires to perform. [*TK*, pp. 8–9]

Obviously these three principles are very rough and ready indeed. However, we also have a wealth of more detailed common–sense principles that anchor our intuitive notion of rationality. Some of these, in turn, are systematized and improved upon by existing theories in logic, evolutionary biology and decision theory. But though the intentional–system theorist can count on some help from these more developed disciplines, he still has a great deal of work to do. Neither singly nor severally do these disciplines tell us what beliefs a given organism or system ought to have, what desires it ought to have, or how it should act, given the beliefs and desires it has. Dennett has no illusions on the point. He portrays intentional-system theory—the general normative theory of rationality—as a discipline in its infancy. When the course of our argument requires some substantive premises about what it would be rational for a system to believe or do, we can follow Dennett's lead and let our common-sense intuitions be our guide.

I have been stressing the role of a normative theory of rationality in Dennett's account of the intentional stance. But there is a second, equally important, component in his view. According to Dennett, when we describe an organism or an artifact as an intentional system, we are making no commitments about the internal physical workings of the system. *Nor are we saying anything about the design or program of the system.* Just as a single program or design description is compatible with indefinitely many physical realizations, so too a single intentional description is compatible with indefinitely many different programs or design descriptions. To view an object as an intentional system, we must attribute to it a substantial range of beliefs and desires—the beliefs and desires it would be rational for such an object to have, given its nature and history. However, we need not assume that the beliefs and desires attributed correspond in any systematic way to internal states characterized either physically or functionally. Dennett makes the point vividly with the example of two robots each designed to be identical to a given person, Mary, when viewed from the intentional stance. The first robot, Ruth, "has internal processes which 'model' Mary's as closely as you like" (*BS*, p. 105). It is functionally identical to Mary, though the two may be quite different physically. Since Mary and Ruth share a common design or program, they will behave identically. Thus any beliefs and desires we attribute to Mary we may attribute also to Ruth, and the attributions will be equally useful in predicting their behavior. The second robot, Sally, has a program which is input-output equivalent to Ruth's, though it uses a quite different computational strategy. "Sally may not be a very good psychological model of Mary," since "Sally's response delays, errors and the like may not match Mary's." But at the level of common-sense descriptions of actions, all three will behave alike. ". . . the ascription of all Mary's beliefs and desires (etc.) to Sally will be just as predictive as their ascription to Ruth so far as prediction of action goes" (*BS*, p. 105). So when we adopt the intentional stance, Mary, Ruth and Sally are indistinguishable.

Dennett, then, is a self-professed instrumentalist about the beliefs and desires we ascribe to an object when we adopt the intentional stance toward it. "... the beliefs and other intentions of an intentional system need [not] be *represented* 'within' the system in any way for us to get a purchase on predicting its behavior by ascribing such intentions to it" (*BS*, p. 277). Rather, these "putative ... states" can be relegated "to the role of idealized fictions in an action-predicting, action-explaining calculus" (*BS*, p. 30). For Dennett, the belief and desire states of an intentional system are not what Reichenbach calls "illata—posited theoretical entities." Rather they are "abstracta—calculation bound entities or logical constructs" (*TK*, p. 13). Their status is analogous to the lines in a parallelogram of forces (*TK*, p. 20). Of course, it is conceivable that some objects which are usefully treated as intentional systems really do have internal states that correspond to the beliefs and desires ascribed to them in an intentional characterization. As some writers have suggested, there might be functionally distinct neural belief and desire stores where each belief and desire is inscribed in an appropriate neural code. Dennett, however, thinks this is not likely to be true for people, animals and other familiar intentional systems.[2] Be this as it may, the important point in the present context is that when we describe an object in intentional-system terms, we are quite explicitly *not* making any commitment about its workings, beyond the minimal claim that whatever the mechanism causally responsible for the behavior may be, it must be the sort of mechanism which will produce behavior generally predictable by assuming the intentional stance.

This completes my sketch of Dennett's notion of intentional systems. Let us now consider what Dennett wants to do with the notion. The principal project Dennett has in mind for intentional systems is "legitimizing" (*BS*, p. xvii), or providing a sort of "conceptual reduction" (*TK*, p. 30) of various notions in common-sense or folk psychology. The sort of legitimizing Dennett has in mind is explained by analogy with Church's Thesis. Church proposed that the informal, intuitive mathematical concept of an "effective" procedure be identified with the formal notion of a recursive (or Turing-machine computable) function. The proposal "is not provable, since it hinges on the intuitive and unformalizable notion of an effective procedure, but it is generally accepted, and it provides a very useful reduction of a fuzzy-but-useful mathematical notion to a crisply defined notion of apparently equal scope and greater power"(*BS*, p. xviii; cf. also *TK*, p. 30). It is

Dennett's hope to provide the same sort of legitimization of the notions of folk psychology by showing how these notions can be characterized in terms of the notions of intentional–system theory. "... the claim that every mental phenomenon alluded to in folk psychology is *intentional–system–characterizable* would, if true, provide a reduction of the mental as ordinarily understood—a domain whose boundaries are at best fixed by mutual acknowledgement and shared intuition—to a clearly defined domain of entities, whose principles of organization are familiar, relatively formal and systematic, and entirely general" (TK, pp. 30–31).

All this sounds reasonable enough—an exciting project, if Dennett can pull it off. The effort looks even more intriguing when we note how broadly Dennett intends to cast his net. It is his aim to show not only that such "program receptive" (BS, p. 29) features of mentality as belief and desire are intentional–system–characterizable, but also that "program resistant features of mentality" like pain, dreams, mental images, and even free will are "captured in the net of intentional systems" (BS, p. xviii). But a dark cloud looms on the horizon, one that will continue to plague us. In much of his work Dennett exhibits an exasperating tendency to make bold, flamboyant, fascinating claims in one breath, only to take them back, or seem to, in the next. Thus, scarcely a page after proclaiming his intention to show that a broad range of common–sense mental phenomena are intentional–system–characterizable and thus legitimized, Dennett proclaims himself to be an eliminative materialist concerning these very same phenomena. Beliefs, desires, pains, mental images, experiences—as these are ordinarily understood "are not good theoretical entities, however well entrenched" (BS, p. xx) the terms 'belief', 'pain', etc. may be in the habits of thought of our society. So "we legislate the putative items right out of existence" (BS, p. xx). How are we to make sense of this apparent contradiction?

There is, I think, a plausible—and uncontradictory—interpretation of what Dennett is up to. The problem he is grappling with is that the fit between our intuitive folk-psychological notions and the intentional–system characterizations he provides for them is just not as comfortable as the fit between the intuitive notion of effective mathematical procedure and the formal notion of Turing computability. Our folk–psychological concepts, "like folk productions generally," are complex, messy, variegated and in danger of incoherence (TK, p. 16). By contrast, notions characterized in terms of intentional–system theory are—it is to be hoped—coherent, sharply drawn and constructed with a self–conscious eye for their subsequent incorporation into science (*TK*, p. 6). The intentional–system analysans are intended to be improvements on their analysanda. What they give us is not an "anthropological" (*TK*, p. 6) portrait of our folk notions (warts and all), but rather an improved version of "the parts of folk psychology worth caring about" (*TK*, p. 30). So Dennett is an eliminative materialist about mental phenomena alluded to in warts–and–all folk psychology; what are intentional–system–characterizable are not the notions of folk psychology, but rather related successor concepts which capture all that's worth caring about.

But now what are we to make of the claim that the intentional system *Ersätze* capture all that's worth caring about in folk psychology? What *is* worth caring about? Dennett concedes that an "anthropological" study of unreconstructed folk notions which includes "whatever folk actually include in their theory, however misguided, incoherent, gratuitous some of it may be," (*TK*, p. 6) would be a perfectly legitimate endeavor. Folk theory may be myth, "but it is a myth we live in, so it is an 'important' phenomenon in nature" (*TK*, p. 6).[3] However, Dennett does not share the anthropologist's (or the cognitive simulator's) interest in the idiosyncracies and contradictions embedded in our folk notions. What is of interest to him, he strongly suggests, is "the proto–scientific quest": "an attempt to prepare folk theory for subsequent incorporation into or reduction to the rest of science," eliminating "all that is false or ill-founded" (*TK*, p. 6). If matters stopped there, we could parse Dennett's "all that's worth caring about" as "all that's worth caring about for the purposes of science." But matters do not stop there. To see why, we will have to take a detour to survey another central theme in Dennett's thinking.

As we have noted, a basic goal of Dennett's theory is to reconcile "our vision of ourselves as responsible, free, rational agents, and our vision of ourselves as complex parts of the physical world of science" (*BS*, p. x). The conflict that threatens between these two visions is a perennial philosophical preoccupation. "... the validity of our conceptual scheme of moral agents having dignity, freedom and responsibility stands or falls on the question: can men ever be truly said to have beliefs, desires, intentions? If they can, there is at least some hope of retaining a notion of the dignity of man; if they cannot, if men never can be said truly to want or believe, then surely they never can be said truly to act responsibly, or to have a conception of justice, or to know the difference between right and wrong" (*BS*, pp. 63–64). Yet many psychologists, most notoriously Skinner, have denied that people have beliefs, desires and other mental states.[4] This threat to our view of ourselves as moral agents does not arise only from rabid behaviorism. Dennett sees it lurking also in certain recently fashionable philosophical theories about the nature of mental states. Consider, for example, the type–type identity theory which holds that every mental-state type is to be identified with a physical-state type—a brain state characterized in physico–chemical terms. What if it should turn out that there simply is *no* physical-state type that is shared by all beings to whom we commonly attribute the belief that snow is white? If we hang on to the type–type identity theory, then this very plausible empirical finding would seem to entail that there is no such mental state as believing that snow is white. Much the same result threatens from those versions of functionalism which hold that "each mental type is identifiable as a functional type in the language of Turing machine description" (*BS*, p. xvi). For "there is really no more reason to believe you and I 'have the same program' in *any* relaxed and abstract sense, considering the differences in our nature and nurture, than that our brains have identical physico–chemical descriptions" (*BS*, p. xvi). So if we adhere to functionalism, a plausible result in cognitive psychology—the discovery that people do not have the same programs—threatens to establish that people do not have beliefs at all.[5]

We can now see one of the principal virtues of Dennett's instrumentalism about intentional systems. Since describing an object as an intentional system entails nothing whatever about either the physico–chemical nature or the functional design of the mechanism that causes the object's behavior, neither neurophysiology nor "sub–personal cognitive psychology" (which studies the functional organization or program of the organism) could possibly show that the object was not an intentional system . Thus if beliefs and desires (or some respectable *Ersätze*) can be characterized in terms of intentional-system theory, we need have no fear that advances in psychology or brain science might establish that people do not really have beliefs and desires. So the viability of our "conceptual scheme of moral agents" is sustained, in this quarter at least.[6]

Now, finally, it is clear how Dennett's preoccupation with moral themes bears on his eliminative materialism. Recall that Dennett proposes to trade our ungainly folk-psychological notions for concepts characterized in terms of intentional systems. The claim is not that the new concepts are identical with the old, but that they are *better*. They are clearer, more systematic, free from the incoherence lurking in folk notions, *and they capture everything in folk psychology that is worth caring about*. One of the things worth caring about, for Dennett, is the suitability of the clarified notions for incorporation into science. However, if he is to succeed in insulating our moral world-view from the threat posed by scientific psychology, then there is obviously something else Dennett must count as worth caring about. The new concepts built from intentional-system notions must be as serviceable as the older folk notions in sustaining our vision of ourselves as persons.

II

In this section I want to examine just how well Dennett's intentional system *Ersätze* mirror the notions of folk psychology. My focus will be on the "program receptive" notions of belief and desire, concepts which should be easiest to purchase "with intentional coin," and my claim will be that the fit between our common-sense notions and Dennett's proffered replacements is a very poor one.[7] Of course, Dennett does not maintain that the fit is perfect, only that intentional-system theory preserves "the parts of folk psychology worth caring about" (*TK*, p. 30). This is the doctrine I am concerned to challenge. On my view, the move to an intentional-system-characterized notion of belief would leave us unable to say a great deal that we wish to say about ourselves and our fellows. Moreover, the losses will be important ones. If we accept Dennett's trade, we will have no coherent way to describe our cognitive shortcomings nor the process by which we may learn to overcome them. Equally unwelcome, the thriving scientific study of the strengths and weaknesses of human reasoning would wither and die, its hypotheses ruled literally incoherent. What is more, the instrumentalism of Dennett's intentional-system notions seems to fly in the face of some deeply rooted intuitions about responsibility and moral agency. Throughout most of what follows, I will cleave to the fiction that we already have a tolerably well worked out normative theory of rationality, or could readily build one, though in the closing pages I will offer some skeptical thoughts about how likely this fiction is.

I begin with the problems posed by irrationality. An intentional system, recall, is an ideally rational system; it believes, wants and does just what it ought to, as stipulated by a normative theory of rationality. People, by contrast, are not ideally rational, and therein lies a devastating problem for Dennett. If we were to adopt his suggestion and trade up to the intentional-system notions of belief and desire (hereafter IS belief & IS desire), then we simply would not be able to say all those things we need to say about ourselves and our fellows when we deal with each other's idiosyncrasies, shortcomings, and cognitive growth.

Consider belief. Presumably no system *ought* to hold contradictory beliefs, and all systems *ought* to believe all the logical truths, along with all the logical consequences of what they believe (cf. *BS*, pp. 11, 20, 44; *TK*, p. 11). But people depart from this ideal in a variety of ways. We generally fail to believe *all* logical consequences of our beliefs—sometimes because the reasoning required would be difficult, and sometimes because we simply fail to take account of one or more of our beliefs. Suppose, for example, that an astronaut set the controls incorrectly and has sent his craft into a perilous spin. One possible explanation of his mistake would be that the on-board computer was down, and he had to hand-calculate the setting for the controls. He made a mistake in the calculation, and thus came to have a mistaken belief about what the setting should be. Another possibility is that, although he knew the craft was in the gravitational field of a nearby asteroid—indeed he could see it through the window—he simply forgot to take this into account in figuring out where the control should be set. There is nothing in the least paradoxical about these explanations. We offer similar explanations all the time in explaining our own actions and those of other people. Indeed, since these explanations are so intimately bound up with our notions of excuse and blame, quick-wittedness, absent-mindedness and a host of others, it boggles the mind to try imagining how we would get on with each other if we resolved to renounce them. But if, following Dennett, we agree to swap the folk notion of belief for the intentional-system notion, then renounce them we must. It simply makes no sense to attribute inferential failings or inconsistent beliefs to an ideally rational system.

Our intuitive grasp on the notion of rational desire is rather more tenuous than our grasp on the analogous notion for belief. Still, there seem to be many cases in which we want to ascribe desires to people which are not rational on any plausible reading of that term. Jones is a successful writer, in good health, with many friends and admirers. But he says he wants to die, and ultimately takes his own life. Smith has a dreadful allergy to chocolate, and he knows it. One taste and he is condemned to a week of painful, debilitating hives. But he *really* wants that chocolate bar at the checkout counter. After staring at it for a minute, he buys it and gobbles it down. Brown collects spiders. They are of no economic value, and he doesn't even think they are very pretty. But it is his hobby. He wants to add to his collection a specimen of a species found only in the desert. So, despite his dislike of hot weather, he arranges to spend his vacation spider hunting in Nevada. By my lights, both Jones' desire and Smith's are simply irrational. As for Brown, "irrational" seems much too strong. Yet it is certainly implausible to say that he *ought* to want that spider. So, on Dennett's account, it is not a rational desire. But idealized intentional systems have all and only the desires they ought to have. Thus if we trade the common-sense notion of want for Dennett's IS want, we simply will not be able to say that Brown wants the spider or that Jones wants to die.

The existence of examples like the ones I have been sketching is not news to Dennett. From his earliest paper on intentional systems to his most recent, he has struggled with analogous cases. Unfortunately, however, he is far from clear on what he proposes to do about them. As I read him, there are two quite differnet lines that he proposes; I will call them the *hard line* and the *soft line*. Neither is carefully spelled out in Dennett's writings, and he often seems to endorse both within a single paper. Once they have been sharply stated, I think it will be clear that neither line is tenable.

The Hard Line

The hard line sticks firmly with the idealized notion of an intentional system and tries to minimize the importance of the gap between IS beliefs and IS desires and their folk-psychological namesakes. The basic ploy here is to suggest that when folk psychology ascribes contradictory beliefs to people or when it insists that a person does not believe some of the consequences of his beliefs, folk psychology undermines its own usefulness and threatens to lapse into incoherence. When this happens, we are forced back to the design stance or the physical stance:

> The presumption of rationality is so strongly entrenched in our inference habits that when our predictions [based on the assumption] prove false, we at first cast about for adjustments in the information possession conditions (he must not have heard, he must not know English, he must not have seen x, . . .) or goal weightings, before questioning the rationality of the system as a

whole. In extreme cases personalities may prove to be so unpredictable from the intentional stance that we abandon it, and if we have accumulated a lot of evidence in the meanwhile about the nature of response patterns in the individual, we may find that a species of design stance can be effectively adopted. This is the fundamentally different attitude we occasionally adopt toward the insane. [*BS*, pp. 9–10]

Here, surely, Dennett is *just wrong* about what we do when predictions based on idealized rationality prove false. When a neighborhood boy gives me the wrong change from my purchase at his lemonade stand, I do not assume that he believes quarters are only worth 23¢, nor that he wants to cheat me out of the 2¢ I am due. My *first* assumption is that he is not yet very good at doing sums in his head. Similarly, when a subject working on one of Wason & Johnson–Laird's deceptively difficult reasoning tasks gets the wrong answer, we are not likely to assume that he didn't understand the instructions, nor that he didn't want to get the right answer. Our *first* assumption is that he blew it; he made a mistake in reasoning.[8] What misleads Dennett here is that he is focusing on cases of counter–intuitive or unfamiliar cognitive failings. When someone seems to have made a mistake we can't readily imagine ourselves ever making, we do indeed begin to wonder whether he might perhaps have some unanticipated beliefs and desires. Or if a person seems to be making enormous numbers of mistakes and ending up with a substantial hoard of bizarre beliefs, we grow increasingly reluctant to ascribe beliefs and desires to him at all. Perhaps we count him among the insane. These facts will assume some importance later on. But they are of little use to the hard–line defense of intentional systems. For it is in the diverse domain of more or less familiar inferential shortcomings that common sense most readily and usefully portrays people as departing from an idealized standard of rationality.

Dennett frequently suggests that we cannot coherently describe a person whose beliefs depart from the idealized standard:

> Conflict arises . . . when a person falls short of perfect rationality, and avows beliefs that either are strongly disconfirmed by the available empirical evidence or are self–contradictory or contradict other avowals he has made. If we lean on the myth that a man is perfectly rational, we must find his avowals less than authoritative: "You *can't* mean—understand—what you're saying!;" if we lean on his right as a speaking intentional system

to have his word accepted, we grant him an irrational set of beliefs. Neither position provides a stable resting place; for, as we saw earlier, *intentional explanation and prediction cannot be accommodated either to breakdown or to less than optimal design, so there is no coherent intentional description of such an impasse.* [*BS*, 20, last emphasis added][9]

In the paper from which the quote is taken, Dennett uses 'intentional description', 'intentional explanation' and the like for both common-sense belief-desire accounts and idealized intentional system accounts. The ambiguity this engenders is crucial in evaluating his claim. On the idealized intentional systems reading it is a tautology that "there is no coherent intentional description of such an impasse." But on the common-sense reading it is simply false. There is nothing at all incoherent about a (common-sense) intentional description of a man who has miscalculated the balance in his checking account!

The fact that folk psychology often comfortably and unproblematically views people as departing from the standard of full rationality often looms large in cases where questions of morality and responsibility are salient. Consider the case of Oscar, the engineer. It is his job to review planned operations at the factory and halt those that might lead to explosion. But one day there is an explosion and, bureaucracy being what it is, three years later Oscar is called before a board of inquiry. Why didn't he halt the hazardous operation? It looks bad for Oscar, since an independent expert has testified that the data Oscar had logically entail a certain equation, and it is a commonplace amongst competent safety engineers that the equation is a sure sign of trouble. But Oscar has an impressive defense. Granted the data he had entails the equation, and granted any competent engineer would know that the equation is a sign of trouble. But at the time of the accident neither Oscar nor anyone else knew that the data logically entailed the equation. It was only six months after the accident that Professor Brain at Cambridge proved a fundamental theorem needed to show that the data entail the equation. Without knowledge of the theorem, neither Oscar nor anyone else could be expected to believe that the data entail the equation.

At several places Dennett cites Quine as a fellow defender of the view that the ascription of inconsistent beliefs is problematic.

To echo a theme I have long cherished in Quine's work, all the evidence—behavioral *and internal*—we acquire for the correctness of one of these ascriptions is not only evidence against the other, but the best sort of evidence. [*Reply*, p. 74]

However, Dennett misconstrues Quine's point. What Quine urges is not that *any* inconsistency is evidence of bad translation (or bad belief ascription), but rather that *obvious* inconsistency is a sign that something has gone wrong. For Quine, unlike Dennett, sees translation (and belief ascription) as a matter of putting ourselves in our subject's shoes. And the self we put in those shoes, we are too well aware, departs in many ways from the standard of optimal rationality. The point can be made vividly by contrasting Oscar, our safety engineer, with Otto, a lesser functionary. Otto is charged with the responsibility of memorizing a list of contingency plans: If the red light flashes, order the building evacuated; if the warning light goes on, turn the big blue valve; if the buzzer sounds, alert the manager. Now suppose that while he is on duty the red light flashes but Otto fails to order an evacuation. There is a strong *prima facie* case that Otto is to be held responsible for the consequences. Either he failed to see the light (he was asleep or not paying due attention), or he did not memorize the contingency plans as he was obligated to, or he has some sinister motive. But, and this is the crucial point, it will be no excuse for Otto to claim that he had memorized the plan, saw the light, and was paying attention, but it just never occurred to him to order the evacuation. It is in these cases of apparently blatant or "incomprehensible" irrationality that we hunt first for hidden motives or beliefs. For, absent these, the subject must be judged irrational in a way we cannot imagine ourselves being irrational; and it is this sort of irrationality that threatens the application of our common-sense notions of belief and desire.

In Dennett's writings there are frequent hints of a second strategy for defending the hard line, a strategy which relies on an evolutionary argument. He cheerfully concedes that he has "left [his] claim about the relation between rationality and evolutionary considerations so open-ended that it is hard to argue against efficiently" (*R*, p. 73). Still, I think it is important to try ringing some arguments out of Dennett's vague meditations on this topic. As I read him, Dennett is exploring a pair of ideas for showing that the gap between IS notions and folk notions is much smaller than some have feared. If he can show this, the hard line will have been vindicated.

The first idea is suggested by a passage (*BS*, pp. 8–9) in which Dennett asks whether we could adopt the intentional stance toward exotic creatures encountered on an alien planet. His answer is that we could, provided "we have reason to suppose that a process of natural selection has been in effect . . . " (*BS*, p. 8). The argument seems to be that natural selection favors true beliefs, and thus will favor cognitive processes which generally yield true beliefs in the organism's natural environment. So if an organism is the product of natural selection, we can safely assume that most of its beliefs will be true, and most of its belief–forming strategies will be rational. Departures from the normative standard required by the intentional stance will be few and far between.

For two quite different reasons, this argument is untenable. First, it is simply not the case that natural selection favors true beliefs over false ones. What natural selection does favor, is beliefs which yield selective advantage. And there are many environmental circumstances in which false beliefs will be more useful than true ones. In these circumstances, natural selection ought to favor cognitive processes which yield suitable false beliefs and disfavor processes which yield true beliefs. Moreover, even when having true beliefs is optimal, natural selection may often favor a process that yields false beliefs most of the time, but which has a high probability of yielding true beliefs when it counts. Thus, for example, in an environment with a wide variety of suitable foods, an organism may do very well if it radically overgeneralizes about what is inedible. If eating a certain food caused illness on a single occasion, the organism would immediately come to believe (falsely, let us assume) that all passingly similar foods are poisonous as well. When it comes to food poisoning, *better safe than sorry* is a policy that recommends itself to natural selection.[10]

The second fault in the argument I am attributing to Dennett is a subtle but enormously important one. As stated, the argument slips almost unnoticeably from the claim that natural selection favors cognitive processes which yield true beliefs in the natural environment to the claim that natural selection favors *rational* belief–forming strategies. But, even if the first claim were true, the second would not follow. There are many circumstances in which inferential strategies which from a normative standpoint are patently invalid will nonetheless generally yield the right answer. The social–psychology literature is rich with illustrations of inferential strategies which stand subjects in good stead ordinarily, but which subjects readily overextend, with unhappy results.[11]

So long as we recognize a distinction between a normative theory of inference or decision making and a set of inferential practices which (in the right environment) generally get the right (or selectively useful) answer, it will be clear that the two need not, and generally do not, coincide. However, in a number of places Dennett seems to be suggesting that there really *is* no distinction here, that by "normative theory of inference and decision" he simply *means* "practices favored by natural selection." This move is at the core of the second idea I see in Dennett for using evolutionary notions to buttress the hard line. (Cf. *R*, pp. 73–74.) And buttress it would! For it would then become *tautologous* that naturally evolved creatures are intentional systems, believing, wanting and doing what they ought, save when they are malfunctioning. Yet Dennett will have to pay a heavy price for turning the hard line into a tautology. For if *this* is what he means by "normative theory of belief and decision," then such established theories as deductive and inductive logic, decision theory and game theory are of no help in assessing what an organism "ought to believe." Natural selection, as we have already noted, sometimes smiles upon cognitive processes that depart substantially from the canons of logic and decision theory. So these established theories and our guesses about how to extend them will be of no help in assessing what an intentional system should believe, desire or do. Instead, to predict from the intentional stance we should need a detailed study of the organism's physiology, its ecological environment and its history. But predicting from the intentional stance, characterized in *this* way, is surely not to be recommended when we "doubt the practicality of prediction from the design or physical stance" (*BS*, p. 8). Nor, obviously, does *this* intentional stance promise to yield belief and desire attributions that are all but co-extensive with those made in common sense.

This is all I shall have to say by way of meeting the hard line head on. I think it is fair to conclude that the hard line simply cannot be maintained. The differences separating the IS notions of belief and desire from their common-sense counterparts is anything but insubstantial. Before turning to Dennett's soft line, we should note a further unwelcome consequence of rejecting folk psychology in favor of intentional-system theory. During the last decade, cognitive psychologists have become increasingly interested in studying the strengths and foibles of human reasoning. There is a substantial and growing literature aimed at uncovering predictable departures from normative standards of reasoning and decision making, almost all of it implicitly or explicitly cast in the idiom of folk psychology.[12] Were we to replace folk notions with their intentional-system analogues, we should have to conclude that all of this work limning the boundaries of human rationality is simply incoherent. For, as Dennett notes, "the presuppositions of intentional explanation . . . put prediction of *lapses* in principle beyond its scope. . ."[13] (*BS*, p. 246).

The Soft Line

In contrast with the hard line, which tries to minimize the size or importance of the difference between folk and IS notions, the soft line acknowledges a substantial and significant divergence. To deal with the problems this gap creates, the soft line proposes some fiddling with the idealized notion of an intentional system. The basic idea is that once we have an idealized theory of intentional systems in hand, we can study an array of variations on the idealized theme. We can construct theories about "imperfect intentional systems" (the term is mine, not Dennett's) which have specified deficiencies in memory, reasoning power, etc. And we can attempt to determine empirically which imperfect intentional system best predicts the behavior of a particular subject or species. Rather than assuming the intentional stance toward an organism or person, we may assume one of a range of "imperfect intentional stances," from which it will make sense to ascribe a less than fully rational set of beliefs and desires. From these various stances we can give intentional descriptions of our cognitive shortcomings and elaborate an empirical science which maps the inferential strengths and weaknesses of humans and other creatures. We can also legitimize our folk-psychological descriptions of ourselves—protecting "personhood from the march of science" (*R*, p. 75)—by appeal to the imperfect-intentional-system theory which best predicts our actual behavior. But *genuine* intentional-system theory (*sans phrase*) would have a definite pride of place among these theories of imperfect intentional systems. For all of the latter would be variations on the basic IS framework.

Dennett, with his disconcerting penchant for working both sides of the street, never flatly endorses the soft line, though it is clear that he has pondered something like it:

> Consider a set T of transformations that take beliefs into beliefs. The problem is to determine the set T_s for each intentional system S, so that if we know that S believes p, we will be able to determine other things that S believes by seeing what the transformations of p are for T_s. If S were ideally rational, every valid transformation would be in T_s; S would believe every logical consequence of every belief (and, ideally, S would have no false beliefs). Now we know that no actual intentional system will be ideally rational; so

we must suppose any actual system will have a T with less in it. But we also know that, to qualify as an intentional system at all, S must have a T with some integrity; T cannot be empty. [*BS*, p. 21]

In the next few sentences, however, Dennett expresses qualms about the soft line:

What rationale could we have, however, for fixing some set between the extremes and calling it *the* set for belief (for S, for earthlings, for ten-year-old-girls)? This is another way of asking whether we could replace Hintikka's normative theory of belief with an empirical theory of belief, and, if so, what evidence we would use. "Actually," one is tempted to say, "people do believe contradictions on occasion, as their utterances demonstrate; so any adequate logic of belief or analysis of the concept of belief must accommodate this fact." But any attempt to *legitimize* human fallibility in a theory of belief by fixing a permissible level of error would be like adding one more rule to chess: an Official Tolerance Rule to the effect that any game of chess containing no more than k moves that are illegal relative to the other rules of the game is a legal game of chess. [*BS*, p. 21]

In a more recent paper, Dennett sounds more enthusiastic about the soft line:

Of course we don't all sit in the dark in our studies like mad Leibnizians rationalistically excogitating behavioral predictions from pure, idealized concepts of our neighbors, nor do we derive all our readiness to attribute desires to a careful generation of them from the ultimate goal of survival. . . . Rationalistic generation of attributions is augmented and even corrected on occasion by empirical generalizations about belief and desire that guide our attributions and are learned more or less inductively. . . .
I grant the existence of all this naturalistic generalization, and its role in the normal calculation of folk psychologists—i.e., all of us. . . . *I would insist, however, that all this empirically obtained lore is laid over a fundamental generative and normative framework that has the features I have described.* [*TK*, pp. 14–15, last emphasis added]

Whatever Dennett's considered view may be, I think the soft line is clearly preferable to the hard line. Indeed, the soft line is similar to a view that I have myself defended.[14] As a way of focusing in on my misgivings about the soft line, let me quickly sketch my own view and note how it differs from the view I am trying to foist on Dennett. Mine is an effort squarely situated in what Dennett calls "the anthropological quest" (*TK*, p. 6). I want to describe as accurately as possible just what we are up to when we engage in the "folk practice" of ascribing beliefs to one another and dealing with one another partly on the basis of these ascriptions. My theory is an elaboration on Quine's observation that in ascribing beliefs to others "we project ourselves into what, from his remarks and other indications, we imagine the speaker's state of mind to have been, and then we say what, in our language, is natural and relevant for us in the state thus feigned" (*Word & Object*, p. 219). As I see it, when we say *S believes that p* we are saying that S is in a certain sort of functionally characterized psychological state, viz., a "belief state." The role of the "content sentence," p, is to specify *which* belief state it is. If we imagine that we ourselves were now to utter p in earnest, the belief we are attributing to S is one *similar* (along specified dimensions) to the belief which would cause our own imagined assertion. One of the dimensions of similarity that figures in belief ascription is the pattern of inference that the belief states in question enter into. When the network of potential inferences surrounding a subject's belief state differs substantially from the network surrounding our own belief that p, we are reluctant to count the subject's belief as a belief *that p*. Thus we will not have any comfortable way of ascribing content to the belief states of a subject whose inferential network is markedly different from ours. Since we take ourselves to approximate rationality, this explains the fact, noted by Dennett, that intentional description falters in the face of egregious irrationality. It also explains the fact, missed by Dennett, that familiar irrationality—the sort we know ourselves to be guilty of—poses no problem for folk psychology.

A full elaboration of my theory would be a long story, out of place here. What is important for our present purposes is to note the differences between my account and what I have been calling Dennett's soft line. These differences are two. First, my story does not portray folk psychology as an *instrumentalist* theory. Belief states are *functional* states which can and do play a role in the causation of behavior. Thus folk psychology is not immune from the advance of science. If it turns out that the human brain does not have the sort of functional organization assumed in our folk theory, then there are no such things as beliefs and desires. Second, the notion of idealized rationality plays *no role at all* in my account. In ascribing content to belief states, we measure others not against an idealized standard but against ourselves. It is in virtue of this Protagorean parochialism that the exotic and the insane fall outside the reach of intentional explanation.

So much for the difference between my view and Dennett's. Why should mine be preferred? There are two answers. First, I think it is simply wrong that we ordinarily conceive of beliefs and desires in instrumentalist terms—as abstracta rather than illata. It is, however, no easy task to take aim at Dennett's instrumentalism, since the target refuses to stay still. Consider:

> Folk psychology is *instrumentalistic*. . . . Beliefs and desires of folk psychology . . . are abstracta. [*TK*, p. 13]

> It is not particularly to the point to argue against me that folk psychology is *in fact* committed to beliefs and desires as distinguishable, causally interacting *illata*; what must be shown is that it ought to be. The latter claim I will deal with in due course. The former claim I *could* concede without embarrassment to my overall project, but I do not concede it, for it seems to me that the evidence is quite strong that our ordinary notion of belief has next to nothing of the concrete in it. [*TK*, p. 15]

> The *ordinary* notion of belief no doubt does place beliefs somewhere midway between being *illata* and being *abstracta*. [*TK*, p. 16]

In arguing for his sometimes instrumentalism Dennett conjures the sad tale of Pierre, shot dead by Jacques in Trafalgar Square. Jacques

> is apprehended on the spot by Sherlock; Tom reads about it in the *Times* and Boris learns of it in *Pravda*. Now Jacques, Sherlock, Tom and Boris have had remarkably different experiences—to say nothing of their earlier biographies and future prospects—but there is one thing they share: they all believe that a Frenchman has committed a murder in Trafalgar Square. They did not all *say* this, not even "to themselves"; *that proposition* did not, we can suppose, "occur to" any of them, and even if it had, it would have had entirely different import for Jacques, Sherlock, Tom and Boris. [*TK*, p. 15]

Dennett's point is that while all four men believe that a Frenchman committed a murder in Trafalgar Square, their histories, interests and relations to the deed are so different that they could hardly be thought to share a single, functionally characterizable state. This is quite right, but it does not force us to view beliefs as abstracta. For if, as my theory insists, there is a *similarity* claim embedded in belief ascriptions, then we should expect these ascriptions to be both vague and sensitive to pragmatic context. For Jacques and Boris both to believe that a Frenchman committed a murder in Trafalgar Square, they need not be in the very same functional state, but only in states that are sufficiently similar for the communicative purposes at hand.

As Dennett notes, one need not be crucially concerned with what "folk psychology is in fact committed to." Since he aims to replace folk psychology with intentional–system notions, it would suffice to show that the instrumentalism of these latter notions is no disadvantage. But here again I am skeptical. It is my hunch that our concept of ourselves as moral agents simply will not sit comfortably with the view that beliefs and desires are mere computational conveniences that correspond in no interesting way to what goes on inside the head. I cannot offer much of an argument for my hunch, though I am encouraged by the fact that Dennett seems to share the intuition lying behind it:

> Stich accurately diagnoses and describes the strategic role I envisage for the concept of an intentional system, permitting the claim that human beings are genuine believers and desirers to survive almost any imaginable discoveries in cognitive and physiological psychology, thus making our status as moral agents well neigh invulnerable to scientific disconfirmation. Not 'in principle' invulnerable, for in a science–fiction mood we can imagine startling discoveries (e.g., some 'people' are organic puppets remotely controlled by Martians) that would upset any particular home truths about believers and moral agenthood you like. . . . [R, p. 73]

Now if our concept of moral agenthood were really compatible with the intentional–system construal of beliefs and desires, it is hard to see why the imagined discovery about Martians should be in the least unsettling. For, controlled by Martians or not, organic puppets are still intentional systems in perfectly good standing. So long as their behavior is usefully predictable from the intentional stance, the transceivers inside their heads sanction no skepticism about whether they really have IS beliefs and IS desires. But Dennett is right, of course. We would not count his organic puppets as believers or moral agents. The reason, I submit, is that the morally relevant concept of belief is not an instrumentalistic concept.

The second reason for preferring my line to Dennett's soft line is that the idea of a *normative* theory of beliefs and desires, which is central to Dennett's view, plays no role in mine. And this notion, I would urge, is one we are best rid of. Recall that from the outset we have been relying on rough and ready intuitions about what an organism ought to believe, desire and do, and assuming that these intuitions could be elaborated and systematized into a theory. But I am inclined to think that this assumption is mistaken. Rather, it would appear that the intuitions Dennett exploits are underlain by a variety of different ideas about what an organism ought to believe or desire, ideas which as often as not pull in quite different directions. Sometimes it is an evolutionary story which motivates the intuition that a belief or desire is the one a well-designed intentional system should have. At other times intuitions are guided by appeal to logic or decision theory. But as we have seen, the evolutionary account of what an organism ought to believe and desire just will not do for Dennett, since it presupposes an abundance of information about the ecological niche and physiological workings of the organism. Nor is there any serious prospect of elaborating logic and decision theory into a suitably general account of what an organism ought to believe and desire. Indeed, apart from a few special cases, I think our intuitions about what an organism ought to believe and desire are simply nonexistent. The problem is not merely that we lack a worked-out normative theory of belief and desire; it runs much deeper. For in general we have no idea what such a normative theory would be telling us. We do not really know what it *means* to say that an organism *ought to have* a given belief or desire. Consider some examples:

Ought Descartes to have believed his theory of vortices?
Ought Nixon to have believed that he would not be impeached?
Ought William James to have believed in the existence of a personal God?
Should all people have perfect memories, retaining for life all beliefs save those for which they later acquire negative evidence?

In each of these cases our grasp of what the question is supposed to *mean* is at best tenuous. The prospects of a *general theory* capable of answering all of them in a motivated way are surely very dim. Worse still, the general theory of intentional systems that Dennett would have us work toward must tell us not only what *people* in various situations ought to believe, but also what other animals ought to believe. Ought the frog to believe that there is an insect flying off to the right? Or merely that there is some food there? Or perhaps should it only have a conditional belief: if it flicks its tongue in a certain way, something yummy will end up in its mouth?

Suppose the fly is of a species that causes frogs acute indigestion. Ought the frog to believe this? Does it make a difference how many fellow frogs he has seen come to grief after munching on similar bugs? A normative theory of desire is, if anything, more problematic. Should I want to father as many offspring as possible? Should the frog?

To the extent that these questions are obscure, the notion of a normative theory of belief and desire is obscure. And that obscurity in turn infects much of what Dennett says about intentional systems and the intentional stance. Perhaps Dennett can dispel some of the mystery. But in the interim I am inclined to think that the normatively appropriate attitude is the skepticism I urged in my opening paragraph.[15]

NOTES

1. References to Dennett's writings will be identified in parentheses in the text. I will use the following abbreviations:

BS = Daniel Dennett, *Brainstorms* (Montgomery, VT: Bradford Books, 1978).

TK = Daniel Dennett, "Three Kinds of Intentional Psychology," forthcoming in a Thyssen Philosophy Group volume edited by R. A. Healey. (The manuscript from which I quote is dated November, 1978.)

R = Daniel Dennett, "Reply to Professor Stich," *Philosophical Books*, 21, 2 (April, 1980).

TB = Daniel Dennett, "True Believers: The Intentional Strategy and Why It Works," forthcoming in a volume of 1979 Herbert Spencer Lectures on the topic of Scientific Explanation (Oxford University Press).

2. For his arguments on this point, cf., "Brain Writing and Mind Reading," (BS, pp. 39–50) and "A Cure for the Common Code," (BS, pp. 90–108).

3. This "anthropological quest," when pursued systematically is the business of the cognitive simulator. Cf., for example, Roger Shank & Robert Abelson, *Scripts, Plans, Goals and Understanding* (Hillsdale, NJ: Lawrence Erlbaum Associates, 1977); also Aaron Sloman, *The Computer Revolution in Philosophy* (Atlantic Highlands, NJ: Humanities Press, 1978), chapter 4.

4. Skinner often muddies the waters by claiming to offer "translations" of common–sense mentalistic terms into the language of behaviorism. But, as Dennett and others have noted, (BS, pp. 53–70) these "translations" generally utterly fail to capture the meaning or even the extension of the common–sense term being "translated."

5. For an elaboration of the point, cf. Thomas Nagel, "Armstrong on the Mind," *Philosophical Review*, 79 (1970) pp. 394–403.

6. An entirely parallel strategy works for those other common–sense mental phenomena which Dennett takes to be essential to our concept of ourselves as persons—e.g., consciousness (BS, p. 269). If we can give an acceptable intentional system *Ersätz* for the folk–psychological notion of consciousness, we need have no fear that advances in science will threaten our personhood by showing that the notion of consciousness is otiose in the causal explanation of our behavior.

7. For some qualms about Dennett's treatment of "program resistant" features of mentality like pains, see my "Headaches," *Philosophical Books*, April, 1980.

8. Cf., P. C. Wason & P. N. Johnson–Laird, *The Psychology of Human Reasoning: Structure and Content* (London: B. T. Batsford, Ltd., 1972).

9. For parallel passages, cf., *TB*, p. 19; *R*, p. 74; *BS*, p. 22.

10. For a detailed discussion of some examples and further references, cf., H. A. Lewis,"The Argument From Evolution," *Proceedings of the Aristotelian Society*, Supplementary Vol. LIII, 1979, also my "Could Man Be an Irrational Animal?" (forthcoming).

11. Cf., Richard Nisbett & Lee Ross, *Human Inference* (Englewood Cliffs, NJ: Prentice–Hall, 1980).

12. E.g., Nisbett & Ross, op. cit., and Wason & Johnson–Laird, op. cit., along with the many studies cited in these books.

13. Dennett appends the following footnote to the quoted sentence: "In practice we predict lapses at the intentional level ('You watch! He'll forget all about your knight after you move the queen') on the basis of loose–jointed inductive hypotheses about individual or widespread human frailties. These hypotheses are expressed in intentional terms, but if they were given rigorous support, they would in the process be recast as predictions from the design or physical stance" (*BS*, p. 246). So the scientific study of intentionally described inferential shortcomings can aspire to no more than "loose–jointed hypotheses" in need of recasting. But cf. *TK*, pp. 11–12, where Dennett pulls in his horns a bit.

14. In "On The Ascription of Content," to appear in A. Woodfield, ed. *Thought and Object*, Oxford University Press.

15. I have learned a good deal from the helpful comments of Bo Dahlbom, Robert Cummins, Philip Pettit and Robert Richardson.

Making Sense of Ourselves

DANIEL C. DENNETT
Tufts University

Stich has (again[1]) given a lively, sympathetic, and generally accurate account of my view and once again he disagrees, this time with more detailed objections and counterproposals. My proposed refinement of the folk notion of belief (via the concept of an *intentional system*) would, he claims, "leave us unable to say a great deal that we now wish to say about ourselves." For this to be an objection, he must mean it would leave us unable to say a great deal we *rightly* want to say—because it is true, presumably. We must see what truths, then, he supposes are placed out of reach by my account. Many of them lie, he says, in the realm of facts about our cognitive shortcomings, which can be given no coherent description according to my account: "if we trade up to the intentional–system notions of belief and desire . . . then we simply would not be able to say all those things we need to say about ourselves and our fellows when we deal with each other's idiosyncracies, shortcomings, and cognitive growth" (p. 48). He gives several examples. Among them are the forgetful astronaut, the boy at the lemonade stand who gives the wrong change, and the man who has miscalculated the balance in his checking account. These three are cases of simple, unmysterious cognitive failure—cases of people *making mistakes*—and Stich claims that my view cannot accommodate them. One thing that is striking about all three cases is that in spite of Stich's summary expression of his objection, these are *not* cases of "familiar irrationality" or cases of "inferential failings" at all. They are not cases of what we would *ordinarily* call irrationality, and since there are quite compelling cases of what we *would* ordinarily call irrationality (and since Stich knows them and indeed cites some of the best documented cases[2]), it is worth asking why he cites instead these cases of miscalculation as proof against my view. I shall address this question shortly, but first I should grant that these are in any case examples of suboptimal behavior of the sort my view is not supposed to be able to handle.

I hold that such errors, as either *malfunctions* or the outcomes of *misdesign*, are unpredictable from the intentional stance, a claim with which Stich might agree, but I go on to claim that there will inevitably be an instability or problematic point in the mere *description* of such lapses at the intentional system level—at the level at which it is the agent's beliefs and desires that are attributed. And here it seems at first that Stich must be right. For although we seldom if ever suppose we can *predict* people's particular mistakes from our ordinary folk-psychological perspective, there seems to be nothing more straightforward than the folk-psychological *description* of such familiar cases. This presumably is part of the reason why Stich chose these cases: they are so uncontroversial.

Let's look more closely, though, at one of the cases, adding more detail. The boy's sign says "LEMONADE—12 cents a glass." I hand him a quarter, he gives me a glass of lemonade and then a dime and a penny change. He's made a mistake. Now what can we *expect* from him when we point out his error to him? That he will exhibit surprise, blush, smite his forehead, apologize, and give me two cents. Why do we expect him to exhibit surprise? Because we attribute to him the belief that he's given me the right change—he'll be surprised to learn that he hasn't.[3] Why do we expect him to blush? Because we attribute to him the desire not to cheat (or be seen to cheat) his customers. Why do we expect him to smite his forehead or give some other acknowledgment of his lapse? Because we attribute to him not only the belief that $25 - 12 = 13$, but also the belief that that's obvious, and the belief that no one his age should make any mistakes about it. While we can't predict his particular error—though we might have made an actuarial prediction that he'd probably make some such error before the day was out—we can pick up the skein of our intentional interpretation once he has made his mistake and predict his further reactions and activities with no more than the usual attendant risk. At first glance then it seems that belief attribution in this instance is as easy, predictive and stable as it ever is.

But now look yet more closely. The boy has made a mistake all right, but *exactly which mistake*? This all depends, of course, on how we tell the tale—there are many different possibilities. But no matter which story we tell, we will uncover a problem. For instance, we might plausibly suppose that so far as all our evidence to date goes, the boy believes:

(1) that he has given me the right change
(2) that I gave him a quarter
(3) that his lemonade costs 12 cents
(4) that a quarter is 25 cents
(5) that a dime is 10 cents
(6) that a penny is 1 cent
(7) that he gave me a dime and a penny change

(8) that $25 - 12 = 13$
(9) that $10 + 1 = 11$
(10) that $11 \neq 13$

Only (1) is a false belief, but how can he be said to believe *that* if he believes all the others? It surely is not plausible to claim that he has *mis-inferred* (1) from any of the others, directly or indirectly. That is, we would not be inclined to attribute to him the inference of (1) directly from (7) and—what? Perhaps he would infer

(11) that he gave me 11 cents change

from (9) and (7)—he *ought to*, after all—but *it would not make sense* to suppose he *inferred* (1) from (11) unless he were under the misapprehension

(12) that 11 cents is the right change from a quarter.

We would expect him to believe *that* if he believed

(13) that $25 - 12 = 11$

and while we *might* have told the tale so that the boy simply had this false belief—and *didn't* believe (8)—(we can imagine, for instance, that he thought that's what his father told him when he asked), this would yield us a case that was not at all a plausible case of either irrationality or even miscalculation, but just a case of a perfectly rational thinker with a single false belief (which then generates other false beliefs such as (1)). Stich rightly does not want to consider such a case, for of course I do acknowledge the possibility of mere false belief, when special stories can be told about its acquisition. If we then attribute (13) *while retaining* (8) we get a blatant and bizarre case of irrationality: someone believing simultaneously that $25 - 12 = 13$, $25 - 12 = 11$ and $13 \neq 11$. This is not what we had supposed at all, but so strange that we are bound to find the conjoined attributions frankly incredible. Something has to give. If we say, as Stich proposes, that the boy "is not yet very good at doing sums in his head" what is the implication? That he doesn't *really* believe the inconsistent triad, that he *sort of* understands arithmetical notions well enough to have the cited beliefs? That is, if we say what Stich says and *also* attribute the inconsistent beliefs, we still have the problem of brute irrationality too stark to countenance; if we take Stich's observation to temper or withdraw the attribution, then Stich is agreeing with me: even the simplest and most familiar errors require us to resort to scare–quotes or other *caveats* about the literal truth of the total set of attributions.

There is something obtuse, of course, about the quest exhibited above for a total belief–set surrounding the error. The demand that we find an inference—even a *mis*–inference—to the false belief (1) is the demand that we find a practice or tendency with something like a rationale, an exercise of which has led in this instance to (1). No mere succession in time or even regular causation is enough in itself to count as an inference. For instance, were we to learn that the boy was led directly from his belief (6) that a penny is 1 cent to his belief (2) that I gave him a quarter, then no matter how habitual and ineluctable the passage in him from (6) to (2), we wouldn't call it *inference*.[4] Inferences are passages of thought for which there is a reason, but people don't make mistakes for reasons. Demanding reasons (as opposed to "mere" causes) for mistakes generates spurious edifices of belief, as we have just seen in (11–13), but simply acquiescing in the attribution of reasonless belief is no better. It is not as if *nothing* led the boy to believe (1); it is not as if that belief was utterly baseless. We do not suppose, for instance, that he would have believed (1) had his hand been empty, or filled with quarters, or had I given him a dollar or a credit card. He does somehow base his mistaken belief on a distorted or confused or mistaken perception of what he is handing me, what I have handed him, and the appropriate relationships between them.

The boy is basically on top of the situation, and is no mere change–giving robot; nevertheless; we must descend from the level of beliefs and desires to some other level of theory to describe his mistake, since no account in terms of his beliefs and desires will make sense completely. At some point our account will have to cope with the sheer senselessness of the transition in any error.

My perhaps tendentious examination of a single example hardly consitutes an argument for my general claim that this will always be the outcome. It is presented as a challenge: try for yourself to tell the total belief story that surrounds such a simple error and see if you do not discover just the quandary I have illustrated.

Mistakes of the sort exhibited in this example are slips in good procedures, not manifestations of an allegiance to a bad procedure or principle. The partial confirmation of our inescapable working hypothesis that the boy is fundamentally rational is his blushing acknowledgment of his error. He doesn't defend his action once it is brought to his attention, but willingly corrects his error. This is in striking contrast to the behavior of agents in the putative cases of genuine irrationality cited by Stich. In these instances, people not only persist in their "errors," but stubbornly defend their practice—and find defenders among philosophers as well.[5] It is at least *not obvious* that there are any cases of systematically irrational behavior or thinking. The cases that have been proposed are all controversial, which is just what my view predicts; no such thing as a cut-and-dried or obvious case of "familiar irrationality." This is not to say that we are always rational, but that when we are not, the cases defy description in ordinary terms of belief and desire. There is no mystery about why this should be so. An intentional interpretation of an agent is an exercise that attempts to *make sense* of the agent's acts, and when acts occur that make no sense, they cannot be straightforwardly interpreted in sense-making terms. Something must give: we allow that the agent either only "sort of" believes this or that, or believes this or that "for all practical purposes," or believes some falsehood which creates a context in which what had appeared to be irrational turns out to be rational after all. (See, e.g., Cohen's suggestions, *op. cit.*) These particular fall-back positions are themselves subject to the usual tests on belief attribution, so merely finding a fall-back position is not confirming it. If it is disconfirmed, the search goes on for another saving interpretation. If there is no *saving* interpretation—if the person in question is irrational—no interpretation at all will be settled on.

The same retreat from the abyss is found in the simple cases of miscalculation and error of which Stich reminds us, but with a few added wrinkles worth noting. In the case of the lemonade seller, we might excuse ourselves from further attempts to sort out his beliefs by just granting that while he knew (and thus believed)[6] all the right facts, he "just forgot" or "overlooked" a few of them temporarily—until we reminded him of them. This has the appearance of being a modest little psychological hypothesis: something roughly to the effect that although something or other was stored safe and sound inside the agent's head where it belonged, its address was temporarily misplaced. Some such story may well in the end be supported within a confirmed and detailed psychological theory,[7] but it is important to note that at the present time we make these hypotheses *simply* on the basis of our abhorrence of the vacuum of contradiction.

For instance, consider absentmindedness—a well-named affliction, it seems. At breakfast I am reminded that I am playing tennis with Paul instead of having lunch today. At 12:45 I find myself polishing off dessert when Paul, in tennis gear, appears at my side and jolts me into recollection. "It completely slipped my mind!" I aver, blushing at my own absentmindedness. But why do I say *that*? Is it because, as I recall, not a single conscious thought about my tennis date passed through my head after breakfast? That might be true, but perhaps no conscious thought that I was going to lunch today occurred to me in the interim either, and yet here I am, finishing my lunch. Perhaps if I *had* thought consciously about going to lunch as usual, that very thought would have reminded me that I wasn't, in fact. And in any case, even if I remember now that it *did* once occur to me in mid-morning that I was to play tennis today—to no avail, evidently—I will still say it subsequently slipped my mind.

Why, indeed, am I eager to *insist* that it completely slipped my mind? To assure Paul that I haven't stood him up on purpose? Perhaps, but that should be obvious enough not to need saying, and if my eagerness is a matter of not wanting to insult him, I am not entirely succeeding, since it is not at all flattering to be so utterly forgotten. I think a primary motive for my assertion is just to banish the possibility that otherwise would arise: I am starkly irrational; I believe both that I am playing tennis at lunch and that I am free to go to lunch as usual. I cannot act on both beliefs at once; whichever I act on, I declare the other to have slipped my mind. Not on any introspective evidence (for I may, after all, have *repeatedly* thought of the matter in the relevant interim period), but on *general principles*. It does not matter how close to noon I have reflected on my tennis date; if I end up having lunch as usual the tennis date *must have* slipped my mind at the last minute.

There is no direct relationship between one's conscious thoughts and the occasions when we will say something has slipped one's mind. Suppose someone asks me to have lunch today and I reply that I can't: I have another appointment then, but for the life of me I can't recall what it is—it will come to me later. Here although in one regard my tennis date has slipped my mind, in another it has not, since my belief that I am playing tennis, while not (momentarily) consciously retrievable, is yet doing some work for me: it is keeping me from making the conflicting appointment. I hop in my car and I get to the intersection: left takes me home for lunch; right takes me to the tennis court; I turn right this time without benefit of an accompanying conscious thought to the effect that I am playing tennis today at lunchtime. It has not slipped my mind, though; had it slipped my mind, I would no doubt have turned left.[8] It is even possible to have something slip one's mind while one is thinking of it consciously! "Be careful of this pan," I say, "it is very hot"—reaching out and burning myself on the very pan I am warning about. The height of absentmindedness, no doubt, but possible. We would no doubt say something like "You didn't think what you were saying!"—which doesn't mean that the words issued from my mouth as from a zombie, but that if I had believed—*really* believed—what I was saying, I *couldn't* have done what I did. If I can in this manner not think what I am saying, I could also in about as rare a case not think what I was thinking. I could think "careful of that hot pan" *to myself*, while ignoring the advice.

There is some temptation to say that in such a case, while I knew full well that the pan was hot, I just forgot for a moment. Perhaps we want to acknowledge this sort of forgetting, but note that it is not at all the forgetting we suppose to occur when we say I have forgotten the telephone number of the taxicab company I called two weeks ago, or forgotten the date of Hume's birth. In those cases we presume the information is gone for good. Reminders and hints won't help me recall. When I say "I completely forgot our tennis date," I don't at all mean I completely forgot it—as would be evidenced if on Paul's arrival in tennis gear I was blankly baffled by his presence, denying any recollection of having made the date.

Some other familiar locutions of folk psychology are in the same family: 'notice', 'overlook', 'ignore', and even 'conclude'. One's initial impression is that these terms are applied by us to our own cases on the basis of direct introspection. That is, we classify various conscious acts of our own as concludings, noticings, and the like—but what about ignorings and overlookings? Do we find ourselves doing these things? Only retrospectively, and in a self-justificatory or self-critical mood: "I ignored the development of the pawns on the queen side" says the chess player, "because it was so clear that the important development involved the knights on the king side." Had he lost the game, he would have said "I simply overlooked the development of the pawns on the queen side, since I was under the misapprehension that the king side attack was my only problem."

Suppose someone asks, "Did you *notice* the way Joe was evading your questions yesterday?" I might answer "yes," even though I certainly did not *think any conscious thoughts* at the time (that I can recall) about the way Joe was evading my questions; if I can nevertheless see that my reactions to him (as I recall them) took appropriate account of his evasiveness, I will (justly) aver that I did notice. Since I did the appropriate thing in the circumstances, I must have noticed, mustn't I?

In order just now for you to get the gist of my tale of absentmindedness, you had to conclude from my remark about "polishing off dessert" that I had just finished a lunch and missed my tennis date. And surely you did so conclude, but did you *consciously* conclude? Did anything remotely like "Hmm, he must have had lunch . . . " run through your head? Probably not. It is no more likely that the boy selling lemonade consciously thought that the eleven cents in his hand was the right change. "Well, if he didn't *consciously* think it, he unconsciously thought it; we must posit an unconscious controlling thought to that effect to explain, or ground, or *be* (!) his belief that he is giving the right change."

It is tempting to suppose that when we retreat from the abyss of irrationality and find a different level of explanation on which to flesh out our description of errors (or, for that matter, of entirely felicitous passages of thought), the arena we properly arrive at is the folk-psychological arena of thinkings, concludings, forgettings, and the like—not mere abstract mental *states* like belief, but concrete and clockable episodes or activities or processes that can be modeled by psychological model-builders and measured and tested quite directly in experiments. But as the examples just discussed *suggest* (though they do not by any means *prove*), we would be unwise to model our serious, academic psychology too closely on these putative illata of folk theory. We postulate all these apparent activities and mental processes *in order to make sense* of the behavior we observe—in order, in fact, to make as much sense as possible of the behavior, especially when the behavior we observe is our own. Philosophers of mind used to go out of their way to insist that one's access to one's own case in such matters is quite unlike one's access to others', but as we learn more about various forms of psycho-pathology and even the foibles of apparently normal people[9], it becomes more plausible to suppose that although there are still some small corners of unchallenged privilege, some matters about which our authority is invincible, each of us is in most regards a sort of inveterate auto-psychologist, effortlessly *inventing* intentional interpretations of our own actions in an inseparable mix of confabulation, retrospective self-justification and (on occasion, no doubt) good theorizing. The striking cases of confabulation by subjects under hypnosis or suffering from various well-documented brain disorders (Korsakoff's syndrome, split brains, various "agnosias") raise the prospect that such virtuoso displays of utterly unsupported self-interpretation are not manifestations of a skill suddenly learned in response to trauma, but of a normal way of life unmasked.[10]

As creatures of our own attempts to make sense of ourselves, the putative mental activities of folk theory are hardly a neutral field of events and processes to which we can resort for explanations when the normative demands of intentional system theory run afoul of a bit of irrationality. Nor can we suppose their counterparts in a developed cognitive psychology, or even their "realizations" in the wetware of the brain, will fare better. Stich holds out the vision of an entirely norm–free, naturalized psychology that can *settle* the indeterminacies of intentional system theory by appeal, ultimately, to the presence or absence of real, functionally salient, causally potent states and events that can be identified and *ascribed content independently of the problematic canons of ideal rationality my view requires.* What did the lemonade seller *really believe*? Or what, in any event, was the *exact content* of the sequence of states and events that figure in the cognitivistic description of his error? Stich supposes we will be able, in principle, to say, even in cases where my method comes up empty–handed. I claim, on the contrary, that just as the interpretation of a bit of *outer,* public communication—a spoken or written utterance in natural language, for instance—*depends on* the interpretation of the utterer's beliefs and desires, so the interpretation of a bit of *inner,* sub–personal cognitivistic machinery must inevitably depend on exactly the same thing: the whole person's beliefs and desires. Stich's method of content ascription depends on mine, and is not an alternative, independent method.

Suppose we find a mechanism in Jones that reliably produces an utterance of 'It is raining' whenever Jones is queried on the topic and it is raining in Jones' epistemically accessible vicinity. It also produces 'yes' in response to 'Is it raining?' on those occasions. Have we discovered Jones' belief that it is raining? That is, more circumspectly, have we found the mechanism that "subserves" this belief in Jones' cognitive apparatus? Maybe—it all depends on whether or not Jones believes that it is raining when (and only when) this mechanism is "on." That is, perhaps we have discovered a weird and senseless mechanism (like the "assent–inducing tumor" I imagined in "Brain Writing and Mind Reading," *Brainstorms*, p. 44) that deserves no intentional interpretation at all—or at any rate not this one: that it is the belief that it is raining. We need a standard against which to judge our intentionalistic labels for the illata of sub–personal cognitive theory; what we must use for this standard is the system of abstracta that fixes belief and desire by a sort of hermeneutical process that tells the best, most rational, story that can be told. If we find that Jones passes the right tests—he demonstrates that he really understands what the supposition that it is raining means, for instance—we may find confirmation of our hypothesis that we have uncovered the mechanistic realization of his beliefs. But where we find such fallings–short, such imperfect and inappropriate proclivities and inactivities, we will *thereby* diminish our grounds for ascribing belief content to mechanisms we find.

It is unlikely, I have said, that the illata we eventually favor in academic psychology will resemble the putative illata of folk theory enough to tempt us to identify them. But whatever illatà we find, we will interpret them and assign content to them by the light of our holistic attribution to the agent of beliefs and desires. We may not find structures in the agent that can be made to line up belief–by–belief with our intentional system catalogue of beliefs for the agent. On Stich's view, and on Fodor's, we would be constrained to interpret this outcome—which all grant is possible—as the discovery that *there were no such things as beliefs after all*. Folk psychology was just false. On my view we would instead interpret this discovery—and a very likely one it is—as the discovery that the concrete systems of representation whereby brains realize intentional systems are simply not *sentential* in character.[11]

Of course sometimes there are sentences in our heads, which is hardly surprising, considering that we are language–using creatures. These sentences, though, are as much in need of interpretation via a determination of our beliefs and desires as are the public sentences we utter. Suppose the words occur to me (just "in my head"): 'Now is the time for violent revolution!'—did I thereby *think* the thought with the content that now is the time for violent revolution? It all depends, doesn't it? On what? On what I happened to believe and desire and intend when I internally uttered those words "to myself." Similarly, even if "cerebroscopes" show that while the boy was handing me my change he was internally accompanying his transaction with the conscious or subconscious expression in his natural language or in Mentalese: 'this is the right change,' that would not settle the correct interpretation of that bit of internal language and hence would not settle the intentional interpretation of his act. And since he has made a mistake, there is no unqualified catalogue of his intentional states and acts of the moment.

So I stick to my guns: even for the everyday cases of error Stich presents, the problems of belief–interpretation encountered by my view *really are there* in the folk–psychological practice, although they often lurk behind our confabulations and excuses. Nor will they go away for Stich's proposed alternative theory of content–ascription. This is *not* to say that such phenomena cannot be given any coherent description. Of course they can be coherently described from either the design stance or the physical stance—a point on which Stich and I agree. So I do not discover any truths of folk theory I must regretfully foreswear.

* * *

In thus resisting Stich's objections, and keeping rationality at the foundation of belief and desire attribution, am I taking what Stich calls the *hard line*, or the *soft line*? The hard line, according to Stich, insists that intentional system theory's idealizing assumption of rationality is actually to be found in the folk practice from which intentional system theory is derived. The soft line "proposes some fiddling with the idealized notion of an intentional system" to bring it more in line with folk practice, which does not really (Stich insists) invoke considerations of rationality at all. These distinct lines are Stich's inventions, born of his frustration in the attempt to make sense of my expression of my view, which is both hard and soft—that is to say, flexible. The *flexible line* insists both that the assumption of rationality is to be found in the folk practice and that what rationality is is not what it appears to be to some theorists—so the idealization will require some "fiddling." What, then, do I say of the ideal of rationality exploited self-consciously by the intentional system strategist and as second nature by the rest of the folk?

Here Stich finds me faced with a dilemma. If I identify rationality with *logical consistency and deductive closure* (and the other dictates of the formal normative systems such as game theory and the calculus of probability) I am embarrassed by absurdities. Deductive closure, for instance, is just too strong a condition, as Stich's case of Oscar the engineer witnesses.[12] If, flying to the other extreme, I identify rationality with *whatever it is that evolution has provided us*, I either lapse into uninformative tautology or fly in the face of obvious counterexamples: cases of evolved manifest irrationality. What then do I say rationality is? I don't say.

Stich is right; for ten years I have hedged and hinted and entertained claims that I have later qualified or retracted. I didn't know what to say, and could see problems everywhere I turned. With that *mea culpa* behind me, I will now take the offensive, however, and give what I think are good reasons for cautiously resisting the demand for a declaration on the nature of rationality while still insisting that an assumption of rationality plays the crucial role I have seen for it.

First, a few words on what rationality is *not*. It is not deductive closure. In a passage Stich quotes from "Intentional Systems" I present the suggestion that "If S were ideally rational . . . S would believe every logical consequence of every belief (and ideally, S would have no false beliefs)" and I make a similar remark in "True Believers." That is, after all, the logically guaranteed resting point of the universally applicable, indefinitely extendable demand that one believe the "obvious" consequences of one's genuine, fully understood beliefs. But Stich's example of Oscar nicely reveals what is wrong with letting sheer entailment expand a rational agent's beliefs, and as Lawrence Powers shows in his important article "Knowledge by Deduction"[13] there is work to be done by a theory of knowledge *acquisition* by deduction: one *comes* to know (and believe) what one *didn't* already know (or believe) by deducing propositions from premises already believed—a familiar and "obvious" idea, but one that requires the very careful exposition and defense Powers gives it. And it is important to note that in the course of making his case for what we might call implication–insulated cognitive states, Powers must advert to neologism and caveat: we must talk about what our agent "pseudo–believes" and "pseudo–knows" (p. 360ff). It puts one in mind, in fact, of Stich's own useful neologism for belief–like states lacking the logical fecundity of beliefs: "sub–doxastic states"[14].

Nor is rationality perfect logical consistency, although the *discovery* of a contradiction between propositions one is inclined to assent to is always, of course, an occasion for sounding the epistemic alarm.[15] Inconsistency, when discovered, is of course to be eliminated one way or another, but making the rooting out of inconsistency the pre–eminent goal of a cognizer would lead to swamping the cognitive system in bookkeeping and search operations to the exclusion of all other modes of activity.[16] Now how can I talk this way about inconsistency, given my account of the conditions for correct belief attribution? Who said anything about inconsistency of *beliefs*? When one enters the domain of considerations about the wise design of cognitive structures and operations, one has left belief proper behind, and is discussing, in effect, structurally identified features with more–or–less apt intentionalistic labels (see "Three Kinds of Intentional Psychology" and *Brainstorms*, pp. 26–27).

If I thus do not identify rationality with consistency and deductive closure, what then could be my standard? If I turn to evolutionary considerations, Stich suggests, "such established theories as deductive and inductive logic, decision theory and game theory" will be "of no help in assessing what an organism 'ought to believe'." This is just not true. The theorist who relinquishes the claim that these formalisms are the final *benchmark* of rationality can still turn to them for help, can still exploit them in the course of criticizing (on grounds of irrationality) and reformulating strategies, designs, interpretations. The analogy is imperfect, but just as one may seek help from a good dictionary, or a good grammar book, in supporting one's criticism of someone's spelling, word choice, or grammar, so may one appeal to the defeasible authority of, say, decision theory in objecting to someone's strategic formulation. One can also reject as wrong—or irrational—the advice one gets from a dictionary, a grammar, a logic, or any other normative theory, however well established.[17]

What of the evolutionary considerations? I am careful *not* to define rationality in terms of what evolution has given us—so I avoid outright tautology. Nevertheless, the relation I claim holds between rationality and evolution is more powerful than Stich will grant. I claim, as he notes, that if an organism is the product of natural selection we can assume that *most* of its beliefs will be true, and *most* of its belief-forming strategies will be rational. Stich disagrees: "it is simply not the case that natural selection favors true beliefs over false ones," because all natural selection favors is beliefs "that yield selective advantage" and "there are many environmental circumstances in which false beliefs will be more useful than true ones." I do not think it is *obvious* that it is *ever* advantageous to be designed to arrive at false beliefs about the world, but I have claimed that there are describable circumstances—rare circumstances—where it can happen, so I agree with Stich on this point: "*better safe than sorry* is a policy that recommends itself to natural selection," Stich says, echoing my claim in "Three Kinds of Intentional Psychology"—"Erring on the side of prudence is a well recognized good strategy, and so Nature can be expected to have valued it on occasions when it came up" (p. 45n).

But does this go any way at all toward rebutting my claim that natural selection guarantees that *most* of an organism's beliefs will be true, *most* of its strategies rational? I think not. Moreover, even if a strategy is, as I grant it very well may be, a "patently invalid" strategy that works most of the time in the contexts it is invoked—does this show it is an *irrational* strategy? Only if one is still clinging to the ideals of Intro Logic for one's model of rationality. It is not even that there are no "established" academic canons of rationality in opposition to the logicians' to which one might appeal. Herbert Simon is duly famous for maintaining that *it is rational* in many instances to *satisfice*—e.g., to leap to possibly "invalid" conclusions when the costs of further calculation probably outweigh the costs of getting the wrong answer. I think he is right, so I for one would not tie rationality to any canons that prohibited such practices. Stich declares:

> So long as we recognize a distinction between a normative theory of inference or decision-making and a set of inferential practices which (in the right environment) generally get the right (or selectively useful) answer, it will be clear that the two need not, and generally do not, coincide. [pp. 53–54]

This is a puzzling claim, for there are normative theories for different purposes, including the purposes of "generally getting the right answer." If one views these as at odds with one another, one makes a mistake. Deductive logic might be held to advise that in the face of uncertainty or lack of information one should simply *sit tight and infer nothing*—bad advice for a creature in a busy world, but fine advice if avoiding falsehood *at all costs* is the goal. It is better to recognize the various uses to which such strategies can be put, and let rationality consist in part of a good sense of when to rely on what. (It is also useful to remind ourselves that only a tiny fraction of all the "rational animals" that have ever lived have ever availed themselves self-consciously of *any* of the formal techniques of the normative theories that have been proposed.)

The concept of rationality is indeed a slippery concept. We agree, it seems, that a system would be improperly called irrational if although its *normal, designed* operation were impeccable (by the standards of the relevant norms), it suffered occasional *malfunctions*. But of course a system that was particularly delicate, particularly prone to uncorrected malfunctions, would hardly be a well-designed system; a system that was foolproof or failsafe would in this regard be better. But which would be better—which would be more rational—all things considered: a very slow but virtually failsafe system, or a very fast but only 90% malfunction-free system? It depends on the application, and there are even normative canons for evaluating such choices in some circumstances.

I want to use "rational" as a general-purpose term of cognitive approval—which requires maintaining only conditional and revisable allegiances between rationality, so considered, and the proposed (or even universally acclaimed) methods of getting ahead, cognitively, in the world. I take this usage of the term to be quite standard, and I take *appeals to* rationality by proponents of cognitive disciplines or practices to require this understanding of the notion. What, for instance, could Anderson and Belnap be appealing to, what could they be assuming about their audience, when they recommend their account of entailment over its rivals, if not to an assumably shared rationality which is such that it is an *open question* which formal system best captures it?[18] Or consider this commentary on the discovery that a compartmentalized memory is a necessary condition for effective cognition in a complex, time–pressured world:

> We can now appreciate both the costs and the benefits of this strategy; *prima facie*, the resulting behavior can be characterized as departures from rationality, but on the assumption that exhaustive memory search is not feasible, such memory organization is advisable overall, despite its costs. Correspondingly, a person's action may seem irrational when considered in isolation, but it may be rational when it is more broadly considered as part of the worthwhile price of good memory management.[19]

The claim is that it is rational to be inconsistent sometimes, not the pseudo–paradoxical claim that it is rational sometimes to be irrational. As the example shows, the concept of rationality is systematically pre–theoretical. One may, then, decline to *identify* rationality with the features of any formal system or the outcome of any process and still make appeals to the concept, and assertions about appeals to it (such as mine), without thereby shirking a duty of explicitness.

* * *

When one leans on our pre-theoretical concept of rationality, one relies on our shared intuitions—when they *are* shared, of course—about what makes sense. What else, in the end, could one rely on? What else would it be *rational* to rely on? When considering what we *ought to do*, our reflections lead us eventually to a consideration of what we *in fact do*; this is inescapable, for a catalogue of our considered intuitive judgments on what we ought to do is both a compendium of what we *do* think, and a shining example (by our lights—what else?) of how we *ought* to think.[20]

Now it will appear that I am backing into Stich's own view, the view that when we attribute beliefs and other intentional states to others, we do this by comparing them *to ourselves*, by projecting ourselves into their states of mind. One doesn't ask: "what ought this creature believe?" but "what would *I* believe if I were in its place?" (I have suggested to Stich that he call his view *idealogical solipsism,* but he apparently feels this would court confusion with some other doctrine.) Stich contrasts his view with mine and claims that "the notion of idealized rationality plays *no role at all*" [Stich's emphasis] in his account. "In ascribing content to belief states we measure others not against an idealized standard but against ourselves." But for the reasons just given, measuring "against ourselves" *is* measuring against an idealized standard.

Now Stich at one point observes that "since we take ourselves to approximate rationality, this explains the fact, noted by Dennett, that intentional description falters in the face of egregious irrationality." He must grant, then, that since we take ourselves to approximate rationality, it is also true that the results of his method and my method will coincide very closely. He, asking "what would I do if . . . ?" and I, asking "what ought he to do . . . ?" will typically arrive at the same account, since Stich will typically suppose that he would do what he ought to do, and I would typically suppose that what he ought to do is what I would do if I were in his shoes. If the methods were actually extensionally equivalent, one might well wonder about the point of the quarrel, but is there not room for the two methods to diverge in special cases? Let us see.

Can it be like this? Stich, cognizant of his lamentable and embarrassing tendency to affirm the consequent, imputes this same tendency to those whose beliefs and desires he is trying to fathom. He does this instead of supposing they might be free from his own particular foible, but guilty of others. Unlikely story. Here is a better one. Having learned about "cognitive dissonance," Stich is now prepared to find both in himself and in others the resolution of cognitive dissonance in the favoring of a self–justifying belief over a less comfortable belief better supported by the evidence. This is a fine example of the sort of empirical discovery that can be used to tune the intentional stance, by suggesting hypotheses to be tested by the attributer, but how would Stich say it had anything to do with *ourselves,* and how would this discovery be put into effective use independently of the idealizing assumption? For, first, is it not going to be an empirical question whether all people respond to cognitive dissonance as we do? If Stich builds this (apparently) sub–optimal proclivity into his very method of attribution, he foregoes the possibility of discovering varieties of believers happily immune to this pathology.

Moreover, consider how such an assumption of sub-optimality would get used in an actual case. Jones has just spent three months of hard work building an addition to his house; it looks terrible. Something must be done to resolve the uncomfortable cognitive dissonance. Count on Jones to slide into some belief that will save the situation. But which one? He might come to believe that the point of the project, really, was to learn all about carpentry by the relatively inexpensive expedient of building a cheap addition. Or he might come to believe that the bold thrust of the addition is just the touch that distinguishes his otherwise hackneyed if "tasteful" house from the run of the neighborhood houses. Or, . . . for many possible variations. But which of these is actually believed will be determined by seeing what he says and does, and then asking: what beliefs and desires would make those acts rational? And whatever delusion is embraced, it must be—and *will* be—carefully surrounded by plausible supporting material, generatable on the counterfactual assumption that the delusion is an entirely rationally held belief. Given what we already know about Jones, we might be able to predict which comforting delusion would be most attractive and efficient for him—that is, which would most easily cohere with the rest of the fabric of his beliefs. So even in a case of cognitive dissonance, where the beliefs we attribute are not optimal by anyone's lights, the test of rational coherence is the preponderant measure of our attributions.

I do not see how my method and Stich's can be shown to yield different results, but I also do not see that they could not. I am not clear enough about just what Stich is asserting. An interesting idea which is lurking in Stich's view is that when we interpret others we do so not so much by *theorizing* about them as by *using ourselves as analogue computers* that produce a result. Wanting to know more about *your* frame of mind, I somehow put myself in it, or as close to being in it as I can muster, and see what I thereupon think (want, do . . .).[21] There is much that is puzzling about such an idea. How can it work *without* being a kind of theorizing in the end? For the state I put myself in is not belief but make-believe belief. If I make believe I am a suspension bridge and wonder what I will do when the wind blows, what "comes to me" in my make-believe state depends on how sophisticated my knowledge is of the physics and engineering of suspension bridges. Why should my making believe I have your beliefs be any different? In both cases, knowledge of the imitated object is needed to drive the make-believe "simulation," and the knowledge must be organized into something rather like a theory.

Moreover, establishing that we do somehow arrive at our interpretations of others by something like simulation and self-observation would not by itself show that the guiding question of our effort is "what would I believe?" *as opposed to* "what ought he to believe?" A wary attributer might exhibit the difference by using the trick of empathy or make-believe to *generate* a candidate set of attributions to *test* against his "theory" of the other before settling on them. Note that the issue is far from clear even in the case of imagined *self*-attribution. What would your state of mind be if you were told you had three weeks to live? How do you think about this? In a variety of ways, probably; you do a bit of simulation and see what you'd say, think, and so on, and you also reflect on what kind of a person you think you are—so you can conclude that a person *like that* would believe—ought to believe—or want such-and-such.

Stich's paper raises many more problems well worth a response from me, but the deadline for this issue of *Philosophical Topics* mercifully intervenes at this point. I close with one final rejoinder. Stich seeks to embarrass me in closing with a series of rhetorical questions about what a frog *ought to believe*—for I have made my determination of what a frog *does* believe hinge on such questions. I grant that such questions are only problematically answerable under even the best conditions,[22] but view that as no embarrassment. I respond with a rhetorical question of my own: does Stich suppose that the exact content of what a frog does in fact believe is any more likely of determination?

NOTES

1. See Stephen Stich's review of *Brainstorms*; "Headaches," *Philosophical Books*, April, 1980, and my reply, ibid.

2. Wason and Johnson-Laird, and Nisbett and Ross (see Stich's notes 8 and 11). See also S. Stich and R. Nisbett, "Justification and the Psychology of Human Reasoning" in *Philosophy of Science*, 1980, Vol. 47, No. 2, pp. 188–202.

3. See J. Weizenfeld "Surprise and Intentional Content," presented at the 3rd Annual meeting of the Society for Philosophy and Psychology, Pittsburgh, March 1977.

4. Cf. Jerry Fodor, "Computation and Reduction" in C. W. Savage, ed., *Perception and Cognition: Issues in the Foundations of Psychology* , 1978, pp. 229–60.

5. E.g., L. Jonathan Cohen, "Can Human Irrationality Be Experimentally Demonstrated?" forthcoming in *Behavioral and Brain Sciences*.

6. I will continue to fly in the face of the examples raised by Vendler et al., about the differences between the objects of knowledge and the objects of belief until I can see that this imprecision is *dangerous*. Perhaps I will be shown this tomorrow, but I haven't been shown it yet.

7. See C. Cherniak, "Rationality and the Structure of Human Memory" (Tufts University Cognitive Science Working Papers WP13, June 1980).

8. Cf. Ryle, "A Puzzling Element in the Notion of Thinking" (1958), a British Academy Lecture reprinted in P. F. Strawson, ed., *Studies in the Philosophy of Thought and Action*, 1968, Oxford University Press.

9. See, especially R. Nisbett and T. DeC. Wilson. "Telling More Than We Can Know: Verbal Reports on Mental Processes," *Psychological Review*, 1977.

10. Michael Gazzaniga and J. E. Ledoux advocate a position along these lines in *The Integrated Mind* (New York: Plenum Press, 1978). For graphic accounts of confabulations in victims of brain disorders, see also Howard Gardner, *The Shattered Mind: the Person After Brain Damage*, Knopf, New York, 1975.

11. See my "Beyond Belief" forthcoming in Andrew Woodfield, ed., *Thought and Object*, Oxford University Press, 1981.

12. Cf. also Jerry Fodor, "Three Cheers for Propositional Attitudes" forthcoming in *Representations*, Bradford Books, 1981.

13. *Philosophical Review*, July 1978, pp. 337–71.

14. "Belief and Sub-Doxastic States," *Philosophy of Science*, December, 1978, pp. 499–518.

15. See R. de Sousa, "How to Give a Piece of Your Mind; or The Logic of Belief and Assent," *Review of Metaphysics*, September 1971, pp. 52–79.

16. See C. Cherniak, "Rationality and the Structure of Human Memory," op. cit., and Howard Darmstadter, "Consistency of Belief," *Journal of Philosophy*, May 20, 1971, pp. 301–10. The point has often been made in different contexts by Marvin Minsky as well.

17. See, e.g., L. Jonathan Cohen, op. cit., and for a dissenting view, see S. Stich and R. Nisbett, "Justification and the Psychology of Human Reasoning," *Philosophy of Science*, June, 1980, pp. 188–202.

18. A. R. Anderson and N. Belnap, *Entailment: the Logic of Relevance and Necessity*, (Princeton: Princeton University Press, 1974).

19. Cherniak, op. cit., p. 23.

20. "Thus, what and how we do think is evidence for the principles of rationality, what and how we ought to think. This itself is a methodological principle of rationality; call it the *Factunorm Principle*. We are (implicitly) accepting the Factunorm Principle whenever we try to determine what or how we ought to think. For we must, in that very attempt, think. And unless we can think that what and how we do think there is correct—and thus is evidence for what and how we ought to think—we cannot determine what or how we ought to think." R. Wertheimer, "Philosophy on Humanity," in R. L. Perkins, ed., *Abortion: Pro and Con*, Schenkman, Cambridge, Mass., 1974, p. 110–111. See also Nelson Goodman, *Fact, Fiction, and Forecast*, 2nd edition, 1965, p. 63.

21. Adam Morton's new book *Frames of Mind* (Oxford University Press, 1980) has much to say on this topic which I have not yet had an opportunity to digest. Hence my tentative and sketchy remarks on this occasion.

22. Cf. Dennett, *Content and Consciousness* (London: 1969, Routledge & Kegan Paul), pp. 83–85.

What Can Be Learned from Brainstorms?

ROBERT CUMMINS
University of Wisconsin-Milwaukee

Brainstorms[†] is a collection of Dennett's essays on the philosophy of mind and psychology. In spite of having been written over a period of years, it hangs together remarkably well, and exhibits a linear development often absent in "regular" books. In addition to being important and good, it is the most entertaining bit of non-fiction I've read in a long while.

The book is divided into four parts:
I. Intentional Explanation and Attributions of Mentality
II. The Nature of Theory in Psychology
III. Objects of Consciousness and the Nature of Experience
IV. Free Will and Personhood.

Parts I–III are a defense of what I hereby dub a "neo–functionalist" theory of mind and psychological explanation. Part IV is more or less what the title leads one to expect.

Brainstorms resists brief summary; I shall therefore rely on a catalogue of characteristic and central claims that I hope will help locate the book on the philosophical map and at the same time provide background for the discussion in Section Two. (1) Propositional attitudes are not mental states. In particular, beliefs and desires are not states—especially not representational states—of the systems that have them. Instead, the idiom of propositional attitudes ('intentional idiom' is Dennett's phrase, though he does not discuss non–propositional cases) finds its place in "intentional systems theory," which seeks to explain, predict and interpret behavior by rationalizing it. Thus, a system has propositional attitudes just in case it is possible to explain/predict/interpret its behavior by attributing propositional attitudes to it (Chapters 1, 3, 6, 14). (2) Homuncular explanations are legitimate provided (a) the homunculi appealed to do not duplicate the capacities they are supposed to explain, and (b) they can be "discharged" by analysis into homunculi whose capacities

[†] Daniel C. Dennett. *Brainstorms: Philosophical Essays on Mind and Psychology.* Montgomery, Vermont: Bradford Books, 1978.

are not intentionally characterized (Chapters 4, 7). (3) The Law of Effect is logically tied to the concept of intelligence: we will not recognize as intelligent a system whose successes do not render more likely whatever leads to them (Chapter 5). (4) Introspective awareness, including awareness of one's "mental images," is simply fallible knowledge of one's semantic intentions (Chapters 2, 9, 10). (5) Dreaming (and, perhaps, experience generally) is a non–conscious process of construction and storage of material for later recall (Chapter 8). (6) Subpersonal cognitive accounts of pain and consciousness are possible, though incoherencies in our intuitions about consciousness and pain make it difficult to produce anything uniquely or completely satisfying (Chapters 2, 9, 11). About an entity realizing such a theory, Dennett writes:

> ... There will be at least the illusion that it is like something to be the entity. In fact it will tell us ... just what it is like. But inside it is all darkness, a hoax. Or so it seems. Inside your skull it is also all darkness.... Can it be said that just as there is some other point of view that *you* have, there is some other point of view that *it* has? [pp. 164–65]

(7) Judgments (or opinions), thought of as semantic intentions or dicta we are disposed to produce, should be sharply distinguished from beliefs. The former are representational states, but do not rationalize behavior as do the latter (Chapters 2, 16). (8) Explanations of novel behavior that rely on response generalization are question–begging because they assume an automatically theory–satisfying notion of "similar behavior" and "similar contingencies/circumstances" (Chapter 4). (9) Since the intentional stance toward something—explaining its behavior *via* intentional characterization—is compatible with both mechanism and indeterminism, so is the moral stance, resting as it does on intentional attributions (Chapters 12, 15). (10) The concept of a person is an idealization; hence, illuminating, sufficient conditions for personhood cannot be given, though a series of nested necessary conditions can be (Chapter 14). (11) Gödel's incompleteness theorem is irrelevant to the capacities of persons or computers, since it applies to abstracta, not to their realizations (Chapter 13).

II

Dennett doesn't raise the mind–body problem in *Brainstorms*; he attempts to solve it (but see his "Current Issues in the Philosophy of Mind," in *The American Philosophical Quarterly*, October, 1978). I think it helps, though, to see his contribution as a response to a particular version of the problem. We seem to have two distinct languages (or sets of general terms) for describing persons—a language of physical characteristics (PL) and a language of mental characteristics (ML).[1] Both work fine. The problem is their almost complete independence of each other. Can both be true of the same thing? Dualists explain the independence by denying unity of subject matter: Mental and physical descriptions are not true of the same things, appearances to the contrary not withstanding. Their problem is explaining mind–body interaction. Monists avoid this problem by insisting on the unity of subject matter. Their problem is to explain how ML and PL descriptions can be true of the same thing. Monists divide over what the "same thing" is, idealists opting for the mental, materialists for the material, and a few for "something else."

Until recently, the favored monist strategy was to explain how ML and PL could be about the same thing by attempting to define one in terms of the other. Idealists attempted to define PL expressions in ML, and materialists attempted to define ML expressions in PL. (The "something elsers" tended to duck the issue, which is, or ought to be, why their view never catches on.) This is what is generally meant by *reductionism* in the philosophy of mind. Reductionism can be tolerant or intolerant depending on whether failure of translation is taken to be a knock on the program or a knock on the recalcitrant idiom. A rather remarkable tendency toward tolerance, in the profession if not in the individual monists themselves, together with massive translation failure, produced a crisis in both monist camps: if persons are really physical (mental), how could there be truths about them not formulatable in PL (ML)? What else could it mean to insist that persons are physical (mental) if not that they are completely describable in PL (ML)? Reductionism appeared to many to be the only alternative to dualism, and it still appears that way to many.

But not to functionalists. Functionalism in the philosophy of mind is exciting precisely because it proposes to save physicalistic monism from an impossible reductionism. Functionalism in the philosophy of mind is, in the first instance, a strategy for reconciling ontological physicalism with anti–reductionism. For example: adding machines are as physically heterogeneous a class of things as one can imagine. The abacus and the electronic calculator have no physics in common that they don't also share with rocks, and hence translating 'x is an adding machine' into PL is hopeless. What adders—physical adders—share is a function, not a physics. We might make a list, relying only on PL specification, but this wouldn't be translation; it would be a demonstration of ontological physicalism for adders.

Until very recently, functionalism was the *only* strategy available for reconciling anti-reductionism with ontological physicalism, but Dennett has introduced another, which I may as well call *intentionalism*. Dennett is a functionalist about mental states, but he thinks that surprisingly little of ML traffics in such things. In particular, he thinks that the idiom of belief, desire, purpose—the idiom of propositional attitudes, in short—does not traffic in mental states.[2] Intentional characterization is legitimate, when it is, in virtue of its explanatory and interpretive success.[3] This much is true of the attribution of mental states, as well, of course. What makes Dennett's view distinctive is its instrumentalist cast: there are no intentional states on his view, only true intentional characterizations.

> Lingering doubts about whether the chess-playing computer *really* has beliefs and desires are misplaced; for the definition of intentional systems I have given does not say that intentional systems *really* have beliefs and desires, but that one can explain and predict their behavior by *ascribing* beliefs and desires to them. [p. 7]

Though Dennett is a bit cagey about it, he is deeply committed to the view that lingering doubts about people are misplaced too: nothing *really* has beliefs and desires. It follows that the viability of one large part of ML—intentional characterization—is neutral with respect to dualism and monism, hence no *problem* for ontological physicalists. If intentionality is the mark of the mental, then the mental (thus far, anyway) is no problem either. Intentionalism thus constitutes a second strategy for defending anti-reductionist monism, and a good part of Dennett's effort is directed to expanding this strategy by assimilating as much of ML as possible to its intentionalist component. (See claims (4), (5) and (6).) There are lots of details to quibble about there, but I don't think it's profitable to pursue them in a review. Instead, I hope to get a kind of fix on Dennett's intentionalism by raising a very general question about it.

What worries me about the intentionalist strategy is that it seems to reduplicate a version of the mind-body problem. Functionalism gives us an account (actually a variety of accounts) of how a certain part of ML–the part that traffics in psychological states—relates to

PL. Call this part of ML *functional state language* (FSL). (In Dennett's terms, functionalism is an account of how the design stance relates to the physical stance.) What's left when we subtract FLS from ML? On Dennett's view, we have (at least) intentional language—IL. Now how does IL relate to FSL? We *seem* to have two largely independent chunks of descriptive machinery that *seem* to apply to the same thing. According to Dennett, they *do* apply to the same thing. Metaphysical dualism isn't allowed as an option here: since IL is supposed to be metaphysically neutral, its relative independence cannot be metaphysically explained. So it *seems* we aren't back to square one (though I shall question that assessment below). But neither are we home free, for we still lack an account of the relation between IL and FSL. Compare functionalism: functionalism "locates" us in PL, as it were, and leads us to see from that perspective how an FSL specification could constitute a characterization of the PL territory "around us." Analogously, intentionalism must locate us in FSL and lead us to see from that perspective how an IL specification could constitute a characterization of our FSL environment. This would allow us to understand the intentional from a physicalist perspective without reducing it, since we already know how to understand (without reduction) FSL from a physicalist perspective.

In Dennett's terms, this amounts to saying how the intentional stance is related to the design stance, but that way of putting it doesn't focus on the problem I want to raise. For while Dennett does tell us something about the relation of the two stances, he doesn't tell us how an inhabitant of FSL–land is to assimilate IL characterizations, and I think only this, or something comparable, would make us understand the intentional.

The characterization in terms of stances tempts us to substitute questions of justification for questions of truth: we ask, "what would justify adoption of the intentional stance?" rather than "in virtue of what sorts of FSL–characterizable facts does (would) an IL characterization truly apply?" Dennett has a good deal to say about the former question, but little if anything to say about the latter.[4] A full-fledged intentionalism must show how intentional idioms can fill the logical space Dennett has created for them. Functionalism went through a comparable stage. No one wants to espouse metaphysical dualism for adders; hence a demonstration of the non–reducibility of 'x is an adder' to the idioms of PL leaves us free to use functional concepts without reducing them or facing charges of dualism. This legitimizes functional characterization, but doesn't explicate it. The second step, still very much in progress, is to see how PL–characterizable facts could make an FSL description true. Once again, calculators come to the rescue: when we design an adder—tell someone how to build one—what we do is give a PL description. Slogging through a design problem of this sort is therefore showing how FSL can truly describe PL–land. Since FSL isn't reducible to PL, it's the sort of thing that has to be done case–by–case. *C'est la vie.*

Well, then, what *would* it take to explicate an IL characterization from an FSL (or PL) perspective? I confess to having a kind of theory (or hunch) about this, which I want to follow for a bit because reflecting on it has convinced me that an instrumentalist treatment of propositional attitudes will ultimately undermine their explanatory value. (Actually, this should come as no surprise: if there are not any, how can they explain anything?)

My hunch is best introduced via some simple reflections on functional interpretation. Suppose we ask what makes a circuit an AND–gate? It is this: there are types of events identified as inputs, and types identified as outputs, and a rule for interpreting these as representations of truth–values, such that the output represents 'true' iff each of the inputs represents 'true'.[5] This is enough to make something an AND–gate, but it isn't enough to make it important to treat it as such. Assuming it is relative dc levels that are interpretable as representations of truth–values, why look at relative dc levels rather than temperature, or mass, or shape? Well, if we hook a lot of these and kindred circuits together in fancy ways, we will have a system whose most striking capacities are explicable only by analyzing them into simple capacities such as the capacity to compute a truth function. Thus, it is the need to explain the capacities of a containing system that makes the truth–functional characterization useful—gives it a role to play. Indeed, only systematic context can make it right to say that it is an AND–gate and not a NAND–gate—or a resistor—and we might put this point by saying that only in an appropriately ritzy neighborhood is it *actually* an AND–gate; otherwise it is only potentially an AND–gate, a would–be AND–gate, the sort of thing that would be an AND–gate in a better neighborhood.

Now my hunch is that what makes intenders, believers, and pretenders is something rather analogous. To understand the intentional is to see that and how something satisfying an FSL description would receive an IL description in the course of explaining the capacities of a containing system—e.g., a community of Gricean communicators. Thus, psychological states are at best would-be intentional states—the sort of thing that would actually be (or count as) an intentional state in a sufficiently ritzy neighborhood. What makes intentional characterization apt, in other words, is something similar to what makes it apt to treat dc levels as representations of truth-values. If this is on the right track, then to understand the intentional we need to know what sort of system would have capacities *requiring* intentional characterization, i.e., how a particular FSL-characterized structure could have such capacities. To see this would be to see how FSL facts could *make* an intentional characterization true.

A paradigm case would be a system consisting (in part) of two components capable of being the *parties* to a Lewis-type convention.[6] (A pair of people in a natural environment is such a system, but perhaps there are others.) The capacities (or some of them) of such a system would require characterization in intentional terms, and a function-analytic explanation of those capacities would entail intentional characterization of the components. Hook a couple of fancy computational engines together in the right way, and you get a system whose capacities are explicable, indeed describable, *only* by construing them as such capacities as the capacity to believe, desire and intend. Thus, 'believer' turns out to be a functional term applying to things with the capacity to believe. Like 'AND-gate,' it will have a (containing) system-relative use, applying to actual believers, and a categorical use, applying to would-be believers—systems that would be believers in a ritzy enough neighborhood. Adapting a term of Stich's, I call capacities that would require intentional characterization in an appropriate context 'sub-doxastic' capacities.[7] A sub-doxastic capacity is what you get when you take out of context a capacity used to analyze an intentionally characterized capacity such as conventional communication or reference.

Notice that this gives us believers, but not beliefs. My theory is neutral over whether beliefs are mental states or not: it all depends on how believers are to be analyzed (or perhaps instantiated), and I've said nothing about that. Still, although I've taken my cue from Dennett's idea that intentional idiom explains and interprets environmental interactions, I don't think I can sustain the rather radical instrumentalism about intentional states that Dennett recommends. After all, when a believer does its stuff, it believes, and this, it seems, must be a state or process of (or in) the believer, just as adding is a state or process in the adder. For surely to say that a believer is believing is, on my account at any rate, to give an intentional characterization of a process or state in the believer. Still, it would be a great mistake to unhook a believer from its containing system, open it up, and look for believings (let alone beliefs). This would be like yanking an AND-gate out of a calculator, and searching for truth-functional computations (or truth-values). Yet this is just what we expect if we demand that the intentional properties of a psychological state or process be derivable from its "psychological" characterization, for psychology (at least as pictured by philosophers) takes as its unit a system whose typical capacities are, at the chosen level of analysis, only sub-doxastic;[8] not actually intentional, but only potentially so.[9]

Let us call this a *contextualist* account of intentionality, though it is really a functionalist account of a property of supra-personal systems. Perhaps some capacities of less-than-whole organisms are actually intentional, but it seems unlikely. Dennett sees no harm in such characterization, but gives no compelling reason for thinking it necessary. My hunch is that, being an instrumentalist about the intentional, he is prepared to use intentional idiom whenever it is useful, whereas I am inclined to use it only when cornered by lack of explanatory or descriptive alternatives. Dennett tends to think the design stance (or even the physical stance) is always an alternative. In a way, this is right: we can choose to operate exclusively in PL, say. But if we do, there are a lot of capacities we won't even be able to describe, let alone explain—that's the anti-reductionist lesson.

For the most part, Dennett resists a functionalist account of propositional attitudes: when we can explain behavior by rationalizing it, the line goes, intentional idiom is appropriate, and that is all there is to say about how intentional idiom relates to the world. I've been claiming, on the other hand, that there is more to be said; that we won't understand propositional attitudes until we know how design facts can force the intentional upon us. It must be admitted, I think, that there is something of this in Dennett as well. On Dennett's view, when we characterize intentionally, we introduce a homunculus, but homunculi need to be discharged eventually.

> Homunculi are *bogeymen* only if they duplicate *entire* the talents they are rung in to explain.... If one can get a team or committee of *relatively* ignorant, narrow-minded, blind homunculi to produce the intelligent behavior of the whole, this is progress.... Eventually this nesting of boxes within boxes lands you with homunculi so stupid... that they can be, as one says, "replaced by a machine." [123–24]

Dennett rightly insists that the homunculi must be "discharged," but he doesn't say *how*. Functionalism tells us how to discharge functions, but not homunculi, unless we assume, contra Dennett, that intentional characterization is functional characterization. Lacking an account of how homunculi (real ones, not sub–doxastic ones) are to be discharged—i.e., lacking an account of how IL relates to FSL—we cannot be at all sure that they will be dischargeable whenever they are useful. Thus, the instrumentalist criterion—usefulness—may be much more liberal than the methodological one (dischargeability). Perhaps Dennett would plump for the methodological criterion if this should turn out to be the case. In any event, Dennett's instrumentalism about intentional characterization will not be entirely persuasive until it is grounded in an account of how homunculi are discharged. We need something sort of analogous to slogging through calculator design. But only sort of: when we design a calculator, we design something that acutally manipulates numerals, but in designing a homunculus, we had best not design something that has and manipulates beliefs, for, on Dennett's view, there aren't any.[10]

NOTES

1. These are not mutually exclusive or jointly exhaustive. There are descriptions that seem to fall into both, and some that seem to fall into neither. But there are plenty of clear cases.

2. He seems committed to the view that intentional idiom generally does not traffic in mental states, but he does not discuss the non–propositional cases such as fearing death. Perhaps he holds that these are really disguised propositional cases.

3. Explanatory: "Why did she castle? To prevent the knight from forking her king and rook." Interpretive: "What is he doing? Trying to attract attention."

4. I'm not persuaded by what Dennett has to say in response to the question of justification. Dennett argues that natural selection guarantees excellence of design, hence rationality, the precondition of intentional explanation and interpretation. Evolution does no such thing: our cognitive capacities may well kill us. Evolution takes a long time. It's *much* too soon to conclude that our cognitive design is adaptive. Insects are doing fine without much rationality.

5. Similarly, what makes something an adder is the fact that each output is interpretable as a numeral representing the sum of the numbers represented by the numerals that are the interpretations of the inputs. See John Haugeland's general characterization of an "intentional black box" in [2].

6. David Lewis, [3]. See also Cummins [1].

7. S. P. Stich [4]. My use of this term may be more like theft and distortion than adaptation.

8. A full–fledged instrumentalism about the intentional would be justified if it turned out that intentional capacities were explicable via intentional instantiations (see Haugeland [2]), for the dimension–shift involved would erase intentional characterization and leave the analyzing of capacities to be carried out in some other idiom.

9. If this is on the right track, then cognitions are not psychological states, though some psychological states may be would-be cognitions. This is what makes AI programs such as Winograd's SHURDLU seem odd. It isn't that, since there aren't any blocks, SHURDLU doesn't know about them. It doesn't know *about* anything. But perhaps it would—perhaps what it does would be knowing about blocks—in a sufficiently ritzy setting. AI abstracts from the setting, philosophers notice the lack of intentionality, and a controversy ensues as to what has been accomplished. Part of this controversy is real enough, for it might be that no surroundings, however fancy, would require intentional characterization of a machine executing SHURDLU. But part of it is just verbal, since standard AI practice is to work with the sub-doxastic intentional idioms.

10. On the "contextualist" alternative, what we need to do is slog through the problem of designing a "community" that has a convention (or something comparable that has capacities requiring intentional characterization). When we do this, I am betting, we will have to design components that function as believers and intenders. It is only in a context like this—one in which intentional analysis is *forced*—that the need for discharging homunculi is *serious*. Dennett's view has it that I have discharged a homunculus (at least one) in designing an adder, since I can treat an adder as an intentional system. It is too easy that way.

REFERENCES

1. Cummins, Robert. "Intention, Meaning and Truth Conditions." *Philosophical Studies* 35 (1979), 345–60.
2. Haugeland, John. "The Nature and Plausibility of Cognitivism." *Behavioral and Brain Sciences* 2 (1978), 215–60.
3. Lewis, David. *Convention*. Cambridge: Harvard University Press (1969).
4. Stich, S. P. "Beliefs and Subdoxastic States." *Philosophy of Science* 45 (1978), 499–518.

Some Varieties of Functionalism

SYDNEY SHOEMAKER
Cornell University

I

I take as my point of departure a procedure for formulating functional definitions which is due to David Lewis.[1] To appreciate the virtues of this procedure one should recall the circularities that have plagued attempts to give behavioral definitions of mental states. Someone who believes that it is raining may be disposed to take an umbrella when he goes out—but only if he wants to keep dry. And someone who wants to keep dry may be disposed to take an umbrella—but only if he believes that it is raining. It appears that to give a behavioral definition of either of these mental states (the belief, or the want), one would have to mention the other; so there appears to be no way of formulating a noncircular dispositional definition of both, or a purely behavioral definition of either. Lewis has shown that the functionalist, unlike the logical behaviorist, can avoid such circularities by making use of the notion of a Ramsey–sentence. One starts off with a theory which incorporates propositions stating all of the causal facts about mental states—about their relations to inputs, outputs, and one another—in terms of which one proposes to define them. One then constructs the Ramsey–sentence of this theory, which says that there is a set of states satisfying the open sentence which results from the replacement of the psychological terms in the original theory by variables (or, on Lewis' version of the procedure, one constructs the "modified Ramsey–sentence," which says that there is a unique such set of states). From the Ramsey–sentence (or modified Ramsey–sentence) one can then extract noncircular definitions of each of the mental terms that figured in the original theory. I shall refer to this as the "Lewis–Ramsey technique." As a first approximation, let us use a version of this procedure recently described by Ned Block.[2] Let T be our psychological theory, so written that all of its psychological terms are predicates. The Ramsey–sentence of T can be written as

$\exists F_1 \ldots \exists F_n \, T(F_1 \ldots F_n)$

If 'F_1' is the variable that replaced 'believes that it is raining' in the formulation of the Ramsey–sentence, and 'F_2' is the variable that replaced 'wants to keep dry', then the following biconditionals will hold:

(1) x believes that it is raining ↔ $\exists F_1 \ldots \exists F_n [T(F_1 \ldots F_n)$ & x has F_1] and

(2) x wants to keep dry ↔ $\exists F_1 \ldots \exists F_n [T(F_1 \ldots F_n)$ & x has F_2].

The functional definition of believing that it is raining will identify this property with the property expressed by the predicate on the right side of the biconditional in (1), and the functional definition of wanting to keep dry will identify this property with that expressed by the predicate on the right–hand side of the biconditional in (2).[3] These predicates quantify over mental properties, or states, but do not mention any specific ones (the Ramsey–sentence having been purged of mental predicates); so no circularity is involved in defining the belief in terms of (1) and the desire in terms of (2).

I am going to assume that for every satisfiable predicate of the form of the right–hand side of (1) and (2) (for short, for every satisfiable functional predicate) there is a property "expressed" by the predicate, i.e., a property something has just in case it satisfies the predicate. (I shall not, in this paper, attempt to make any distinction between properties and states (state types); in some contexts I find 'property' more natural, while in others I prefer 'state'—but nothing of substance will turn on the difference.) Should we say that every property expressible by such a predicate is a functional property? To avoid trivializing the notion of a functional property we will have to make some restrictions. Suppose that our "theory" is "Someone is in pain just in case he has a sensation that hurts." From this we can construct a "functional predicate," namely '$\exists F [\forall y(y$ is $F \leftrightarrow y$ has a sensation that hurts) & x is F]$', which is necessarily coextensive with 'x is in pain'. Supposing that we allow that the property expressed by this predicate is none other than the property of being in pain, we still will not want to count *this* as showing that the property of being in pain is a functional property. This suggests the following restriction: in order to express a functional property, such a predicate must not contain any predicate which is necessarily coextensive with the functional predicate itself (nor, to cover our bets, may it contain predicates from which such a predicate can be constructed truth–functionally). Henceforth I will restrict the term 'functional predicate' to predicates that satisfy this condition.

It may seem obvious that we want a much stronger restriction, namely that the functional predicate must contain no mental predicates whatever. But while this is a reasonable restriction to make when our concern is with the functional definition of mental states or properties, it is not one we want to make in characterizing the general notion of a functional property. Consider the property, possessed by certain drugs, of being an anti-depressant. Presumably this ought to count as a functional property, whether or not it is possible to eliminate mental predicates (such as 'depressed', 'in good spirits', etc.) from the *definiens* of its functional definition.

But now let us focus our attention again on the functional definition of mental states. Sometimes it is said that pain, for example is functionally definable if it is definable "in terms of its causal relations to inputs, outputs, and other mental states."[4] But suppose that pain were definable in terms of its causal relations to inputs, outputs, and certain beliefs and desires, but that those beliefs and desires were not definable in any such way. In that case being in pain would be a functional property, in a sense, but what functionalists have meant in claiming that it is a functional property would not be true. What they have meant is that it is expressible by a functional predicate which contains no mental predicates whatever, and not merely that it is expressible by one that contains no predicate which is necessarily coextensive with 'is in pain'; and if the other mental properties by relation to which it is defined include beliefs and desires, this requires that those properties likewise be expressible by such functional predicates. Let us say that a mental state is functionally definable in the weak sense just in case it is definable in terms of its causal relations to inputs, outputs, and other mental states, regardless of whether those other mental states are so definable. And let us say that a state (mental or otherwise) is functionally definable in the strong sense just in case it is expressible by a functional predicate that contains no mental predicates (or mental terminology) whatever. States that are functionally definable in the strong sense I will call 'SS–functional states'; and it is functional states in this sense which functionalism takes mental states to be.

II

Now let us consider the relationship between functional properties, or states, and what are sometimes called their "realizations." Let '$\exists F_1 \ldots \exists F_n [T(\ldots F_j \ldots) \& x \text{ has } F_j]$' be a functional predicate which contains no mental terminology, i.e., one that expresses a SS–functional property. Let us pretend, in fact, that the functional property expressed by this is identical to the property of being in pain, and that 'F_j' is the variable that replaced the predicate 'is in pain' in forming the Ramsey–sentence of the psychological theory from which this predicate was derived. And now suppose that we find a person A, and a set of physical predicates 'P_1' ... 'P_n', such that if we replace 'F_1' ... 'F_n' in our functional predicate with 'P_1' ... 'P_n,' respectively, and remove the initial quantifiers (since there are no longer any variables for them to bind), the resulting physical predicate is true of A. There are now two different physical properties which might naturally be said to "realize" in A the property of being in pain. First, there is that named by 'P_j'—perhaps this might be something like 'has C–fibers firing.' Second, there is the property expressed by the physical predicate 'T(... P_j ...) & x has P_j)'.

Before we go on we must correct an inadequacy in our current formulation. Presumably "T(... P_j ...)" will be a general proposition about how states P_1 ... P_n relate causally to one another and to inputs and outputs, in whatever creatures these states occur. It will have the same form as the psychological theory from which our Ramsey–sentence was derived; to expose a little more of its form, let us rewrite it as "$\forall x[T(... P_j x ...)]$", where the variable 'x' takes persons as values. But must this general proposition be true, i.e., must these states behave as it says wherever and whenever they occur, in order for it to be true that in the case of person A the having of P_j realizes the property of being in pain? Suppose as before, that 'P_j' abbreviates 'has C–fibers firing,' and suppose that there are creatures whose brains are wired differently than A's, so that in them C–fiber firings do not have the characteristic causes and effects of pain. In that case "$\forall x[T(... P_j x ...)]$" will be false. But on the assumption that being in pain is a functional property derived from theory T, this should have no bearing on whether A has pain in virtue of having C–fibers firing (i.e., having P_j); all that should be required for the latter is that *A's* brain should be wired in such a way that *in him* C–fiber firings have the required sorts of causes and effects. What we want as a first conjunct of our physical predicate is not the proposition '$\forall x[T(... P_j x ...)]$', but rather a predicate— 'T(... $P_j x$ ...)', or 'Tx' for short—which results from the removal from that proposition of the universal quantifier binding the variable 'x'; this predicate will be true of a person just in case the person is as all subjects of P_j would have to be in order for "$\forall x[T(... P_j x ...)]$" to be true, but it can be true of a person without that general proposition being true. For the same reason, our functional predicate should be rewritten as '$\exists F_1 ... \exists F_n[T(... F_j x ...) \& P_j x]$'

or (for short) '$\exists F_1 \ldots F_n\, (Tx\, \&\, F_j x)$', and the physical predicate which results from replacing 'F_1' ... 'F_n' with 'P_1' ... 'P_n' will read 'T(... $P_j x$ ...) & $P_j x$' or (for short) 'Tx & $P_j x$'.

Now let us return to the notion of physical realization. As I said earlier, there are two different physical properties that might be said to be the realization in A of the property of being in pain. There is P_j, i.e., having C–fibers firing. Whether A is in pain depends on whether he has P_j, and clearly his having P_j is in some sense constitutive of his being in pain, as opposed to being a cause of it. But this is true only because A has the property expressed by 'Tx'; this can be thought of as a determinate form of the property: *being physically constituted in such a way that P_j plays the causal role definitive of pain*. So the physical property of A which is unconditionally sufficient for being in pain is not P_j by itself, but rather the conjunctive property expressed by 'Tx & $P_j x$'. I will say that the latter property is a total *realization* of being in pain, and that P_j is a *core realization*.

A common functionalist claim is that the same mental state can be physically realized in a variety of different ways. This can be put by saying that there can be indefinitely many different physical properties which are total realizations of the same functional property. So while having a given total realization of a functional property is sufficient for having that property, it is not necessary for it—that same functional property could be instantiated in virtue of the instantiation of some quite different total realization of it. Some writers have said that it is also true that the same physical state can realize different functional properties at different times, or in different circumstances, or in different creatures.[5] This is true if 'realize' means 'be a core realization of', but it is false if it means 'be a total realization of'. Supposing that in us C–fiber firing is a core realization of pain, there might be creatures, with brains wired differently from ours, in which C–fiber firing is a core realization of some altogether different mental state—say the desire to fly to the moon. But in no such creature could a physical property which in us is a total realization of the property of being in pain be a realization of any other mental property, or fail to be a realization of that one.

I shall have more to say about the distinction between core realizations and total realizations in the next section. First, however, I should say something about the relationship between functionalism (as understood here) and materialism. Some early formulations of functionalism suggested that it is incompatible with materialism.[6] The fact that functional states are "multiply realizable" implies that a functional state cannot be identical to any particular physical realization of it; and on the assumption that materialism requires such identities, this implies that materialism is false if functionalism is true. But it should be apparent by now that if functionalism is true, *and* if all of the total realizations of functional states that actually occur are physical states, then materialism is true on any reasonable interpretation of what it says. (It is perhaps worth observing that if materialism really did require the identities which functionalism holds to be unavailable, it would be refuted by the existence of such horological properties of clocks and watches as those expressed by 'keeps accurate time', 'is five minutes slow', and 'registers five o'clock'; for these, like mental properties as conceived by the functionalist, are multiply realizable and not identifiable with any of their physical realizations.)

A natural suggestion is that a functional property can be identified with the property which is the disjunction (perhaps infinite) of all of its total realizations. Now it *may* be that all possible total realizations of mental properties (or of functional properties generally) are physical properties, and in that case each functional property will be identical to a physical property—assuming that it is permissible to speak of infinite disjunctions. But it cannot be excluded a priori that it is possible that functional states should have realizations that are wholly or partially nonphysical (perhaps involving, as Putnam once imagined, the operation of "bundles of ectoplasm"). And if that is a possibility, then the disjunctive property with which such a functional state is identifiable will have some nonphysical disjuncts, and so cannot be said to be a physical property. But even if this is so, if it is nevertheless true that only the physical disjuncts of such properties are ever instantiated in the actual world—or, in other words, if all actual realizations of functional properties are physical—then materialism will be true. If one interprets materialism as requiring that all properties be identical to physical properties, and if one also allows for uninstantiated properties and holds that the disjunction of any two properties is a property, one is in effect taking materialism to hold, not only that there are no nonphysical entities, but that it is logically impossible that there should be any. And that, surely, is a much stronger claim than the materialist is committed to simply in virtue of being a materialist.

III

While the functionalist approach I favor employs a procedure for formulating functional definitions which is due to David Lewis (the "Lewis–Ramsey technique"), the view I end up with is importantly different from Lewis'. To bring out the differences and (I hope) illuminate the virtues of my account, I shall briefly discuss Lewis' recent paper "Mad Pain and Martian Pain."[7]

Lewis wants an account of pain that allows for the possibility of a certain sort of "madman"—a man whose pain differs radically from ours in its causes and effects. The madman's pain has none of the typical causes and effects of normal human pain; instead, it is caused by "moderate exercise on an empty stomach," it "turns his mind to mathematics, facilitating concentration on that but distracting him from anything else," it causes him to "cross his legs and snap his fingers," and so on.[8] The madman is not in the least motivated to prevent pain or to get rid of it. Lewis also wants his account to allow certain imaginary Martians to have pain, precisely because they have states that have the typical causes and effects of pain, despite the fact that the physical realization of pains in the Martians is totally different from that in us. In the case of a Martian, what plays the causal role played in us by C–fiber firing is "the inflation of many smallish cavities in his feet."[9] According to Lewis, the case of the madman shows that pain is only contingently connected with its causal role, while the case of the Martian shows that it is only contingently connected with its physical realization.

Lewis remarks that "[a] simple identity theory straightforwardly solves the problem of mad pain," but it "goes just as straightforwardly wrong about Martian pain."[10] We are to suppose, then, that the madman's pain has the same physical realization as ours—that it is realized in some physical state, let it be C–fiber firing, with which a "simple" identity theory might want to identify pain. Such a simple identity theory is wrong because it cannot account for the pain of the Martians, who lack C–fibers altogether. On the other hand, according to Lewis, "[a] simple behaviorism or functionalism goes the other way: right about the Martian, wrong about the madman."[11] We are to conclude from this that the madman does not have any state that satisfies the (best possible) functional characterization of pain.

What we need, according to Lewis, is a mixed theory. Briefly, his account is as follows. The concept of pain "is the concept of a state that occupies a certain causal role, a state with certain typical causes and effects."[12] Whatever does occupy that causal role is pain. If "the state of having neurons hooked up in a certain way and firing in a certain pattern"[13] is the state apt for causing and being caused in relevant ways, then that neural state is pain. But it is only contingent that that state is pain. "Pain might not have been pain."[14] Lewis says that the concept of pain is "a *non-rigid* concept," and that 'pain' is a non-rigid designator.[15] Not only can 'pain' designate different things in different possible worlds; it can designate different things in different "populations" in the actual world. What is pain for a given population is what occupies the relevant causal role for that population. Since (we will suppose) what occupies the causal role in our population is C-fiber firing, and since (we will stipulate) Lewis' madman is a member of our population, the madman is in pain when his C-fibers are firing—for when his C-fibers are firing he has the state which, in the relevant population, has the typical causes and effects definitive of pain, even though in him (an atypical member of this population) this state does not have these causes and effects. The Martians, however, are a different population. In that population what occupies the causal role definitive of pain is the inflation of tiny cavities in the feet, so in that population it is that state, and not C-fiber firing, which is designated by 'pain'. (We are not talking, of course, about what the *Martian* word 'pain' (if there is one) designates; we are talking about what Martian states fall within the extension of *our* word 'pain'.) Lewis' account does give the result he wants: it allows both his Martian and his madman to have pain. But we have to consider the cost.

Lewis does not say much about what constitutes a "population." He does say that "an appropriate population should be a natural kind—a species, perhaps."[16] But species can accommodate freaks—otherwise Lewis' madman could not be a member of our species. One wonders what Lewis would say of a Martian freak (progeny of Martian parents) who is physically indistinguishable from one of us, or a human freak (progeny of human parents) who is indistinguishable from a Martian. (Perhaps the Martians are so different from us, physiologically, that such freaks are biologically impossible—but if so we can pose the difficulty by imagining some Venusians who are not quite so different.) If Lewis holds that the Martian freak lacks pain, because it lacks the state which among Martians plays the causal role definitive of pain, he will hold a view which it ought to be difficult for a materialist to stomach—that a creature could fail to be in pain despite being physically indistinguishable from a creature which is in pain. This puts the property of being in pain in the company of such manifestly non-intrinsic properties as that of being a Baptist inhabitant of a state whose Governor is a Methodist, and offhand this seems to be just the sort of property it is not. On the other hand, if Lewis assigns the Martian freak to our population because of his physical similarity to us, it becomes unclear on what basis his madman is assigned to our population; would the madman not belong to our population, and not be in pain, if somewhere else (on Venus, say) there were a race of creatures physically just like him, among whom some physical state utterly different from C–fiber firing plays the causal role of pain, and C–fiber firing does not?

But even if these difficulties can somehow be met, it seems to me that the attractiveness of Lewis' position is considerably diminished once we apply to it the distinction, made in section II, between "core realizations" and "total realizations" of a functional state or property. Lewis' madman is supposed to have a state which in typical members of our population, but not in him, plays the causal role of pain, and it is natural to express this by saying that the madman has a state which in our population "realizes" pain, or is the (or a) "realization" of pain. But this, we now see, is ambiguous; it can mean that the madman has a state which is, in our population, the (or a) core realization of pain, or it can mean that he has a state which in our population is the (or a) total realization of pain. If the latter were meant, there would certainly be no objection to saying that the madman has pain—although there would be a question as to how Lewis can consistently characterize the madman as someone who "is not in a state that occupies the causal role of pain for him" (I will return to this shortly). But if this is how the example is to be understood, then the admission that the madman has pain poses no threat to a "simple" functionalism, and provides no grounds for the claim that we must go to a "mixed theory" of the sort Lewis proposes. It also provides no grounds for Lewis' belief that 'pain' is a non–rigid designator. Lewis expresses the latter belief by saying that "pain might not have been pain," and presumably would say that the state that "is" pain in the Martian (and us) might not have been pain. But if 'is' means 'is the total realization of', this will surely not be true—or at any rate, one would suppose that Lewis' functionalist intuitions would lead him to deny it. On the other hand, this will be true if 'is' means 'is the core realization of'; in creatures who are "hooked up" differently than us, so that in them the standard causes and effects of C–fiber firing are utterly different than they are in us, C–fiber firing would not be a core realization of pain, even though it is so in us. And I think that the most natural reading of Lewis' example is that according to which the madman has a state which in us is a core realization of pain, but does not have the total realization of which that state is the core—and does not have any other total realization of pain. This goes with his characterization of the madman as someone who is "hooked up wrong." But now the question is, why should we allow that the madman has (or could have) pain? It would be sheer confusion to say that he must have pain because he has a state which is a realization of pain; this would involve an equivocation on the notion of realization. And Lewis would have to agree that the inductive argument "C-fiber firing is invariably accompanied by pain in us; the madman has C-fiber firing; therefore (probably) the madman has pain" is worthless, given that we know that the madman is hooked up differently than we are. (If that argument were cogent, we could use an analogous inductive argument, based on the fact that in us pain is always accompanied by C-fiber firing, to show that the Martians do not have pain!) Of course, given Lewis' theory we would have a basis for assigning pain to the madman; for the madman belongs to our population, and he has the state which in our population is the (core) realization of pain—or, as Lewis puts it, he is in the state which occupies the causal role of pain for most members of that population (notice that 'occupies the causal role of' shares the ambiguity of 'realizes'). What I am suggesting is that once we are clear that the madman is not supposed to have any total realization of pain, the assignment of pain to him has no plausibility independently of Lewis' theory, and so cannot be used to support it.

Near the beginning of his paper Lewis remarks of his madman case that "my opinion that this is a possible case seems pretty firm. If I want a credible theory of mind, I need a theory that does not deny the possibility of mad pain."[17] Now I think that Lewis' initial description of the case can be read in such a way as to make reasonable Lewis' conviction that the case is possible. But I think that this reading, unlike the interpretation which Lewis subsequently puts on the case, is compatible with the madman's having a total realization of pain (as functionally defined, *à la* Lewis, in terms of a "common-sense" psychological theory)—and on such a reading, as we have seen, the claim that mad pain is possible does not support Lewis' view that 'pain' is a non-rigid designator, that pain is population-relative, and that we need a "mixed theory." Since Lewis doesn't say which of the typical causes and effects of pain are to be taken as defining, the fact that the madman's pain—or rather, the state of him which supposedly realizes pain—does not have certain of the typical causes and effects of pain, and has other causes and effects which are not typical, does not by itself imply that it does not have those that are defining. Perhaps the proper conclusion from the possibility of mad pain is that the defining causal role of pain is other than its total causal role, and other than what one might initially suppose it to be. Moreover, there is an ambiguity in the notion of "playing a causal role." To say that a state plays the causal role of pain may mean that it actually has causes and effects of certain kinds, or it may mean that it is "apt" for causing and being caused in certain ways. And the truth of the latter is compatible with the falsity of the former. There are various ways in which a creature could have a state which is apt for causing and being caused in certain ways without that state's having, when instantiated in that creature, the relevant causes and effects. To mention just one, it may be that the generalizations that comprise "common–sense psychology" are studded with 'probably's and 'normally's, and that instead of saying that pain has such and such causes and effects, they say that it "tends" to be caused by certain sorts of events, and "tends" to cause, in conjunction with certain other states, certain effects. If one holds this, one will also hold that it is possible for there to be, as a sort of statistical fluke, a creature who has states whose nature it is to tend to have such and such causes, but in whom these states seldom if ever do have such causes and effects. But if this is how we think of the madman, we will be thinking of him as having a physical makeup such that certain conditions (the typical causes of pain) are likely to cause his C–fibers to fire, and such that his C–fibers firing is likely to have certain behavioral effects (the typical behavioral effects of pain). But we will also be supposing that in his case the likely does not happen—he is a statistical fluke, analogous to the fair coin which comes up heads a thousand times in a row. Of course, this is not compatible with Lewis' subsequent characterization of the madman as some one who is "hooked up" differently than the rest of us, presumably in such a way that C–fiber firing does not even have the tendency to cause the typical effects of pain, or to be caused by its typical causes. My point is simply that Lewis' initial characterization of mad pain is such that the admission of its possibility does not imply that there can be pain in the absence of total realizations of pain (as functionally defined), and so does not support the claim that a "simple" functionalism must give way to a "mixed theory."

IV

Ned Block has distinguished two main varieties of functionalism, analytical functionalism, or what Block calls 'Functionalism' (with a capital 'F'), and 'Psychofunctionalism'.[18] These two versions of functionalism do not differ in the sorts of ontological claims they make. Both assert that mental states are identical to SS–functional states (i.e., states expressible by functional predicates containing no mental vocabulary). Nor, I assume, need there be any difference in the modal status they assign to these claims; both can agree with Kripke that identity propositions are metaphysically necessary (assuming that the terms involved are rigid designators). But whereas analytical functionalism views the enterprise of formulating functional definitions as an a priori one, one of conceptual analysis, Psychofunctionalism views it as an empirical enterprise. While both can use the Lewis–Ramsey technique for constructing functional definitions, they will seek different sorts of theories as the bases for constructing their definitions. The analytical functionalist seeks to extract his definition from a "theory" consisting of analytic or conceptual truths about the relations of mental states to inputs, outputs and other mental states. For the Psychofunctionalist, on the other hand, the definitions are to be extracted from the best theory provided by empirical psychology.

It may be that we should distinguish three rather than two versions of functionalism. David Lewis is often classified as an analytical functionalist. But Lewis characterizes the theory from which the functional definitions are to be derived as consisting of "common sense platitudes" about the mental—and while he suggests that at least some of these have the flavor of analyticity about them, it is by no means clear that he wants to include only those platitudes that could be claimed to be analytic. At any rate, there is a possible view which says that mental states are identical to functional states which are definable, by the Lewis–Ramsey technique, in terms of a commonsense psychological theory (sometimes referred to as "folk psychology"), as opposed to a scientific one, but which does not claim that the propositions in that common–sense theory have the status of analytic or conceptual truths. But this seems to me an unpromising view. Assuming that our "common sense platitudes" are synthetic, if one of them should be contradicted by scientific findings we presumably would not want to include it in the theory to which the Lewis–Ramsey technique is applied; we do not want to define our mental terms in terms of a *false* theory. And if our functional "definitions" are not meant to capture the meaning, or sense, of the mental terms, why should the information included in them be limited to facts that are common knowledge? We might say that the analytical functionalist looks for functional characterizations that give the "nominal essence" of mental states, while the Psychofunctionalist looks for functional characterizations that give the "real essence" of such states; what is unclear is what sort of essence the "common sense functionalist" would be looking for. At any rate, in what follows I shall ignore "common sense functionalism," and shall concentrate my attention on analytical functionalism and psychofunctionalism.

There is, however, a version of functionalism which someone could hold without holding either analytical functionalism or Psychofunctionalism—although it could be held together with one or the other of these, or even with both. One might label this view 'minimal functionalism'. But that name isn't really appropriate, since it is a view which some proponents of analytical functionalism and Psychofunctionalism will want to reject. My procedure in the remainder of this paper will be as follows. I shall first characterize this sort of functionalism, and make some observations about it. I shall then consider the relative merits of analytical functionalism and Psychofunctionalism, first on the assumption that this other sort of functionalism is true, and then on the assumption that this other sort of functionalism is false.

V

Properties have two main sorts of (what I shall call) causal features. One sort are causal potentialities; a property has a causal potentiality in virtue of being such that its instantiation in a thing contributes, when combined with the instantiation of certain other properties, to the possession by that thing of a certain causal power. For example, one of the causal potentialities of the property of having a sharp edge consists in the fact that if coinstantiated with the property of being made of steel, this property bestows on its possessor the power of being able to cut wood and various other substances. The second sort of causal feature has to do with the ways in which the instantiation of a property can be caused; a property's having a causal feature of this sort amounts to its being such that its instantiation in a thing will be caused by the instantiation of such and such other properties in things standing in such and such relations to the thing. Every property has many, perhaps in some cases uncountably many, causal features of each of these kinds.

If we could specify all of the causal features of a property in a set of propositions of finite length, then using that set of propositions as our "theory" we could use the Lewis–Ramsey technique to construct a functional predicate which is true of a thing, in all worlds having the same causal laws as the actual world, just in case it has that property. The functional property expressed by that predicate could be called the "functional correlate" (or the "actual world functional correlate") of that property. There is, however, no guarantee that such a finite specification of the causal features of a property is possible. Nevertheless, there is a natural extension of the notion of a functional property which will enable us to speak of each property as having associated with it a functional property which is its functional correlate. It is obviously true of finite sets of causal features that if all of the members of the set can belong to the same property, there is a functional property which something has just in case it has a property having all of the causal features in the set. I propose that we extend the notion of a functional property by stipulating that this is true of infinite and uncountable sets of causal features as well; the functional property corresponding to such a set will be the property of having a property having all of the causal features in the set. This allows there to be functional properties that are not expressible in functional predicates. And if we may speak of the totality of the causal features of any property (and I see no reason why we should not be able to) then we may say that corresponding to any property P there is a functional property, its functional correlate, which something has just in case it has a property having the totality of the causal features possessed by P.

Mental properties, just like others, have infinitely, perhaps uncountably, many causal features. Some of these are ones that no analytic functionalist or Psychofunctionalist would want to mention in his functional definition of the property. For example, if pain can be realized (as earlier) in a certain physiological state $T \& P_j$, and if the coinstantiation of that physiological state with another physiological state P* results in a rise in body temperature, then one of the causal features of pain is that its coinstantiation with T and P* results in a rise of body temperature. This causal feature belongs essentially to the functional property which is the functional correlate of the property of being in pain, but it is presumably without conceptual or psychological significance.

What the causal features of a property are depend on what causal laws hold. If the same properties can be governed by different causal laws in different possible worlds, then there will be worlds in which something has a property without having its functional correlate, and perhaps vice versa. In that case properties cannot in general be identified with their functional correlates. However, a number of philosophers have recently offered causal accounts of property identity.[19] On all of these accounts, it is necessary and sufficient for the identity of properties A and B in the actual world that A and B share all of the same causal features. This amounts to the requirement that properties in the actual world are identical just in case they have the same functional correlate. I have argued elsewhere that a similar condition holds for the "transworld" identification of properties: property P in world w is the same as property P' in world w' just in case P has in w just the causal features that P' has in w'.[20] Or, in other words, P in w is the same as P' in w' just in case the functional correlate of P in w is the same as the functional correlate of P' in w'. I shall refer to this as the causal theory of properties—for short, CTP.

If CTP is true, then every property will be identical to its functional correlate, and every property will be a functional property. And if this is true of properties in general, it will be true of mental properties in particular. However, to say that every mental property is a functional property is not yet to say what functionalism asserts, namely that every mental property is an SS-functional property. Earlier I characterized SS-functional properties as those that are functionally definable in the strong sense, i.e., are expressible by functional predicates containing no mental terminology. Now that I have broadened the notion of a functional property, a corresponding broadening of the notion of an SS-functional property is called for. Let us say that a causal feature of a property is an SS-causal feature if there is an SS-functional property which something has just in case it has a property having that feature—or, in other words, if it can be specified without the use of mental terminology. If all of the members of a set (even of an uncountable set) of causal features are SS-causal features, then the functional property something has just in case it has a property having all of the causal features in that set is an SS-functional property. The "minimal" functionalism mentioned earlier is the view that (a) every mental property is identical to its functional correlate, and (b) the functional correlate of every mental property is an SS-functional property. Since to hold this is to hold that CTP holds for mental properties, I shall refer to it as CTP-functionalism. But while it is obvious that (a) follows from CTP, it is not at all obvious that (b) does; and therefore it is not obvious that CTP–functionalism is a consequence of CTP. I believe that it is a consequence, but I shall not attempt to demonstrate this here. I shall, however, make some remarks about the relationship between the two, which will bring out what must be shown if this is to be demonstrated.

It is clear, I think, that CTP–functionalism does follow from the conjunction of CTP and the version of materialism which says that every property is a physical property, where this is understood as implying that every property has a physical description. On the latter assumption, all of the causal features of mental properties can be specified in physical and "topic neutral" terms, and this means that all are SS–causal features, and thus that the functional correlate of a mental property is an SS–functional property; so if (as CTP says) every property is identical to its functional correlate, every mental property is an SS–functional property.

If we understand materialism as the weaker thesis that all actual realizations of mental states (but not necessarily all possible realizations) are physical, then it is easy to see that from materialism and CTP it follows that for each mental state there is an SS–functional state which is (as a matter of metaphysical necessity) sufficient for its existence, and is such that in the actual world having the mental state is "nothing over and above" the having of that SS–functional state. Let us here understand 'realization' in such a way that if a property P can be construed as the disjunction of properties Q and R, then Q and R are both realizations of P. On the version of materialism now under consideration, while there may be possible worlds in which mental states are realized nonphysically, this does not happen in the actual world. This means that every mental property is construable as a disjunction of properties, and that each of these disjunctions contains as disjunct a physical property (itself, no doubt, a disjunction of properties) such that (a) its instantiation is sufficient for the instantiation of that mental property, and (b) in the actual world it is by having that physical property that something has the mental property. By the argument of the preceding paragraph, if CTP is true, then all of the physical disjuncts of mental properties are SS–functional properties.

To establish the stronger claim that CTP–functionalism follows from CTP even on the assumption that nonphysical realizations of mental states are possible and sometimes occur, and even on the antimaterialist view that *only* nonphysical realizations of mental states are possible, we would have to show the logical impossiblility of the following sort of situation. Suppose that $a_1 \ldots a_n$ and $b_1 \ldots b_n$ are two sets of irreducibly nonphysical properties, and that the a's can be paired with the b's in such a way that for any such pair $\{a_j, b_j\}$, the members of the pair differ in some of the their causal features but share all of the same SS–causal features. If a_j has the causal feature of being caused to exist in x by x's having a_i and physical state P, then b_j will have not this but the counterpart feature of being caused to exist in x by x's having b_i and physical state P; and in virtue of this, both will share an SS–causal feature expressible by a predicate of the form 'α is such that $\exists F[\ldots F \ldots \& (\forall x)$ (x's having F and P causes x to have α)]'. And if a_j has the causal feature that in conjunction with a_k it causes physical state of affairs P*, then b_j will have not this but the counterpart feature that in conjunction with b_k it causes P*; and in virtue of this, both will share an SS–causal feature expressible by a predicate of the form 'α is such that $\exists F[\ldots F \ldots \& (\forall x)$ (x's having α and F causes P*)]'. Let us call such a pair of properties 'functional counterparts'. Let us suppose further that there are two individuals A and B which are exactly alike in all respects (and so in all of their physical properties), except that A's repertoire of possible properties includes the a's and not the b's, while B's repertoire includes the b's but not the a's, and A has a given a-property a_j just in case B has its functional counterpart b_j. Let us speak of individuals related as A and B are as 'functional twins'. Finally, let us suppose that $a_1 \ldots a_n$ are mental states and that $b_1 \ldots b_n$ are not. Thus B, although indistinguishable in its behavior and physical makeup from A, would altogether lack the mental states that A has.

The situation just described is compatible with CTP; since functional counterparts would differ in their causal features, although not in their SS–causal features, they would satisfy CTP's requirement that different properties differ in their causal features. But the situation is of course not compatible with CTP–functionalism. So if the situation is possible, CTP–functionalism does not follow from CTP. To me it seems obvious that this situation is not possible. But I know of no way of arguing for this that does not involve invoking epistemological principles that are at best no less controversial than the claim they would be used to establish. For example, it would be easy enough to show that a mindless creature who was a functional twin of a minded one would be absolutely indistinguishable, by any logically possible observation or test, from the minded one. It is tempting (at least to me) to argue that it follows from this that on the assumption that functional twins are possible we are reduced to total scepticism about the possibility of knowledge of other minds, and that this amounts to a *reductio ad absurdum* of the assumption. But such an argument requires some such principle as the following: if state of affairs S is in principle indistinguishable from state of affairs S', which is incompatible with it, and if it is logically possible that state of affairs S' should obtain, then it is impossible to know that state of affairs S obtains. And there are plenty of contemporary epistemologists who would deny that principle.[21] So while I think that CTP–functionalism should seem plausible to anyone to whom CTP seems plausible, I do not claim to be able to establish conclusively that the latter entails the former.

VI

Let us suppose for the moment that CTP and CTP–functionalism are true. I have said that CTP–functionalism is compatible with either analytic functionalism or Psychofunctionalism. But supposing that we accept the former, what reason could we have for accepting either of the latter?

What distinguishes the CTP–functionalist who accepts analytic functionalism from one who rejects it is not their ontological views, but their views about the semantics of mental terms. Both hold that mental states are identical to functional states, and they need not differ as to what functional states a given mental state is identical to. But CTP–functionalism does not, as such, offer any account of how mental terms latch onto the particular functional states they designate. The analytic functionalist offers an explanation of this along the following lines. Each mental term has analytically associated with it its functional definition, which gives its meaning and specifies the "nominal essence" of the mental state it designates. Although the functional property or state picked out by this definition will have, according to CTP–functionalism, infinitely (perhaps uncountably) many causal features, only a tiny and finite subset of these will be mentioned in the analytic functional definition. What makes the others essential to the functional property is the fact that they are connected by nomological necessity (and so, according to CTP, by metaphysical necessity) with those that are mentioned.

An account along these lines is at least a possible explanation of how a property–term connects with its designatum. There are many terms in the language, such as 'poisonous' and 'mousetrap', for which only such an account is plausible, and the analytic functionalist holds that the same is true of words like 'pain' and 'desire'.

If Psychofunctionalism offers an alternative account of the semantics of mental terms, presumably it will be one along the following lines. Mental terms refer in basically the same way as Kripke and Putnam have held that natural-kind terms like 'gold' and 'water' refer. Such terms apply to certain paradigms and to whatever other things share with those paradigms a scientifically discoverable "real essence". In the case of gold or water, we turn to the science of chemistry to determine what the real essence is. The Psychofunctionalist, as I am now construing him, holds that just as chemistry can tell us the real essence of gold or water, psychology (once it is developed further) can tell us the real essence of pain, anger, belief, desire and thought. Whereas on analytical functionalism the infinitely many causal features of pain belong to the property designated by 'pain' in virtue of their nomological connections with the causal features which are mentioned in the analytic definition of 'pain', according to Psychofunctionalism these features belong to that property in virtue of their nomological connections with a real essence, presently unknown but in principle discoverable by the science of psychology.

A CTP–functionalist who rejects analytical functionalism would not necessarily have to accept Psychofunctionalism. But if he did not, I think that his account of the semantics of mental terms would have to be similar to that just ascribed to the Psychofunctionalist. The difference would be that whereas the Psychofunctionalist sees mental terms as standing for natural kinds whose natures are to be discovered by psychology, this third sort of functionalism sees them as standing for natural kinds whose natures are the subject matter of some other science—most likely physiology. The materialist version of this view would be a version of the psychophysical identity theory, which says that mental properties (states) just are certain physiological properties (states). This is a version of what I have elsewhere called the 'parochial view' about the nature of mental states and the semantics of mental terms. To distinguish it from Psychofunctionalism, which could also be called a parochial view (it makes having *our* "depth psychology" essential to having mental states), let us refer to it as 'physiological parochialism'.

One thing that analytic functionalism and Psychofunctionalism are agreed on is that there are conceivable creatures in whom mental states have very different physical realizations than they do in us—thus both could agree on the conceivability of David Lewis' Martians, whose pains are realized in the inflation of tiny cavities in the feet. Of course, it may turn out to be nomologically impossible given the physical laws that obtain in the actual world (and so metaphysically impossible, if CTP is true), that any functional property with which either sort of functionalist would hold that pain is identifiable could be realized in such a way. What both of these sorts of functionalism are agreed upon, however, is that the mere fact that a creature's physical states are radically different from ours does not in itself preclude them from being realizations of mental states. So both the analytical functionalist and the Psychofunctionalist are persuaded by reflection on (*prima facie*) possible cases that no simple form of the psychophysical identity theory can be true, and that physiological parochialism is false. In Ned Block's terminology, both hold that physiological parochialism is "chauvinistic"—that there are possible circumstances in which it would require us to deny mental states to creatures that have them.

The argument which leads both analytical functionalists and Psychofunctionalists to reject physiological parochialism as chauvinistic might be called the 'argument from science fiction'—it is an argument from our "semantic intuitions" about, i.e., what it seems natural to say about, certain conceivable situations. I want now to suggest that if the argument from science fiction provides a good reason for rejecting physiological parochialism, it provides an equally good reason for favoring analytical functionalism over Psychofunctionalism.

Presumably the psychological theory which the Psychofunctionalist envisages as giving us the real essence of mental states will not consist exclusively or primarily of common-sense platitudes; presumably it will go into some detail about the nature of the underlying psychological processes and mechanisms involved in perception, memory, information processing, and the like. But what reason is there for thinking that these underlying processes and mechanisms must be the same in all creatures having mental states? In other words, what reason is there for thinking that all creatures having mental states must have the same "depth psychology"? As far as I can see, there is no reason for thinking that this is so, and there is good reason for thinking that it is not. As I have said, the analytical functionalist and the Psychofunctionalist agree that the physical differences between Lewis' Martians and us do not in themselves preclude their having the same sorts of mental states we have—or rather, that they preclude this only if they preclude the Martians having the right sorts of functional states. But now suppose that we are investigating the Martians' "psychology" (I put the word 'psychology' in scare quotes, so as not to beg the question as to whether the functional states we assign to them in order to explain their behavior, and which we find to be realized in their physiology, are genuine mental states or not). And let us suppose that not only do the Martians have states which satisfy the best functional definitions of mental states that any analytic functionalist has been able to come up with, but also that if we take their states to be the mental states which satisfy these functional definitions in us then all of the facts that empirical psychology will discover prior to (say) 1985 are true of them—except, of course, those having to do with their relations to neurophysiological states. In other words, if we purge scientific psychology as it will exist in 1985 of whatever mistaken claims it will contain, and also of whatever neurophysiology it will contain, then the remaining theory will do equally well as a theory about human mental states and as a theory about Martian "mental states." For convenience, let us suppose that we make this discovery in 1985. From that time on there are two groups of psychologists at work, one studying us and the other studying the Martians. And let us suppose that for each theoretical issue that is put to experimental test, the issue is decided one way by the experiments on us, and in a different and incompatible way by the experiments on the Martians. Ultimately the psychologists decide that while it requires highly sophisticated experiments to detect the difference, the underlying mechanisms and processes operating in the Martians are radically different from those operating in us—for short, their depth psychology is radically different from ours. To repeat, the difference does not have to do primarily with the radical difference there is (by hypothesis) between the Martian physiology and ours. Indeed, we can suppose that subsequently we find creatures who are superficially very much like us physiologically but who have the Martian "depth psychology," and still other creatures who are superficially very much like the Martians in the physiology but who have the human (Earthling) depth psychology. What we are imagining is that the best possible scientific psychological theory true of human mental states is not true of the Martians—although there is true of them a theory which, relative to our psychological knowledge in 1985, could (epistemically) be the best psychological theory true of us.

The Psychofunctionalist (as I understand his position) has to say that in the case just imagined the Martians don't have such mental states as pain, desire, belief, etc. Here I can only appeal to intuition.

It seems to me that this view is obviously wrong—that it is ruled out by the understanding we all tacitly have of our mental vocabulary. Psychofunctionalism is exposed by this thought experiment as being, like physiological parochialism, a "chauvinist" view about the mental.[22]

It may be helpful to compare this bit of science fiction with a comparable story about gold. Let us suppose that at some time, it will have to be considerably earlier than 1985, we find (on Mars, say), samples of a metallic substance which passes all of the layman's and jeweler's tests for being gold, and obeys all of the laws which the chemistry of the time has established to be true of gold. Subsequently we find that the microstructure of this substance is entirely different from that of our paradigms of gold, and that it is a compound rather than an element. I share the intuition of Kripke and Putnam that this substance is not gold. Of course, if we had become habituated to calling it 'gold', that usage might stick; but in that case the word 'gold' would have become ambiguous—the stuff in question would not fall within the extension of our present word 'gold' although it would fall within the extension of one of the senses that word would have in the imagined situation. But I, for one, have no inclination to say that words like 'belief', 'desire', and 'pain' would be used ambiguously if applied to us and to my imaginary Martians. It is perfectly consistent to accept the Kripke–Putnam account of the semantics of natural kind terms like 'gold' and 'water' while rejecting such an account for mental terms. The notion of a natural kind is not the most luminous of notions; but I do not think we should be bothered if we are required to say that pains, like poisons and mousetraps, are not a natural kind, and lack a scientifically determinable essence.

I should mention that there is an understanding of Psychofunctionalism on which it is compatible with analytical functionalism—on the assumption that CTP-functionalism is true. If Psychofunctionalism incorporates a Kripke–Putnam account of the semantics of mental terms, then it is incompatible with analytical functionalism. But if it holds merely that there is a scientifically discoverable essence of mental states, and that there is in principle available a psychological theory from which functional definitions of mental states could be derived by the Lewis–Ramsey technique, then it is perfectly compatible with analytical functionalism. The analytical functionalist might put the matter as follows: While it is not in any way analytically or conceptually necessary, it may for all we know be nomologically necessary, that in order to satisfy the analytic functional definitions of the various mental states, the states in question must be governed by certain psychological laws which require that they stem from, or involve, certain specific sorts of underlying psychological processes and mechanisms. In other words, it may be that Lewis' Martians, or rather my recent version of them, whose underlying depth psychology is radically different from ours, are a nomological impossibility. If, as a matter of nomological fact, there is only one possible depth psychology which is compatible with the common–sense psychology from which our analytic definitions are derived, then functional definitions extracted from that psychology may be said to express the real, scientifically determinable, essence of mental states. To be sure, the functional predicates extracted from that theory will not be equivalent in meaning to those extracted from the common–sense theory. The predicate that expresses the scientific definition of pain will be very different, and presumably much more complex, than that which expresses the analytic definition. But, assuming CTP–functionalism, this does not prevent these from expressing the same functional property. What we will have are different ways of picking out the same functional property; it will be picked out by two different finite subsets of the infinite set of causal features that "define" the property, and both subsets will determine the same total set because it is in each case a matter of nomological necessity—and so, according to CTP, metaphysical necessity—that whatever has that subset of features has that total set.

It is worth observing that if physiological parochialism is divorced from the Kripke–Putnam account of the semantics of mental terms, and is merely the view that mental states are identical to the functional counterparts of certain physiological states (roughly, those which in us are total realizations of the best possible analytic functional definitions of those states), then on the assumption that CTP is true, physiological parochialism is compatible with analytical functionalism and Psychofunctionalism. For it is compatible with the latter views that in fact the only nomologically possible realizations of the functional states with which they identify mental states are the physiological states which realize them in us. Given CTP, the only nomologically possible realizations will also be the only metaphysically possible realizations. And it would seem that a functional state can be identified with the disjunction of its metaphysically possible realizations.

VII

Now let us consider how things stand if CTP and CTP–functionalism are rejected. To reject CTP is to allow that the causal features of properties can vary from one possible world to another, and thus that a property cannot be identified with its functional equivalent. In other words, it is to hold that the same properties can be governed by different causal laws in different possible worlds. To reject CTP–functionalism is to hold (assuming that one does believe in the possibility of "functional twins," *à la* section V) that this is true of mental properties and states in particular.

First of all, if CTP–functionalism is false, it seems very unlikely that analytic functionalism and Psychofunctionalism can *both* be true. Suppose that analytical functionalism is true, and suppose further, as we did at the end of section VI, that in the actual world the causal laws are such that it is nomologically impossible for a creature's states to satisfy the "correct" analytic functional definitions without conforming to a certain depth psychology. In the actual world, then, mental states have a certain scientifically determinable essence. As we have seen, if CTP–functionalism were true then in these circumstances both analytical functionalism and Psychofunctionalism would be true—both the best analytic definition of a functional state and the best scientific definition of it would pick out the same functional state, namely the functional counterpart of that state. But if CTP and CTP–functionalism are false, and mental properties have different causal features in different possible worlds, then of course it will not follow from the fact that the best analytic definition and the best scientific one are nomologically equivalent in the actual world that they are nomologically equivalent in all possible worlds, and so it will not follow that they are metaphysically equivalent.

But another point of importance merges here. If CTP is false, then from the supposition that in the actual world it is nomologically necessary that whatever creatures have mental states (of the sorts we have) must have the same depth psychology, it does not follow that this is true in all possible worlds. Assuming, then, that there is a depth psychology which all "minded" creatures in the actual world share, if we use the Lewis–Ramsey technique to define functional states or properties in terms of this theory, then while each of these will be coextensive with some mental property in the actual world (and in all worlds nomologically like it), we cannot infer from this, if CTP is false in the case of mental properties, that this coextensiveness holds in all metaphysically possible worlds—as it must do if the mental properties are to be identified with the functional ones. If analytical functionalism is true, but CTP is not, then there seems no reason in principle why there should not be worlds in which the depth psychologies underlying mental states are very different from the one we are supposing there to be in the actual world, and also worlds in which there is no *one* depth psychology, but rather different ones for different species of minded creatures (as I suggested earlier may well be the case in the actual world). And it is hard to see why this shouldn't be a possibility quite apart from whether analytical functionalism is true. Psychofunctionalism is often advanced as an empirical thesis. But it is hard enough to see how it could be discovered empirically that it is nomologically impossible for there to be more than one depth psychology in the actual world. And if we assume the falsity of CTP, it is even harder—I think it is quite impossible—to see how it could be discovered empirically that the one nomologically possible depth psychology in the actual world is also the only nomologically possible depth psychology in all possible worlds in which there are mental states.

One possible out for the Psychofunctionalist who rejects CTP is to hold that while there are possible worlds in which the causal laws, and so the causal features of properties, are different from what they are in the actual world, these are worlds in which mental properties do not exist (or, at any rate, cannot be instantiated). This would enable him to identify mental properties with their functional correlates, and so would amount to holding CTP–functionalism while rejecting CTP as a general view about properties. Assuming (as I do in this section) that CTP does not hold in general, it is hard to see what reason there could be for thinking that it holds in the special case of mental properties. Certainly there seems to be little prospect of its being an empirical discovery (say of psychology) that this is so; it is not easy to see how empirical data could support the conclusion that certain properties can only be instantiated in worlds nomologically equivalent to this one.

In the absence of some a priori reason why we should hold CTP–functionalism without holding CTP, the prospect of Psychofunctionalism being true seems even dimmer on the supposition that CTP is false than on the supposition that it is true. On the other hand, analytic functionalism can live equally well with CTP and with its denial. If CTP is false, then there may be logically or metaphysically possible realizations of the best analytic functional definitions which are not nomologically possible, given the laws that hold in the actual world. In that case, the functional properties picked out by the analytic functional definitions will not be metaphysically coextensive with, and so cannot be identical to, the actual–world functional correlates of the corresponding mental properties. But it is no part of the thesis of analytic functionalism that such an identity holds; analytical functionalism is compatible with CTP–functionalism, as we have already noted, but it does not imply it.

VIII

I have not, in this paper, offered any reason for thinking that any version of functionalism is true. My primary aim has been to clarify some of the different versions (no doubt there are more than I have distinguished) and the relations between them. But I think that it emerges from this clarification that some versions have less prospect of being established than others. Reflection on the nature of properties, or on the notion of a property, may give us reason to accept CTP–functionalism, and reflection on our mental concepts may give us reason to accept analytical functionalism. But there is no prospect of Psychofunctionalism being established by unaided philosophical analysis. And even if philosophical analysis is supplemented by empirical research in psychology, the prospects of Psychofunctionalism being established seem nonexistent unless CTP–functionalism can be established, and dim even if it can be.[23]

NOTES

1. See Lewis' "Psychophysical and Theoretical Identification," *Australasian Journal of Philosophy*, 27 (1975), 291–315. See also Ned Block's "Troubles with Functionalism," in *Perception and Cognition, Issues in the Foundations of Psychology* (ed. by C. Wade Savage, *Minnesota Studies in the Philosophy of Science*, Vol. IX [Minneapolis, 1978]), and Block's introduction to his anthology *Readings in Philosophy of Psychology*, Vol. I (Harvard University Press, Cambridge, Mass.: 1980).

2. Ned Block, "Are Absent Qualia Impossible?" *The Philosophical Review*, LXXXIX, No. 2 (April, 1980), p. 257, footnote 1.

3. Of course, no functionalist would maintain that each different belief and each different want must be defined separately; in the case of belief, for example, the functionalist will want a definition of 'S believes that P' which holds for all values of 'P'.

4. See, for example, Block, "Are Absent Qualia Impossible?", p. 257.

5. See, for example, Ned Block and Jerry Fodor, "What Mental States are Not," (*The Philosophical Review*, LXXXI [1972], 159–81), p. 163.

6. See especially Hilary Putnam, "The Mental Life of Some Machines," in Putnam's *Mind, Language and Reality, Philosophical Papers, Volume 2* (Cambridge, 1975).

7. Forthcoming in Block (ed.), *Readings in Philosophy of Psychology*, Vol. I. Hereafter I shall refer to this as 'MP&MP'.
8. MP&MP, p. 216.
9. Ibid.
10. Ibid., p. 217.
11. Ibid.
12. Ibid., p. 218.
13. Ibid.
14. Ibid.
15. Ibid.
16. Ibid., p. 220.
17. Ibid., p. 216.
18. See Block, "Troubles with Functionalism."
19. See Peter Achinstein, "The Identity of Properties," *American Philosophical Quarterly* 11 (1974), and David Armstrong, *A Theory of Universals, Universals & Scientific Realism*, Vol. II (Cambridge, 1978). See also my "Causality and Properties," in Peter van Inwagen (ed.), *Time and Cause* (Dordrecht, Holland, 1980).
20. See my "Causality and Properties."
21. See, for example, Alvin I. Goldman, "Discrimination and Perceptual Knowledge," *The Journal of Philosophy*, LXXIII (1976), 771–91.
22. Cf. Ned Block, "Troubles with Functionalism," pp. 310–14, especially his remarks on "cross–world psychology."
23. I wish to thank the National Endowment for the Humanities for support during the period in which this paper was written.

Functionalism, Qualia, and Intentionality

PAUL M. CHURCHLAND
PATRICIA SMITH CHURCHLAND
University of Manitoba

Functionalism—construed broadly as the thesis that the essence of our psychological states resides in the abstract causal roles they play in a complex economy of internal states mediating environmental inputs and behavioral outputs—seems to us to be free from any fatal or essential shortcomings. Functionalism-on-the-hoof is another matter. In various thinkers this core thesis is generally embellished with certain riders, interpretations, and methodological lessons drawn therefrom. With some of the more prominent of these articulations we are in some disagreement, and we shall turn to discuss them in the final section of this paper. Our primary concern, however, is to *defend* functionalism from a battery of better-known objections widely believed to pose serious or insurmountable problems even for the core thesis outlined above. In sections I and II we shall try to outline what form functionalism should take in order to escape those objections.

I. *Four Problems Concerning Qualia*

'Qualia' is a philosophers' term of art denoting those intrinsic or monadic properties of our sensations discriminated in introspection. The quale of a sensation is typically contrasted with its causal, relational, or functional features, and herein lies a problem for functionalism. The quale of a given sensation—pain, say—is at best contingently connected with the causal or functional properties of that state; and yet common intuitions insist that said quale is an essential element of pain, on some views, *the* essential element. Functionalism, it is concluded, provides an inadequate account of our mental states.

Before addressing the issues in greater detail, let us be clear about what the functionalist need not deny. He need not and should not deny that our sensations have intrinsic properties, and he should agree as well that those properties are the principal means of our introspective discrimination of one kind of sensation from another. What he is committed to denying is that any particular quale is *essential* to the identity of any particular type of mental state. Initially they may seem to be essential, but reflection will reveal that they do not have and should not be conceded that status. In what follows we address four distinct but not unrelated problems. Each problem is manageable on its own, but if they are permitted to band together for a collective assault, the result is rather confusing and formidable, in the fashion of the fabled Musicians of Bremen. With the problems separated, our strategy will be to explain and exploit the insight that intrinsic properties *per se* are no anathema to a functionalist theory of mental states.

A. The Problem of Inverted/Gerrymandered Qualia

This problem is just the most straightforward illustration of the general worry that functionalism leaves out something essential. The recipe for concocting the appropriate intuitions runs thus. Suppose that the sensations having the quale typical of pain in you play the functional role of pleasure sensations in someone else, and the quale typical of pleasure sensations in you are had instead by the sensations that have the functional role of pain in him. Functionally, we are to suppose, the two of you are indistinguishable, but his pleasure/pain qualia are simply inverted relative to their distribution among your own sensations, functionally identified. A variation on the recipe asks us to imagine someone with an inverted distribution of the color qualia that characterize your own visual sensations (functionally identified). He thus has (what you would introspectively identify as) a sensation of red in all and only those circumstances where you have a sensation of green, and so forth.

These cases are indeed imaginable, and the connection between quale and functional syndrome is indeed a contingent one. Whether it is the quale or the functional syndrome that determines type–identity qua psychological state, we must now address. The intuitions evoked above seem to confound functionalist pretensions. The objection to functionalism is that when the inversion victim has that sensation whose functional properties indicate pleasure, *he is in fact feeling pain*, functional properties notwithstanding; and that when the victim of a spectrum inversion says, "I have a sensation of green" in the presence of a green object, *he is in fact having a sensation of red*, functional properties notwithstanding. So far as type–identity of psychological states is concerned, the objection concludes, sameness of qualitative character dominates over sameness of functional role.

Now there is no point in trying to deny the possibilities just outlined. Rather, what the functionalist must argue is that they are better described as follows. "Your pains have a qualitative character rather different from that of his pains, and your sensations-of-green have a qualitative character rather different from that of his sensations-of-green. Such internal differences among the same psychological states are neither inconceivable, nor even perhaps very unusual." That is to say, the functionalist should concede the juggled qualia, while continuing to reckon type-identity in accordance with functional syndrome. This line has a certain intuitive appeal of its own, though rather less than the opposing story, at least initially. How shall we decide between these competing intuitions? By isolating the considerations that give rise to them, and examining their integrity.

The "pro-qualia" intuitions, we suggest, derive from two main sources. To begin with, all of us have a strong and entirely understandable tendency to think of each type of psychological state as constituting a *natural kind*. After all, these states do play a vigorous explanatory and predictive role in everyday commerce, and the common-sense conceptual framework that comprehends them has all the features and functions of a sophisticated empirical theory (see Wilfrid Sellars, 1956; and Paul Churchland, 1979). To think of pains, for example, as constituting a natural kind is to think of them as sharing an *intrinsic nature* that is common and essential to *every* instance of pain. It is understandable then, that the qualitative character of a sensation, the only non-relational feature to which we have access, should present itself as being that essential element.

Our inclination to such a view is further encouraged by the fact that one's introspective discrimination of a sensation's qualitative character is far and away the most immediate, most automatic, most deeply entrenched, and (in isolation) most authoritative measure of what sensations one has. In one's own case, at least, the functional features of one's sensations play a minor role in one's recognition of them. It is as if one had a special access to the intrinsic nature of any given type of sensation, an access that is independent of the purely contingent and causal features that constitute its functional role.

Taken conjointly, these considerations will fund very strong intuitions in favor of qualia as *the* determinants of type-identity for psychological states. But though natural enough, the rationale is exceptionally feeble on both points.

Take the first. However accustomed or inclined we are to think of our psychological states as constituting natural kinds, it is vital to see that it is not a semantic or conceptual matter, but an objective *empirical* matter, whether or not they do. Either there is an objective intrinsic nature common to all cases of, e.g., pain, as it occurs in humans, chimpanzees, dogs, snakes, and octopi, or there is not. And the fact is, the functionalist can point to some rather persuasive considerations in support of the view that there is not. Given the physiological and chemical variety we find in the nervous systems of the many animals that feel pain, it appears very unlikely that their pain states have a common physical nature underlying their common functional nature (see Hilary Putnam, 1971). It remains possible that they all have some intrinsic *non*–physical nature in common, but dualism is profoundly implausible on sheer evolutionary grounds. (The evolutionary process just *is* the diachronic articulation of matter and energy. If we accept an evolutionary origin for ourselves, then our special capacities must be construed as the capacities of one particular articulation of matter and energy. This conclusion is confirmed by our increasing understanding of the nervous system, both of its past evolution and its current regulation of behavior.) In sum, the empirical presumption *against* natural–kind status for psychological states is substantial. We should not place much trust, therefore, in intuitions born of an uncritical prejudice to the contrary. Such intuitions may reflect ordinary language more or less faithfully, but they beg the question against functionalism.

The facts of introspection provide no better grounds for thinking sensations to constitute natural kinds, or for reckoning qualia as their constituting essences. That the qualitative character Q of a psychological state S should serve as the standard ground of S's introspective discrimination is entirely consistent with Q's being a non–essential feature of S. The black and yellow stripes of a tiger serve as the standard ground on which tigers are visually discriminated from other big cats, but the stripes are hardly an essential element of tigerhood: there are albino tigers, as well as the very pale Himalayan tigers. The telling question here is this: why should the qualia of our familiar psychological states be thought any different? We learn to pick out those qualia in the first place, from the teeming chaos of our inner lives, only because the states thus discriminated are also the nexus of various generalizations connecting them to other inner states, to environmental circumstances, and to overt behaviors of interest and importance to us. Had our current taxonomy of introspectible qualia been *un*successful in this regard, we would most certainly have thrown it over, centered our attention on different aspects of the teeming chaos within, and recarved it into a different set of similarity classes—a set that *did* display its objective integrity by its many nomic connections, both internal and external. In short, the internal world comes pre-carved into observational kinds no more than does the external world, and it is evident that the introspective taxonomies into which we eventually settle are no less shaped by considerations of explanatory and causal coherence than are the taxonomies of external observation.

It is therefore a great irony, it seems to us, that anyone should subsequently point to whatever qualia our introspective mechanisms have managed tenuously to fix upon as more-or-less usable indicators of nomologically interesting states, and claim *them* as constituting the *essence* of such states. It is of course distantly possible that our mechanisms of introspective discrimination have lucked onto the constituting essences of our psychological states (assuming, contrary to our earlier discussion, that each type *has* a uniform natural essence), but a priori that seems about as likely as that the visual system lucked onto the constituting essence of tigerhood when it made black–on–yellow stripes salient for distinguishing tigers.

Therefore, it seems very doubtful that the type–identity of any psychological state derives from its sharing in any uniform natural essence. Moreover, even if it does so share, it seems entirely unlikely that introspection provides any special access to that essence. Consequently, this beggars the intuition which sustains the inverted–qualia objections.

The preceding investigation into the weight and significance of factors determining type–identity of psychological states does more than that, however. It also enriches the competing intuition, namely, that the type–identity of psychological states is determined by functional characteristics. To repeat the point made earlier, since the taxonomy of observational qualia constructed by the questing child *follows* the discovered taxonomy of states as determined by interesting causal roles, it is evident that sameness of functional role dominates over differences in qualitative character, so far as the type–identity of psychological states is concerned. That a single category, unified by functional considerations, can embrace diverse and disparate qualitative characters has a ready illustration, ironically enough, in the case of pain.

Consider the wide variety of qualia wilfully lumped together in common practice under the heading of pain. Compare the qualitative character of a severe electric shock with that of a sharp blow to the kneecap; compare the character of hands dully aching from making too many snowballs with the piercing sensation of a jet engine heard at very close range; compare the character of a frontal headache with the sensation of a scalding pot grasped firmly. It is evident that what unites sensations of such diverse characters is the similarity in their functional roles. The sudden onset of any of them prompts an involuntary withdrawal of some sort. Our reaction to all of them is immediate dislike, and the violence of the dislike increases with the intensity and duration of the sensation. All of them are indicators of physical trauma of some kind, actual or potential. All of them tend to produce shock, impatience, distraction, and vocal reactions of familiar kinds. Plainly, these collected causal features are what unite the class of painful sensations, not some uniform quale, invariant across cases. (For a general account of the intentionality of our sensations, in which qualia also retreat into the background, see Paul Churchland, 1979: ch. 2.)

The converse illustration is formed by states having a uniform or indistinguishable qualitative character, states which are nevertheless distinguished by us according to differences in their functional roles. For example, our emotions have a certain qualitative character, but it is often insufficient to distinguish which emotion should be ascribed. On a particular occasion, the felt knot in one's soul might be mild sorrow, severe disappointment, or gathering despair, and which of these it is—really is—would depend on the circumstances of its production, the rest of one's psychological state, and the consequences to which it tends to give rise. Its type–identity need not be a mystery to its possesser—he has introspective access to some of the context which embeds it—but the identification remains unmakeable on qualitative grounds alone. Similarly, a therapist may be needed, or a thoughtful friend, to help you distinguish your decided unease about some person as your hatred for him, envy of him, or simple fear of him. The felt quality of your unease may be the same for each of these cases, but its causes and effects would be significantly different for each. Here again, functional role is the dominant factor in the type–identity of psychological states.

The reason that functional role dominates introspectible qualitative differences and similarities is not that the collected laws descriptive of a state's functional relations are analytically true, or that they exhaust the essence of the state in question (though withal, they may). The reason is that the common–sense conceptual framework in which our psychological terms are semantically embedded is an *empirical theory*. As with theoretical terms generally, their changeable position in semantic space is fixed by the set of theoretical laws in which they figure. In the case of folk psychology, those laws express the causal relations that connect psychological states with one another, with environmental circumstances, and with behavior. Such laws need not be seen, at any given stage in our growing understanding, as *exhausting* the essence of the states at issue, but at any given stage they constitute the best-founded and most authoritative criterion available for identifying those states.

We conclude against the view that qualia constitute an essential element in the type-identity of psychological states. Variations within a single type are both conceivable and actual. The imagined cases of qualia inversion are of interest only because they place directly at odds intuitions that normally coincide: the non-inferential impulse of observational habit against the ponderous background of theoretical understanding. However, the qualitative character of a sensation is a relevant mark of its type-identity only insofar as that character is the uniform concomitant of a certain repeatable causal syndrome. In the qualia-inversion thought experiments, that uniformity is broken, and so, in consequence, is the relevance of those qualia for type-identity, at least insofar as they can claim a *uniform* relevance across people and across times.

B. The Problem of Absent Qualia

The preceding arguments may settle the qualia-inversion problem, but the position we have defended is thought to raise in turn an even more serious problem for functionalism (see Ned Block and Jerry Fodor, 1972; and Block, 1978). If the particular quale a sensation has contributes nothing to its type-identity, what of a "psychological" system functionally isomorphic with us, whose functional states have no qualia whatever? Surely such systems are possible (nomically as well as logically), runs the objection. Surely functionalism entails that such a system feels pain, warmth, and so on. But since its functional states have no qualitative character whatever, surely such a system *feels nothing at all*. Functionalism, accordingly, must be false.

This argument is much too glib in the contrast it assumes between functional features (which supposedly matter to functionalism) and qualitative character (which supposedly does not). As the functionalist should be the first to admit, our various sensations are introspectively discriminated by us on the basis of their qualitative character, and any adequate psychological theory must take this fact into account. How might functionalism do this? Straightforwardly. It must require of any state that is functionally equivalent to the sensation–of–warmth, say, that it have some instrinsic property or other whose presence is detectable by (= is causally sufficient for affecting) our mechanisms of introspective discrimination in such a way as to cause, in conceptually competent creatures, belief–states such as the belief that I have a sensation–of–warmth. If these sorts of causal relations are not part of a given state's functional identity, then it fails to be a sensation–of–warmth on purely functional grounds. (Sydney Shoemaker makes much the same point in Shoemaker, 1975. We do not know if he will agree with the points that follow.)

So functionalism *does* require that sensations have an intrinsic property that plays a certain causal role. But it is admittedly indifferent as to precisely what that intrinsic property might happen to be for any given type of sensation in any given person. So far as functionalism is concerned, that intrinsic property might be the spiking frequency of the signal in some neural pathway, the voltage across a polarized membrane, the temporary deficit of some neurochemical, or the binary configuration of a set of DC pulses. So long as it is one of these properties to which the mechanisms of introspective discrimination happen to be keyed, the property fills the bill.

"But *these* are not qualia!" chorus the outraged objectors. Are they not indeed. Recall the characterization of qualia given on the first page of this paper: " . . . those intrinsic or monadic properties of our sensations discriminated in introspection." Our sensations are anyway token–identical with the physical states that realize them, so there is no problem in construing a spiking frequency of 60 hertz as an intrinsic property of a certain sensation. And why should such a property, or any of the others listed, *not* be at the objective focus of introspective discrimination? To be sure, they would be *opaquely* discriminated, at least by creatures with a primitive self–conception like our own. That is to say, the spiking frequency of the impulses in a certain neural pathway need not prompt the non–inferential belief, "My pain has a spiking frequency of 60 Hz"; it may prompt only the belief, "My pain has a searing quality." But withal, the property you opaquely distinguish as "searingness" may be precisely the property of having 60 Hz as a spiking frequency.

There are many precedents for this sort of thing in the case of the intrinsic properties of material objects standardly discriminable in observation. The redness of an object turns out to be a specific reflectance triplet for three critical wavelengths in the EM spectrum. The pitch of a singer's note turns out to be its frequency qua oscillation in air pressure. The warmth of a coffee cup turns out to be the vibrational energy of its molecules. The tartness of one's lemonade turns out to be its high relative concentration of H^+ ions. And so forth.

These chemical, electromagnetic, and micromechanical properties have been briskly discriminated by us for many millennia, but only opaquely. The reason is that we have not possessed the concepts necessary to make more penetrating judgments, and our mechanisms of sensory discrimination are of insufficient resolution to reveal on their own the intricacies uncovered by other means. Unambiguous perception of molecular KE, for example, would require sensory apparatus capable of resolving down to about 10^{-10} metres, and of tracking particles having the velocity of rifle bullets, millions of them, simultaneously. Our sensory apparatus for detecting and measuring molecular KE is rather more humble, but even so it connects us reliably with the parameter at issue. Mean molecular kinetic energy may not seem like an observable property of material objects, but most assuredly it is. (For a working-out of these themes in detail, see Paul Churchland, 1979.)

Similarly, spiking frequency may not seem like an introspectible property of sensations, but there is no reason why it should not be, and no reason why the epistemological story for the faculty of inner sense should be significantly different from the story told for outer sense. Qualia, therefore, are not an ineffable mystery, any more than colors or temperatures are. They are physical features of our psychological states, and we may expect qualia of some sort or other in any physical system that is sufficiently complex to be functionally isomorphic with our own psychology. The qualia of such a robot's states are not "absent." They are merely *unrecognized* by us under their physical/electronic description, or as discriminated by the modalities of outer rather than inner sense.

We may summarize all of this by saying that the functionalist need not and perhaps should not attempt to deny the existence of qualia. Rather, he should be a realist about qualia—in particular, he should be a *scientific* realist.

It is important to appreciate that one can be reductionistic about qualia, as outlined above, without being the least bit reductionistic about the taxonomy of states appropriate to psychological theory.

Once qualia have been denied a role in the type–identity of psychological states, the path described is open. If this line on qualia is correct, then it vindicates Ned Block's prophecy (1978: p. 309) that the explication of the nature of qualia does not reside in the domain of psychology. On the view argued here, the nature of specific qualia will be revealed by neurophysiology, neurochemistry, and neurophysics.

C. The Problem of Distinguishing States With Qualia From States Without

One could distinguish many differences between the sensations and the propositional attitudes, but one particular difference is of special interest here. A sensation–of–warmth, for example, has a distinct qualitative character, whereas the belief–that–Tom–is–tall does not. Can functionalism account for the difference?

Yes it can. The picture to be avoided here depicts sensations as dabbed with metaphysical paint, while beliefs remain undabbed and colorless. The real difference, we suggest, lies less in the objective nature of sensations and beliefs themselves, than in the nature of the introspective mechanisms used to discriminate and identify the states of each class. This hypothesis requires explanation.

How many different types of sensation are there? One hundred? One thousand? Ten thousand? It is difficult to make an estimate, since most sensations are arrayed on a qualitative continuum of some sort, and it is to some extent arbitrary where and how finely the lines between different kinds are drawn. It is plain, however, that the number of distinct continua we recognize, and the number of significant distinctions we draw within each, is sufficiently small that the brain can use the following strategy for making non–inferential identifications of sensations.

Consider the various physical properties which in you are characteristic of the repeatable brain state that realizes a given sensation. Simply exploit whichever of those physical properties is accessible to your innate discriminatory mechanisms, and contrive a standard habit of conceptual response ("lo, a sensation of warmth") to the property–evoked activation of those mechanisms. While this strategy will work nicely for the relatively small class of sensations, it will not work at all well for the class of beliefs, or for any of the other propositional attitudes. The reason is not that the brain state that realizes a certain belief *lacks* intrinsic properties characteristic of it alone. Rather, the reason is that there are far too many beliefs, actual and possible, for us to have any hope of being able to discriminate and identify all of them on such a one–by–one basis. The number of possible beliefs is at least a denumerable infinity, and the number of possible beliefs expressible in an English sentence of ten words or less is still stupendous. Assuming a vocabulary of 10^5 words for English, the number of distinct strings of ten words or less is 10^{50}. Assuming conservatively that only one string in every trillion trillion is grammatically and semantically well–formed, this still leaves us over 10^{25} distinct sentences. Even if there were a distinct and accessible monadic property for each distinct belief–state, therefore, the capacity of memory is insufficient to file all of them. Evidently the brain must use some more systematic strategy for discriminating and identifying beliefs—a strategy that exploits in some way any belief's unique combinatorial structure.

But this is a very complex and sophisticated matter, requiring the resources of our higher cognitive capacities, capacities tuned to the complex relational, structural, and combinatorial features of the domain in which the discriminations are made. Unlike the sensation case, no narrow range of stimulus/response connections will begin to characterize the mechanisms at work here.

Sensations and beliefs, accordingly, must be introspectively discriminated by entirely distinct cognitive mechanisms, mechanisms facing quite different problems and using different strategies for their solutions. Sensations are identified by way of their intrinsic properties; beliefs are identified by way of their highly abstract structural features. It should not be wondered at then, that there is a subjective contrast in the nature of our awareness of each.

D. The Differentiation Problem

This problem arises because we are occasionally able to discriminate between qualitatively distinct sensations where we are ignorant of any corresponding functional differences between them, and even where we are wholly ignorant of the causal properties of both of them, as when they are new to us, for example. These cases are thought to constitute a problem in that functional considerations should bid us count the states as type–identical, whereas by hypothesis, they are type–distinct (see Block, 1978: p. 300).

The objection has two defects. First, sheer ignorance of functional differences need not bind us to counting the sensations as functionally identical. The functionalist can and should be a realist about functional properties. Functional identities are not determined by what we know or do not know, but by what is actually out there in the world (or, *in* there, in the world). Second, the objection begs the question against functionalism by assuming that a discriminable qualitative difference between two sensations entails that they are type–distinct qua psychological states. We have already seen that this inference is wrong in any case: pains display a variety of qualitative characters, but because of their functional similarities, they still count as pains.

In short, we can and do make discriminations among our sensations in advance of functional understanding. But whether the discriminations thus made mark a difference of any importance for the taxonomy of psychological theory is another question. In some cases they will; in other cases they will not. What decides the matter is whether those qualitative differences mark any causal or functional differences relevant to the explanation of psychological activity and overt behavior.

So long as introspectible qualia were thought to be ineffable, or epiphenomenal, or dualistic, or essential for type–identity, one can understand the functionalist's reluctance to have anything to do with them. But once we have seen how the functionalist can acknowledge them and their epistemic role, within a naturalistic framework, the reluctance should disappear. For the taxonomy of states appropriate for psychological theory remains dictated entirely by causal and explanatory factors. Qualia are just accidental hooks of opportunity for the introspective discrimination of *dynamically* significant states.

II. The Problem of Non–Standard Realizations

Some of the issues arising here have already been broached in the section concerning absent qualia. However, novel problems arise as well, and organization is best served by a separate section. All of the problems here begin with the functionalist's central contention that the functional organization necessary and sufficient for personhood is an abstract one, an organization realizable in principle in an indefinite variety of physical systems. Such liberalism seems innocent enough when we contemplate the prospect of humanoid aliens, biomechanical androids, and electromechanical robots whose physical constitutions are at least rough parallels of our own. Who could deny that C3PO and R2D2 are persons? But our liberal intuitions are quickly flummoxed when we consider bizarre physical systems which might nevertheless realize the abstract causal organization at issue, and such cases move one to reconsider one's generosity in the more familiar cases as well.

The following discussion will explore but two of these non-standard "persons": Ned Block's "Chinese Nation" (Block, 1978), and John Searle's "Chinese-speaking room" with the monolingual anglophone locked inside it (Searle, 1980). Block is concerned with the absence of *qualia* from states posing as sensations, and Searle is concerned with the absence of *intentionality* from states posing as propositional attitudes.

Block's example will be examined first. He has us imagine a certain Turing machine T_m, which is realized in the population of China, as follows. Each citizen enjoys a two-way radio link to a certain robotic device with sensory transducers and motor effectors. This robot is the body of the simulated person, and it interacts with its collective brain thus: it sends a sensory input message I_j to every citizen and subsequently receives a motor output message O_i from exactly one citizen. Which citizen sends what output is determined as follows. Overhead from a satellite some state letter S_k is displayed in lights for all to see. For each possible state letter S_k there is assigned a distinct subset of the population. In the rare event when S_k is displayed *and* input I_j is received, one person in the S_k group to whom I_j has been assigned performs this pre-assigned task: she sends to the robot the unique output message O_i antecedently assigned to her, radios the satellite to display the state letter S_p antecedently assigned to her, and then subsides, waiting for the next opportunity to do exactly the same thing in exactly the same circumstances.

As organized above, each citizen realizes exactly one square of the machine table that specifies T_m. (A machine table is a matrix or checkerboard with state letters heading the columns and input letters heading the rows. Any square is the intersection of some S_k and I_j, and it specifies an output O_i and a shift to some state S_p, where possibly p = k.) Block asks us to assume that T_m adequately simulates your own functional organization. One is likely to grant him this, since any input–output function can in principle be simulated by a suitable Turing machine. In pondering an apparently fussy detail, Block wonders, "How many homunculi are required?" and answers, "Perhaps a billion are enough; after all, there are only about a billion neurons in the brain" (p. 278). Hence his choice of China as the potential artificial brain.

Finally, Block finds it starkly implausible to suppose that this realization of T_m has states with a qualitative character like pains, tastes, and so on. It is difficult not to agree with him. His homunculi do not even interact with one another, save indirectly through the satellite state letter, and, even less directly, through the adventures of the robot body itself. The shimmering intricacies of one's inner life are not to be found here.

The way to avoid this criticism is just to insist that any subject of beliefs and sensations must not only be "Turing–equivalent" to us (that is, produce identical outputs given identical inputs), it must be computationally equivalent to us as well. That is, it must have a system of inner states whose causal interconnections mirror those in our own case. This is not an arbitrary restriction. Folk psychology is, and scientific psychology should be, realistic about our mental states, and mere parity of gross behavior does not guarantee parity of causal organization among the states that produce it. The computational organization displayed in the Chinese Turing machine is not even distantly analogous to our own. If it were analogous to our own, worries about absent qualia could be handled as outlined in section I, part B, above.

There is a further reason why it is not arbitrary to demand a computational organization more along the lines of our own, and we may illustrate it by examining a further defect in Block's example. It is demonstrable that no T_m realized as described in the population of China could possibly simulate your input–output relations. There are not nearly enough Chinese—not *remotely* enough. In fact, a spherical volume of space centered on the Sun and ending at Pluto's orbit packed solidly with cheek–to–cheek Chinese (roughly 10^{36} homunculi) would still not be remotely enough, as we shall show.

Being realized on a one–man/one–square basis, the Chinese T_m can have at most 10^9 distinct possible outputs, and at most $10^9/S$ distinct possible inputs, where S is the total number of distinct state letters. That is, T_m has rather less than 10^9 possible inputs.

How many distinct possible inputs characterize your own functional organization? Since the present argument requires only a lower limit, let us consider just one of your retinas. The surface of your retina contains roughly 10^8 light sensitive cells, which we shall assume (conservatively) to be capable of only two states: stimulated or unstimulated. Good eyesight has a resolution limit of about one foot at a distance of a mile, or slightly less than one arc–minute, and this angle struck out from the lens of the eye subtends about six microns at the retina. This is roughly the distance between the individual cells to be found there, so it is evident that individual cells, and not just groups, can serve as discriminative atoms, functionally speaking.

If we take distinct stimulation patterns in the set of retinal cells as distinct inputs to the brain, it is evident that we are here dealing with

2 to the (10^8) power distinct inputs. This is an appallingly large number. Since $2^{332} \approx 10^{100}$ (a googol), $2^{10^8} \approx 10^{30,000,000}$ distinct possible inputs from a single retina! Since a one–man/one–square Turing machine must have at least as many homunculi as possible inputs, any such realization adequate to the inputs from a single retina would require no less than $10^{30,000,000}$ distinct homunculi. However, there are only about 10^{80} distinct atoms in the accessible universe. Small wonder the Chinese nation makes an unconvincing simulation of our inner lives, but we should never have acquiesced in the premise that a Turing machine thus realized could even begin to simulate your overall functional organization. The Chinese robot body can have at most a mere 30 binary input sensors, since $2^{30} \approx 10^9$, and the number of inputs cannot exceed 10^9.

This argument does not depend on inflated estimates concerning the retina or its input to the brain. (It might be objected that retinal cell stimulation is not independent of the state of its immediate neighbor cells, or that the optic nerve has only 800,000 axons.) If your retina contained only 332 discriminatory units, instead of 10^8, the number of distinct inputs would still be 2^{332}, or roughly 10^{100}: ninety–one orders of magnitude beyond the capacity of the Chinese nation, and twenty orders of magnitude beyond the atoms in the universe. Nor have we even begun to consider the other dimension of the required machine table: the range of states, S, of the brain which receives these inputs, a brain which has at least 10^{10} distinct cells in its own right, each with about 10^3 connections with other cells. Our estimate of the number of distinct states of the brain must be substantially in excess of $10^{30,000,000}$, our number for the retina.

Our conclusion is that *no* brute–force one–device/one–square realization of a Turing machine constructible in this universe could even begin to simulate your input–output organization. Even the humblest of creatures are beyond such simulation. An unprepossessing gastropod like the sea slug *Aplysia Californica* has well in excess of 332 distinct sensory cells, and thus is clearly beyond the reach of the crude methods at issue. This does not mean that the human input/output relations cannot be represented by an abstract Turing machine T_m. What it does mean is that any *physical* machine adequate to such simulation *must* have its computational architecture and executive hardware organized along lines vastly different from, and much more unified and efficient than, those displayed in Block's example. That example, therefore, is not even remotely close to being a fair test of our intuitions. Quite aside from the question of qualia, the Chinese Turing machine couldn't simulate an earthworm.

This weakness in the example is not adequately made up by allowing, as Block does at one point (p. 284), that each homunculus might be responsible for a wide range of inputs, each with corresponding outputs. On this modification, each homunculus would thus realize, dispositionally, many machine–table squares simultaneously. Suppose then that we make each Chinese citizen responsible for one billion squares peculiar to him. This raises the number of distinct inputs processable by the system to 10^9 citizens × 10^9 squares = 10^{18} possible inputs, still well short of the $10^{30,000,000}$ we are striving for. Well, how many squares must each citizen realize if the nation as a whole *is* to instantiate some Turing machine adequate to handle the required input? The answer is, of course, $10^{(30,000,000-9)}$ squares each. But how will each citizen/homunculus handle this awesome load? *Not* by being a simple one-device/one-square Turing machine in turn, as we have already seen. No physical simulation adequate to your input–output relations, therefore, can avoid having the more unified and efficient modes of computational organization alluded to in the last paragraph, even if they only show up as modes of organization of its various subunits. Any successful simulation of you, that is, must somewhere display a computational/executive organization that is a much more plausible home for qualitative states than Block's example would suggest.

But can a number of distinct persons or near–persons collectively constitute a further person? Apparently so, since the system consisting of your right hemisphere and left hemisphere (and your cerebellum and thalamus and limbic system, etc.) seems to do precisely that. Further attempts to construct homunculi–headed counter–examples to functionalism should perhaps bear this fact in mind.

The argument of the preceding pages does not, of course, show that the specific details of *our* computational organization are essential to achieving the informational capacity required. And this raises a question we might have asked anyway: if we do require of any subject of sensations, beliefs, and so forth, that it be functionally equivalent to us in the strong sense of "computationally equivalent," do we not then run the opposite danger of allowing too *few* things to count as sites of mentality? (see again Block, p. 310ff.) If we restrict the application of the term 'mentality' to creatures having sensations, beliefs, intentions, etc., we will indeed have become too restrictive. Yet the functionalist need not pretend that our internal functional organization exhausts the possible kinds of mentality. He need only claim that our kind of internal functional organization is what constitutes a psychology of *beliefs, desires, sensations,* and so forth. He is free to suggest that an alien functional organization, comparable only in sophistication to our own, could constitute an alien psychology of quite different internal states. We could then speak of Martian mentality, for example, as well as of human mentality.

Still, it might be wondered, what is the shared essence that makes both of us instances of the now more general term, 'mentality'? There need be none, beyond the general idea of a sophisticated control center for complex behavior. One of the functionalist's principal theses, after all, is that there are no natural essences to be found in this domain. If he is right, it is folly to seek them. In any case, it is question–begging to demand that he find them.

On the other hand, there may yet prove to be some interesting natural kind, of which both we and the Martians are variant instances: some highly abstract thermodynamic kind, perhaps. In that case, orthodox functionalism would be mistaken in one of its purely negative theses. On this matter, see the final section of this paper.

Let us now turn to John Searle's worries about meaning and intentionality. The states at issue here are beliefs, thoughts, desires, and the rest of the propositional attitudes. On the functionalist's view, the type–identity of any of these states is determined by the network of relations it bears to the other states, and to external circumstances and behavior. In the case of the propositional attitudes, those relations characteristically reflect a variety of logical and computational relations among the propositions they "contain." We can thus at least imagine a computer of sufficient capacity programmed so as to display an economy of internal states whose interconnections mirror those in our own case. The simulation would create the required relational order by exploiting the logical and computational relations defined over the formal/structural/combinatorial features of the individual propositional states.

Searle has no doubt that such a simulation could, in principle, be constructed. His objection to functionalism is that the states of such a system would nevertheless lack meaning and intentionality: "... no purely formal model will ever be sufficient by itself for intentionality because the formal properties are not by themselves constitutive of intentionality" (Searle, 1980: p. 422). His reasons for holding this position are illustrated in the following thought–experiment.

Imagine a monolingual anglophone locked in a room with (a) a substantial store of sequences of Chinese symbols, and (b) a set of complex transformation rules, written in English, for performing operations on sets and sequences of Chinese symbols. The occupant periodically receives a new sequence of Chinese symbols through a postal slot. He applies his transformation rules dutifully to the ordered pair, ⟨new sequence, old store of sequences⟩, and they tell him to write out a further sequence of Chinese symbols, which he sends back out through the postal slot.

Now, unknown to the occupant, the large store of sequences embodies a rich store of information on some one or more topics, all written in Chinese. The new sequences sent through the door are questions and comments on those topics. The transformation rules are a cunningly devised program designed to simulate the thought processes and conversational behavior of a native speaker of Chinese. The symbol-sequences the occupant sends out are "responses" to the queries and comments received. We are to suppose that the transformation rules are well-devised, and that the simulation is as convincing as you please, considered from the outside.

However convincing it is, says Searle, it remains plain that the room's occupant does not understand Chinese: he applies transformation rules, and he understands those rules, but the sequences of Chinese symbols are meaningless to him. Equally clear, claims Searle, is that the system of the room-and-its-contents does not understand Chinese either. Nothing here understands Chinese, save those sending and receiving the messages, and those who wrote the program. No computational state or output of that system has any meaning or intentionality save as it is interpretively imposed from without by those who interact with it.

However, concludes Searle, this system already contains everything relevant to be found in the physical realization of any purely formal program. If meaning and intentionality are missing here, they will be missing in any such attempt to simulate human mental activity. Instantiating a program could not be a sufficient condition of understanding,

> Because the formal symbol manipulations by themselves don't have any intentionality; they are quite meaningless; they aren't even *symbol* manipulations, since the symbols don't symbolize anything. In the linguistic jargon, they have only a syntax but no semantics. Such intentionality as computers appear to have is

solely in the minds of those who program them, those who send in the input and those who interpret the output. [Ibid., p. 422]

The set of commentaries published in the same issue provides many useful and interesting criticisms of Searle's argument, and of his conclusion as well. The critical consensus is roughly as follows. If the system of the room–plus–contents is upgraded so that its conversational skills extend beyond a handful of topics to include the entire range of topics a normal human could be expected to know; and if the system were supplied with the same inductive capacities we enjoy; and if the "belief store" were integrated in the normal fashion with some appropriately complex goal structure; and if the room were causally connected to a body in such a fashion that its inputs reflected appropriate sensory discriminations and its outputs produced appropriate behavior; then the system of the room–plus–contents jolly well would understand Chinese, and its various computational states—beliefs that p, desires that q—would indeed have meaning and intentionality, in the same way as with a normal Chinese speaker.

Searle is quite willing to consider upgradings of the kind described—he attempts to anticipate them in his paper—but he is convinced they change nothing relevant to his case. As it emerges clearly in his "Author's Response" (pp. 450–56), of central importance to his argument is the distinction between

> ... cases of what I will call *intrinsic intentionality*, which are cases of actual mental states, and what I will call *observer–relative ascriptions* of intentionality, which are ways that people have of speaking about entities figuring in our activities but lacking intrinsic intentionality. [p. 451] [The latter] are always dependent on the intrinsic intentionality of the observers. [p. 452]

Examples of the latter would be the words and sentences of one's native tongue. These have meaning and intentionality, allows Searle, but only insofar as they bear certain relations to our beliefs, thoughts, and intentions—states with intrinsic intentionality. A simulation of human mentality grounded in a formal program may yield states having this derivative observer–relative brand of intentionality, concedes Searle, but they cannot have intrinsic intentionality. And since they lack a feature essential to genuine mental states, they cannot be genuine mental states, and to that extent the simulation must be a failure.

As we see it, this criticism of functionalism is profoundly in error. It is a mistake to try to meet it, however, by continuing with the strategy of trying to upgrade the imagined simulation in hopes of finally winning Searle's concession that at last its states have achieved intrinsic intentionality. The correct strategy is to argue that our own mental states are just as innocent of "intrinsic intentionality" as are the states of any machine simulation. On our view, all ascriptions of meaning or propositional content are relative—in senses to be explained. The notion of "intrinsic intentionality" makes no more empirical sense than does the notion of position in absolute space. We shall try to explain these claims.

There are basically just two ways in which one can assign propositional content to the representational states of another organism. An example of the first is the translation of a foreign language. An example of the second is the calibration of an instrument of measurement or detection.

In the case of translation, one assigns specific propositional contents to the alien representations because one has found a general mapping between the alien representations and our own such that the network of formal and material inferences holding among the alien representations closely mirrors the same network holding among our own representations. Briefly, their collected representations display an *intensional structure* that matches the intensional structure displayed by our own.

The story is essentially the same when we are assigning propositional content to an alien's thoughts, beliefs, etc. It matters naught whether the alien's representation is overt, as with a sentence, or covert, as with a belief. We assign a specific content, p, to one of the alien's representations, on the strength of whatever assurances we have that his representation plays the same abstract inferential role in his intellectual (computational) economy that the belief-that-p plays in ours. And what goes for aliens goes also for one's brothers and sisters.

This is not to say that the representational states of other humans have content only insofar as others interpret them in some way. After all, the set of abstract inferential relations holding among the representations in someone's intellectual economy is an objective, non-relational feature of that person. But it does mean that the content, call it the *translational content*, of any specific representation of his *is a matter of the inferential/computational relations it bears to all the rest of his representations*. There can be no question of an isolated state or token possessing an intrinsic translational content; it will have a specific translational content only if, and only insofar as, it enjoys a specific set of relations to the other elements in a *system* of representations.

Contrast translational content with what is naturally termed *calibrational content*. The repeatable states of certain physical systems are more-or-less reliable indicators of certain features of their environment, and we may assign content (e.g., 'The temperature is 0°C'.) to such states (e.g., a certain height in a column of red alcohol) on the strength of such empirical connections. This goes for the human system as well. The various states we call 'perceptual beliefs' can be assigned contents in this manner, as a function of which type of environmental circumstance standardly triggers their occurrence. In fact, if a system has any systematic responses to its environment at all, then calibration can take place even where translation cannot—either because the system simply lacks the internal economy necessary for translational content, or because the intensional structure of that economy is incommensurable with our own. Furthermore, calibrational content may regularly *diverge* from translational content, even where translation is possible. Consider an utterance which calibrates as 'There is thunder', but which translates as 'God is shouting'; or one which calibrates as 'This man has a bacterial infection', but which translates as 'This man is possessed by a pink demon'.

Accordingly, Searle is right to resist the suggestion that merely hooking up the room-system, via some sensors, to the outside world, would supply a unique meaning or content to the room's representational states. Genuine mental states do indeed have a content or intentionality that is independent of, and possibly quite different from, their calibrational content. (The reader will notice that this entails that it is just possible that all or most of our beliefs are false—that their translational contents may be systematically out of agreement with their actual calibrational contents. For an extended exploration of this real possibility, see Paul Churchland, 1979: ch. 2. On this matter see also Stephen Stich, this issue.) That independent intentionality is their *translational content*. But this content falls well short of being the "intrinsic intentionality" Searle imagines our states to have. Translational content is not environmentally determined, nor is it observer-relative, but it is most certainly a *relational* matter, a matter of the state's inferential/computational relations within a system of other states. Accordingly, it is entirely possible for translational content to be possessed by the states of a machine—the realization of a purely formal program.

What more than this Searle imagines as fixing the content of our mental states, we are unable to surmise. He floats the distinction between intrinsic intentionality and other kinds by means of illustrative examples (p. 451); he hazards no palpable account of what intrinsic intentionality consists in; and the intuitions to which he appeals can be explained in less mysterious ways, as outlined above. To conclude, there is simply no such thing as intrinsic intentionality, at least as Searle conceives it. Functionalists need not be concerned then that computer simulations of human mentality fail to display it.

We complete this section by underscoring a contrast. In the first half of this section we conceded to the critic of functionalism that our mental states have qualia, but we argued that the states of a machine simulation could have them as well. In this second half we have conceded to the critic of functionalism that the states of certain machine simulations must lack intrinsic intentionality. But we insist that our own states are devoid of it as well.

III. Functionalism and Methodology

Despite the defenses offered above, we do wish to direct certain criticisms against functionalism. The criticisms are mainly methodological rather than substantive, however, and we shall here provide only a brief summary, since they have been explained at length elsewhere.

A. Conceptual Conservatism

No functionalist will suppose that the functional organization recognized in the collected lore of folk psychology exhausts the functional intricacies that make up our internal economy. All will agree that folk psychology represents only a partial, and in some respects even a superficial, grasp of the more complex organization that empirical psychology will eventually unravel. Even so, there is a decided tendency on all sides to suppose that, so far as it goes, folk psychology is essentially correct in the picture it paints, at least in basic outlines. Empirical psychology will add to it, and explain its principles, most expect, but almost no one expects it to be overthrown or transmogrified by such research.

This sanguine outlook is not unique to functionalists, but they are especially vulnerable to it. Since the type–identity of mental states is held to reside, not in any shared physical or other natural essences, but in the structure of their causal relations, there is a tendency to construe the generalizations connecting them as collectively *stipulating* what it is to be a belief, a desire, a pain, and so forth. Folk psychology is thus removed from the arena of empirical criticism.

This is unfortunate, since the "denaturing" of folk psychology does not change its epistemic status as a speculative account of our internal workings. Like any other theory, it may be radically false; and like any other deeply entrenched theory, its falsity is unlikely to be revealed without a vigorous exploration of that possibility.

A functionalist can of course accept these points without danger to what is basic in his position. Nevertheless, they are worth making for two reasons. First, eliminative materialism is not a very widespread opinion among adherents of functionalism, despite being entirely consistent with their view. And second, there are very good reasons for doubting the integrity of folk psychology, in its central structures as well as in its peripheral details (see Paul Churchland, 1979: ch. 5; 1981a; also, Patricia Churchland, 1980a; 1980b; and look for Stephen Stich's *The Case Against Belief*, in progress).

B. Top–Down Versus Bottom–Up

Given that the essence of our psychological states resides in the set of causal relations they bear to one another, etc., and given that this abstract functional organization can be realized in a nomically heterogeneous variety of substrates, it is fair enough that the functionalist should be more interested in that abstract organization than in the machinery that realizes it. With the science of psychology, it is understanding the "program" that counts; an understanding of such hardwares as may execute it is secondary and inessential.

This much is fair enough, but so long as we are so profoundly ignorant of our functional organization as we are at present, and ignorant of where to draw the line between "hardware" and "program" in organisms, we cannot afford to be so casual about or indifferent to the neurosciences as the preceding rationale might suggest. If we wish to unravel the functional intricacies of our internal economy, one obvious way to go about it is to unravel the intricacies of the physical system that executes it. This "bottom–up" approach is not the only approach we might follow, but it does boast a number of advantages: it is very strongly empirical; it is not constrained by the preconceptions of folk psychology; it has the capacity to force surprises on us; it permits a non–behavioral comparison of cognitive differences across species; it enjoys direct connections with evolutionary ethology; and at least in principle it *can* reveal the functional organization we are looking for.

Neuroscience is an awkward and difficult pursuit, however, and there is an overwhelming preference among philosophers, psychologists, and artificial intelligence researchers for a more "top-down" approach: hypothesize functional systems ("programs") and test them against our molar behavior, as conceived within common sense. This is entirely legitimate, but if the functionalist is moved by the argument from abstraction to ignore or devalue the bottom-up approach, his methodology is dangerously conservative and one-sided. (We have discussed these shortcomings at length in Patricia Churchland, 1980a, 1980c; and in Paul Churchland, 1981a, 1981b, 1980.)

C. Reductionism

Thanks to the argument from abstraction, functionalists tend to be strongly anti-reductionist. They deny that there can be any general characterization of what makes something a *thinker* that is expressible in the language of any of the physical sciences. Given the variety of possible substrates (biological, chemical, electromechanical) that could realize a thinking system, it is difficult not to agree with them. But it does not follow, from multiple instantiability *per se*, that no such general characterization is possible. It follows only that the required characterization cannot be expressed in the theoretical vocabulary peculiar to any one of the available substrates. It remains entirely possible that there is a level of physical description sufficiently abstract to encompass all of them, and yet sufficiently powerful to fund the characterization required.

As it happens, there is indeed a physical theory of sufficient generality to encompass the activity of all of these substrates, and any others one might think of. The theory is thermodynamics—the general theory of energy and entropy. It has already supplied us with a profoundly illuminating characterization of what the nineteenth century called "vital activity," that is, of the phenomenon of life. And it is far from unthinkable that it might do the same for what this century calls "mental activity." (For a brief exploration of these ideas, see Paul Churchland, 1981b.) The theoretical articulation of such a characterization would be a very great achievement. It would be unfortunate if the search for it were impeded by the general conviction that it is impossible, a conviction born of the anti-reductionist urgings of a false orthodoxy among functionalists.

REFERENCES

Block, Ned. "Troubles with Functionalism." *Minnesota Studies in the Philosophy of Science*, Vol. IX: pp. 261–325. Edited by C. Wade Savage. Minneapolis: University of Minnesota Press, 1978.

Block, Ned and Fodor, Jerry. "What Mental States Are Not." *The Philosophical Review*, LXXXI (1972): 159–81.

Churchland, Patricia Smith. (1980a). "A Perspective on Mind–Brain Research." *The Journal of Philosophy*, LXXVII, 4 (April, 1980): 185–207.

———— (1980b). "Language, Thought, and Information Processing." *Noûs* 14 (1980): 147–69.

———— (1980c). "Neuroscience and Psychology: Should the Labor Be Divided?" *The Behavioral and Brain Sciences*, III, 1 (March, 1980): 133.

Churchland, Paul M. (1979). *Scientific Realism and the Plasticity of Mind*. Cambridge: Cambridge University Press, 1979.

———— (1980). "Plasticity: Conceptual and Neuronal." *The Behavioral and Brain Sciences*, III, 1 (March, 1980): 133–34.

———— (1981a). "Eliminative Materialism and the Propositional Attitudes." *The Journal of Philosophy* (LXXVIII, 2 February, 1981): 67–90.

———— (1981b). "Is *Thinker* a Natural Kind?" *Dialogue* (forthcoming, 1981).

Putnam, Hilary. "The Nature of Mental States." *Materialism and the Mind–Body Problem*, pp. 150–61. Edited by David Rosenthal. New Jersey: Prentice–Hall, 1971.

Searle, John. "Minds, Brains, and Programs." *The Behavioral and Brain Sciences*, III, 3 (September, 1980): 417–57.

Sellars, Wilfrid. "Empiricism and the Philosophy of Mind." *Minnesota Studies in the Philosophy of Science*, Vol. I. Edited by Herbert Feigl and Michael Scriven. Minneapolis: University of Minnesota Press, 1956. Reprinted in Sellars, *Science, Perception, and Reality*. London: Routledge & Keegan Paul, 1963: 127–96.

Shoemaker, Sydney. "Functionalism and Qualia." *Philosophical Studies* 27 (1975): 291–315.

Stich, Stephen. *The Case Against Belief*. In progress.

Functionalism, Psychology, and the Philosophy of Mind

K. V. WILKES
St. Hilda's College, Oxford

I

A great deal has been claimed for functionalism; in my view, considerably more than it can or should try to deliver. To overestimate its scope renders it vulnerable to a number of objections which cannot easily or plausibly be evaded,[1] so that it is easy to conclude by *under*estimating its power and potential in its true and proper domain. In this paper I sketch my own version of the scope and limits of functionalism, arguing both for the promise of its scope and the extent of its limitations.

First, though, some ground–clearing: a few preliminary remarks which I hope will be recognized as obvious and trivial. (i) To describe a theory as 'functionalist' is elliptical shorthand; 'being a function' is as such an incomplete predicate. Functions are functions *of* things: cutting is the function of a knife, herding sheep that of a sheepdog, and seeing (*vide* Aristotle) is the job of the optical apparatus. Functions are thus functions of structures, and often of complex structures at that. Further, some structures physically cannot perform certain tasks—meringues can't carve joints. It often therefore proves unwise in psychology to concentrate exclusively upon the functional design of the systems examined, because the applicability of many predicates will often depend, as Gunderson puts it,[2] not so much on how the robot is programmed but rather upon how the program is roboted. To keep this important, if obvious, point in mind I shall throughout the rest of the paper talk not of 'functionalism' but of 'S–F theory', where 'S–F' stands for 'structural–functional'. This point has implications to which we shall return.

(ii) An equally obvious remark: not all functions as initially described are such as to be realizable *per se* by specific and identifiable structures. Before we get to structures suitable for theoretical purposes (i.e., structures that are not only identifiable and reidentifiable, but which were worth picking out and adding to our theoretical ontology in the first place), the functions in question may need to be dissected into their constituent functions, and these in turn may need further subdivision until, maybe sooner and maybe later, we come across structures competent to perform them. Perception is a case in point. It is merely unhelpful to be told (*pace* Aristotle this time) that it is "the optical apparatus" which performs the function of seeing. If we attempted to individuate "the optical apparatus" as a system capable of realizing this function, we would need to range all over the brain: from the retina to the visual cortex, then *via* bits of the temporal and parietal lobes, pulling in certain functions of the frontal lobes as well; and whatever else we may have, we do not have here a well–defined system. Instead, we need to break down the function of seeing into its constituent sub–functions. Let us consider just two of these, the functions of analysis and synthesis performed by the striate cortex (Area 17) and the prestriate cortex (Areas 18 and 19) respectively. The analysis performed by the striate cortex presupposes the activity of columns of simple cells specific to only precisely–defined sorts of stimuli; some respond to moving edges, others to lines with a particular alignment, others to colour contrasts, and so forth. The complex and hypercomplex cells of Areas 18 and 19 react to increasingly elaborate stimulus configurations, thereby synthesizing into a complex *Gestalt* the atomic data supplied by the simple cells of Area 17. Thus we find a step–by–step dissection of the global function of seeing; first into a set of processes that include the processes of analysis and synthesis, and then a break–down of these processes into sub–processes which columns of cells are thought to realize.

(iii) It follows from this that the structures to which various functions are assigned will themselves be structured systems; and hence that they can in turn be subjected to a *S–F* analysis. This will be so whether we find ourselves at the level of the visual cortex, of Area 18, or of cell–columns. The function or functions which the theory assigns to these structures becomes their "behavior" or output, the production of which is to be explained; functions competent to produce this output need to be postulated and assigned to subsystems of the structure or dissected into constituent functions and then so assigned. This point also has implications to which we shall return.

(iv) From (ii) and (iii) above it should be clear that the structure–function distinction does not divide the brain and its operations into two neat categories. It depends upon the depth and detail of the analysis whether Area 17, for example, is taken as being "the" structure which performs the function of analysis, or whether it is rather seen as the locale of a set of constituent functions for which different kinds of neural structures are sought. Within a given theory, and at a chosen level of analysis, the structure–function distinction may be clear enough; but from a different theoretical background or from the perspective of a coarser or a finer–grained analysis it may be lost to sight.

II

So much for preliminaries. I turn now to my first main contention, arguing for the *limitations* of S–F theory. The contention, crudely and dogmatically stated, is that S–F theory has little if anything to do with our everyday descriptions, explanations and predictions of human or animal behavior, and consequently that it tells us nothing about ordinary–language ascriptions of mental terms. Thus if by the phrase 'the philosophy of mind' we understand the analysis of everyday mental terms à la Ryle or Wittgenstein, then S–F theory has nothing to say to it. But if we enlarge the scope of the philosophy of mind to incorporate the philosophy of psychology, then S–F theory, inasmuch as it provides the most promising framework for research in psychology, falls squarely into its purview. This is an important point, for several writers have suggested that functional analyses are analyses of the meanings of mental terms[3] or that they tell us what mental states are; and if by 'mental' they mean the everyday battery of ordinary language psychological terms, this is seriously mistaken. Although several writers have noted that there will be a difference between the psychologist's and the layman's ontology and conceptual apparatus,[4] the full implications of this insight have not yet been absorbed. I shall try here to underline the differences between the two kinds of psychological explanation, from which it should become clear just how irrelevant S–F theory is to the understanding of ordinary–language ascriptions of mental terms.

The central point is that there is no useful sense of the term 'theory' whereby everyday psychological explanation suggests or contains a theory of the mind[5]; so *S–F theory* could not be expected to fit it. There are several reasons for denying to common–sense explanation the status of theory. First and foremost, our everyday mental terms have more work to do than have scientific terms. Although they share with the latter the tasks of describing, explaining and predicting, they have countless other roles as well: to warn, threaten, assess, applaud, praise, blame, discourage, urge, wheedle, sneer, hint, imply, insult . . . and so on. The conceptual apparatus of common–sense psychology stands to that of scientific

149

psychology as a multi-purpose tool stands to a spanner. Second, and a related point: even if we consider those functions which common-sense and scientific psychology do share (description, explanation and prediction) we find that the everyday *explananda*, and hence inevitably the *explanantia*, are substantially and significantly different from those of the science. For cognitive psychology is seeking to identify and explain the pervasive, fundamental capacities that underlie the purposive behavior of humans and animals; it asks, for example, how we can store visual or verbal information in short-term or long-term memory; how we perceive; how we set about solving problems of various kinds; and so forth. It looks for what is basic and common to organisms which in turn must be classified into relevant kinds: humans, primates, vertebrates, octogenarians, pre-linguistic children, aphasics. Every science must devise a taxonomy of the events that fall within its domain of discourse, and hence has to devise a descriptive vocabulary of observational and theoretical predicates. Since events can be very variously described, not every description of an action or a capacity for action will be a description in the domain of psychology. Similarly, psychology must create its own taxonomy of subjects, the agents of the behaviors picked out; and then one way of characterizing the rest of the enterprise is to portray it as searching for the most perspicuous taxonomies of theoretical and explanatory postulates in terms of which the behavior as described, of the agents as described, might be explicable.

In ordinary life, on the other hand, we are typically and characteristically interested primarily in the individual and dateable actions of specific people in particular circumstances, and it is our everyday needs, interests, preoccupations and styles of life that determine the descriptions under which we classify action and agent. We want to know why Fred became a Catholic, whether John will dislike David, why Sheila went to France rather than to Italy. Usually our explanations and predictions will not, and are not intended to, generalize to different people or altered circumstances; our reasons for predicting that John will dislike David may be quite irrelevant to our estimation of the likelihood of Peter finding Jeremy uncongenial. Now of course we do at times both seek and employ generalizations about agents; we may ask what makes people join the National Front;[6] or explain someone's attitude towards his distant wife by saying either "out of sight, out of mind" or, "absence makes the heart grow fonder." But if we compare such generalizations as these with the general laws sought by cognitive psychology, considering in particular the impossibility of filling out the *ceteris paribus* clauses in the everyday generalizations and the consequent near–irrelevance of counter–examples, then we can see that this limited interest in general statements cannot help to turn common–sense psychology into a theory. And the interest is indeed limited; the primary concern of everyday explanation, and the domain where it is most at home and is able to produce subtle, accurate, ambitious and sophisticated analyses of human motivation, is the sphere of the unique actions of specific individuals in well–nigh unrepeatable circumstances.

Since the *explananda* differ so much from those of science, the *explanantia* will evidently do so too. To account for the fact that X ɸ–ed at time *t* in circumstances C we typically need to cite one or more of his beliefs or assumptions, show what he wanted to gain by doing just this in those circumstances by ascribing to him a specific intention or desire, in short, to display his reasons for ɸ–ing then. Furthermore, such an account will be offered to an interlocutor who not only fails to understand some feature of the action, but who can usually be supposed to possess a lot of information already about the agent, the action and the circumstances in question. It is trivial to point out that we tailor our descriptions and explanations to the needs and information of our audience; but this trivial point, when applied to everyday psychological explanations, means that such explanations are irredeemably and essentially context–relative. There is thus a double influence of context: first because what we are examining is a unique action done in a particular time and place by a specific individual, and second because our explanations are tailored to the particular problems of the audience. Hence the way we describe the action will depend upon the interest that our interlocutors have in it (e.g., the difference between 'he put out his arm' and 'he signaled'); and what we cite in our explanation will depend just as crucially upon what we take our audience to know or not to know as upon what, if anything, we take to have been going through the agent's mind as he acted. Thus "the same action" may be explained on two different occasions by the citation of quite different beliefs, desires or intentions.

Some of this is certainly reflected, albeit to a very slight extent, in scientific explanation. All accounts presuppose that the reader has adequate background knowledge, and will fail of their purpose if this presupposition is unfounded; so explanations are in this sense audience–relative. However, the audience to which psychological analyses are relativized is the body of fellow–psychologists, co-workers in the field, and no further than that—for experiments conducted in California must be so described that they can be repeated and assessed in Tokyo. Further, the first kind of context-relativity—that the *explanandum* is a specific dated action of an individual in a particular context—has no reflection in scientific psychology. And this alone is enough to give us a gross divergence in the kinds of things that are cited as *explanantia*; for to account for X's ϕ-ing at t in C we will need to cite his belief *that p*, or his desire *for x*, or his intention *to* ψ, whereas if we are trying to explain how people in general are capable of doing things such as holding strings of digits in short-term memory, no such beliefs, desires or intentions are relevant. Instead we should be looking for *explanantia* common to all those capable of performing the task, such as processes of storing and retrieving information. We abstract from specificities of context and seek for what is common, hence the explanatory items will most certainly not prove to be individual propositional attitudes.

The fact that common-sense explanation is essentially context-dependent, whereas scientific explanation is committed to abjuring reliance on idiosyncracies of context, helps make intelligible another dramatic and important distinction between the conceptual frameworks of each. Context-independence requires that the terms used in description and explanation be clear, unambiguous, and where possible well-defined (instrumentally, operationally, what you will). More general constraints upon scientific theory require further that the conceptual apparatus be as economical and non-redundant as possible; theories seek to explain the maximum in terms of the minimum. So cognitive psychology seeks a stripped-down, precise conceptual framework in which the categorial status of each referent is clear and defined. But nothing remotely like this is to be found in everyday psychology, where our ordinary mental terms display riotous overlap, alluring vagueness, categorial ambiguity, and rich shades of nuance. The overlap is what makes books like Roget's *Thesaurus* possible: for example, instead of ascribing a belief to an agent we could often ascribe instead a memory, an opinion, an assumption, a prejudice; or something held, taken for granted, known or recalled. Vagueness can be illustrated by the concept of belief again: is it a *belief* that I have two hands, or should it rather be described as something I take for granted? When a dog is barking beneath a tree, can we say that he *believes* that a cat is up it? As for categorial ambiguity, consider how freely we reify almost any mental phenomenon at the drop of a hat:

he visualized, she formed a mental image, her elbow hurt, he had a pain in his elbow, he believes that there is life on Mars, she holds the belief that there is. Our mental life seems to be an excellent example of a Heraclitean flux (cf. William James: "Consciousness is nothing jointed; it flows") which we can divide up as we will and which rarely suggests or prescribes any single method of categorial division. Finally, nuance can often be conveyed by a specific choice of terms; when I report that he remembers that p, my words will not carry the implications that may be suggested by saying (sneer in the voice, perhaps) that he believes that p. These features of our everyday mental vocabulary are not regrettable deficiencies, however, and so are not features which should, ideally, be eliminated; for they give us versatility and flexibility adequate for our varied linguistic purposes in everyday life. Because of rich overlap, because of indefinable shades of nuance, and because there is categorial and ontological indifference we can, *before* a specific audience and *about* a specific action, convey accurately, precisely and economically equally specific explanations of experience and behavior. Put another way, it is the uniqueness of the action and the explanatory context that renders precise and accurate (in context!) our best and most perspicuous accounts of the doings of ourselves and others. Context–relativity lends to everyday explanation the precision that in scientific explanation must derive from the clarity and definitiveness of the concepts used.

If all this is indeed so—and the foregoing strikes me as boringly obvious rather than as a substantial or a contestable thesis—then it is evidently impossible to regard the referents of ordinary terms as states of which a S–F theory might be true or false. For consider what would be required if we did try to force them into the functionalist straitjacket; if, as Dennett suggests,[7] we thought of common–sense psychology as that which provides the most general and abstract formulations of the *explananda* with which cognitive psychology must cope. The likelihood is (and this emerges clearly from the literature) that the non–scientist takes it for granted that familiar notions like beliefs, and desires or pro–attitudes of some kind, pick out the correct *explanantia* and hence that the S–F theorist's flow–chart must make room for these. However, if we select 'belief' as the right explanatory notion,[8] then clearly we cannot also include in the model such things as assumptions, memories, opinions, convictions etc.; all these concepts overlap, to a greater or a lesser degree, with the concept of belief, and thus would quarrel for room with the box in the flow–chart marked 'beliefs'. Hence these concepts must not figure in the functional map; nevertheless, since they overlap only partly with 'belief', the notion of belief itself must be modified to scoop up what it would otherwise be leaving out. Thus the meaning of 'belief' must be enlarged, or at least drastically modified; and we will need to delineate carefully what is then meant by the term, for it will have become technical and unfamiliar. Then we will need to perform the same exercise with the term 'desire' (or with whatever pro-attitude concept has been selected) in order to avoid competition from 'wish', 'long for', 'want', 'incline' and 'prefer'.

So, then, we proceed; but what reason can there be for thinking that this exercise can be done, except inefficiently, from an armchair? Why, in short, is this the abstract-and-general layer of cognitive psychology rather than bad a priori pseudo-science? The question becomes particularly pointed when we reflect that in this exercise we must also be settling a priori the fundamental *explananda* for cognitive psychology; for the choice of *explanantia*—'beliefs' and 'desires', for example—goes hand in hand with, and makes no sense without, a firm grip on an equally clear taxonomy of the sorts of behavior that we are trying to explain. However, it seems evident from the philosophical literature that the *explananda* envisaged are the familiar actions picked out by everyday psychology, the action-types that for various reasons attract our interest, and not, usually, the basic cognitive capacities which psychology seeks to explain; moreover, even if it is acknowledged that it must be such abilities as learning, perception, problem-solving, pattern-recognition etc. that provide the *explananda*, it is still a moot point whether a taxonomy of these abilities that derives from familiarity with the language will indeed coincide with the taxonomy thought to be the most perspicuous, fruitful, comprehensive and economical from the viewpoint of the laboratory. Consider the difference between the layman's, and the physicist's, understanding of the terms 'force', 'mass' and 'energy'; this parallel is, incidentally, an instructive one, for *vis-à-vis* the physical world the philosopher retains no trace of the imperialism that now seems to dominate his relationship to psychology: Mill's description of philosophy as "the scientific study of the mind" undeservedly lingers on.[9]

To sum up, my contention in this section is that the philosopher who regards some ordinary-language 'theory' as something which is to provide the most abstract and the most general framework within the terms of which cognitive psychology should set to work must find himself caught between two uncomfortable stools. If he does his concept-clarifying work properly, considering the various constraints upon the taxonomies of *explananda* and *explanantia* and being rightly suspicious of the intuitive obviousness of the classifications of actions and of mental states which his familiarity with ordinary language suggests to him, then his work is better done in a laboratory than a study, and he will find himself moved so far from common-sense psychology that he can no longer claim that it is *this* which provides the most abstract-level framework for the science. Once ordinary-language concepts have been adopted, they then have to be adapted—modified, tidied up, extended or restricted—in short, denaturalized: baked in the theoretical kiln until they bear as little resemblance to their parent concepts as do the physicists' notions of force, mass and energy. That is all clearly a scientific enterprise. On the other hand, inasmuch as the philosopher clings to folk psychology and thinks to find in that the 'theory' which cognitive psychology should work with and from, so will he be the more deceived: not only does the everyday conceptual framework contain no theory, not only do the elements of that framework suffer from redundancy, categorial obscurity and ineliminable vagueness, but above all there is no justification for the supposition that common sense can provide the most general and abstract level of cognitive psychology; we do not make the same assumption about common sense and the physical sciences.

S–F theory cannot therefore fit the pattern of our everyday psychological explanations. And, failing to fit, it can tell us nothing about our ordinary-language mental terms: neither what mental states are, nor what mental terms mean.

III

My second main contention is about the *scope* of S–F theory when it is correctly regarded as a theory for the science of cognitive psychology. Its potential cannot be fully realized unless we recall a claim made earlier: the structures are quite as important to the enterprise of constructing the theory as are the functions—the hardware, as well as the software, counts. Too much emphasis seems to me to have been given to the "top-down" strategy in psychology; i.e., the strategy whereby cognitive psychologists and workers in computer simulation (plus any philosophers competent to assist) concentrate on the Kantian question 'how is X (perceiving, remembering, learning) possible?' and then go on to devise functionalist flow-charts that map the requirements selected. Of course it is true that they can and must do this; and so long as it is explicitly recognized that the capacities examined (problem–solving, pattern–recognizing etc.) may not tally more than roughly with the capacities talked about in everyday explanation in the same words, then I have no quarrel with the strategy. However, as soon as one gets an inch beyond this—as soon as one tries to choose between alternative flow–charts or attempts to provide the most perspicuous and precise description for the boxes listed in the blueprint—then it is both inefficient and shortsighted to neglect the contribution that comes from examination of the hardware.

The cognitive psychologist who attempts to devise a theory—and hence a taxonomy for his *explananda*, a theoretical ontology, and an economical but comprehensive set of theoretical and observational terms—must acknowledge *two* distinguishable constraints. First, and obviously, he wants a theory competent to account for the complete range of human behavior (as described and classified in his taxonomy); he therefore seeks a list of capacities both as *explananda* and as postulates in terms of which his *explananda* can be analyzed. This, as I have suggested above, will not be a simple matter, and the alluring categories offered by everyday psychology may be a hindrance rather than a help. Then second, not only must he produce a theory adequate to explain the fundamental abilities of purposive creatures, but his theory should also describe the way that humans and animals do *in fact* operate (I am obviously rejecting an exclusively instrumentalist view of scientific theory). Put another way, his theory may prove compatible with all the data and succeed in predicting behavior, and still be wrong; put yet another way, he wants a theory which it makes sense to suppose the brain is designed to realize; put more precisely, he must try to devise a theory with an ontology that can itself be analyzed and dissected at a more micro level. The point can be illustrated by considering the different methodologies used in artificial–intelligence work and computer–simulation research. Workers in artificial intelligence want to construct computers to carry out certain tasks (computing, pattern–recognizing) speedily and efficiently, with no essential reference to the way the human being may or may not perform the same tasks. Evidently, if they get stuck—and pattern–recognition is a case in point—they may turn to the neurosciences to see whether a model of human performance could be adapted for their work; currently they are particularly interested in the structure and function of neural nets. But efficient performance is the primary goal. Those working in computer simulation, on the other hand, are interested only in modeling human performance at some level of description; in other words, should there be several rival programs, each of which appears capable of modeling the human output, the best will be the one approximating most closely to the operations of the human brain. Analogously, then, the cognitive psychologist wants a theory that the human brain can and does actually realize.

Speculation arising from the "top–down" strategy cannot proceed far without consideration of the hardware. People and calculators add, cats and mousetraps catch mice[10]; and there is a (boring) level of description at which each of the two pairs do these things 'in the same way'. But at any interesting level of description they clearly function in highly different ways; in fact, there could be dozens of functionally dissimilar devices that could be used for mouse–catching. Similarly there may be many rival flow–charts that purport to explain how humans perceive, learn to recognize patterns, memorize digits; we need some principled means for sorting out the likely from the improbable, and consideration of the hardware is easily the best bet. Programming computers with the candidate models can indeed help to sort them out with respect to their efficiency in accounting for behavior; if a computer designed to recognize various tokens of the letter 'A' indeed does so, then that tells us that the theory suggested is at least adequate to do the job required of it. But there remains the question whether that theory identifies (at a given level of description) the way the brain does it; and that question will remain unanswered so long as the "top–down" strategy is pursued exclusively.

There is a more interesting reason, too, for bringing in consideration of the hardware early. Functional isomorphism holds, or fails to hold, only at particular levels of description. Two systems X and Y may ϕ "in the same way" in that they ϕ by running through processes a, b, c and d; but the way that subsystems of X and Y manage to achieve a, b, c and d may differ completely. Men and machines both wash clothes by soaking, soaping, rinsing and drying them, but the soaking, soaping etc. is accomplished so differently by the two systems that the functional isomorphism here is a trivial and uninteresting surface isomorphism. In abstraction from the hardware—from consideration of what the brain can and cannot do—cognitive psychology cannot hope to get far beyond a range of alternative abstract and global flow–charts; and research into the brain not only helps one to select between the candidate theories on offer, but itself may supply hypotheses about what functions should or should not be postulated. Not only may it do so; it has, frequently and to good effect. (A fact somewhat neglected by S–F theorists.) The question of the "top–down" versus the "bottom–up" strategies is often seen in overly simple terms: it is regarded as a question of starting *either* from the abstract flow–chart of the cognitive psychologists *or* from the nuts and bolts of cellular composition and activity, and the gulf between these looms large. However, it is not only possible but also profitable to study the activities and structures of brain masses: the cerebellum, the hippocampus, Broca's area, the left prefrontal lobe, the angular gyrus, Brodmann's area 18, and so forth. Such investigations of course point both ways: neurophysiology is interested in explaining how these complex structures fulfill their functions, psychology hopes to postulate or to discover what roles and functions these brain masses do in fact perform. The main point to be made here is that very often psychologists *discover* from neuroscientists the functions that certain subsystems in the brain fulfill—it is certainly not always a question of the "top-down" cognitive psychologist prescribing to the neuroscientist a set of functions which the latter must seek structures to realize. Indeed, it is just in this domain of research that we may expect to fill out the flow–charts at a level more detailed and penetrating than the abstract models hypothesized by the "top-down" strategist; and from animal studies and studies of humans with various kinds of brain damage or deficiency much has been discovered that could not conceivably have been predicted by psychology alone. For example: surprising and unexpected facts about the cerebral organization of language comprehension and production, and of perception, have emerged from the examination of patients with the brain lesions that cause aphasia, alexia and agnosia; damage to specific parts of the brain can systematically cause apparently unrelated abilities to fail together, thus indicating that their cerebral organization has more in common than we might have thought, whereas abilities that seem prima facie highly similar are unaffected, thereby indicating that their cerebral organization has less in common than intuition would suggest. Because this is an important point, I shall substantiate it with a few examples.

There are many forms of alexia. 'Pure' alexia—alexia without agraphia—often occurs when damage to the brain involves the splenium. The patient typically cannot read, but his writing ability remains. He can however, 'read' words spelled out in building-blocks if he is allowed to touch them, or words traced on his skin. His capacity for visual recognition remains otherwise unimpaired, with one curious exception: he cannot name colors on sight (though he can match and sort them easily). Pure alexia provides an excellent example of abilities we would expect to stand or fall together (reading and writing; the visual recognition of colors and objects; reading by sight and by touch) not doing so, and abilities that seem intuitively distinct (recognizing words and colors) proving to share some important cerebral organization.

"Gerstmann's syndrome" classically involves the disruption of four abilities. Patients with this syndrome cannot write and cannot calculate (neither on paper nor in their heads), although they can read both words and numbers with good comprehension; they suffer from right–left disorientation; and, finally they have finger agnosia: i.e., if the experimenter held up his fourth finger, the patient could not single out *his* fourth finger, and if the third finger on one hand was touched, he could not identify the corresponding finger on the other hand.

Other well–documented forms of alexia include: literal alexia (blindness for individual letters but not necessarily for words), verbal alexia (where letters but not words are recognized), alexia for words but not for numbers or musical notation, alexia for words in the patient's native language but not for those in a foreign one, and 'paralexia', a condition which makes the patient unable to read a word like 'puppy' but competent to produce a near miss: 'small dog'.

The point could be illustrated equally easily if we took not alexia but aphasia, agnosia or apraxia; abilities that to intuition seem evidently related prove to be distinct, in that one can be totally lost while the other is preserved, while *prima facie* unrelated capacities fall together, thus indicating significant shared cerebral organization. What concerns us particularly is that these findings naturally compel neuroscientists to devise explanations for the data, and such explanations require substantial hypotheses about the S–F organization of the brain; but they could never have emerged from the "top-down" strategy.[11] Because of the unfortunate fact that strokes, accidents, tumors and decay can all selectively impair the workings of the brain, there is no shortage of subjects. Moreover—a highly important, if more technical point—whether one is studying brain damage or the normal functioning of the human or animal brain there are now sophisticated new techniques by means of which cerebral functioning can be displayed: for example, the use of micropipettes to inject procion yellow dye into a *single* neuron, so that the dye diffuses into that cell's branches without spreading to adjacent cells; microelectrodes with tips of 0.4 microns in diameter which can record the electric potential of one neuron; chemical stimulation which has now joined electric stimulation as a method of activating specific sites in the brain; and the ability to measure the extent and location of cerebral activity throughout the brain by discovering the rate and location of blood flow[12]. In short, the "top-down" strategists seem to underestimate the achievements and the promise of neuroscientific research.

The plain fact is that there is really no priority at issue—no choice between strategies. The process of inquiry is one of continuous mutual adjustment: sometimes the "top–down" strategist postulates a function which provides for the neuroscientist an *explanandum* upon which he can get to work, at other times the function specified proves to be one which the brain almost certainly cannot realize, and then the psychologist needs to look elsewhere. Meanwhile the neuropsychologist studying brain regions and structures is often in a position to inform the psychologist that, almost certainly, there is a function F performed at a relatively global level in the processes of, for instance, perception. (It is from such mutual cooperation that we might one day expect to crack the puzzle of memory storage; at the moment dozens of rival psychological theories abound, postulating up to 25 different types of memory–storage system, or just *STM* and *LTM*, or 'primary' and 'secondary' memory, or 'episodic' and 'semantic' memory, or 'sensory' and 'iconic' memory; there are stimulus–stimulus versus stimulus–response, single–process versus two–process theories. Meanwhile on the neuroscientific side the main candidates appear to be the synaptic–structure theories and the intracellular–chemistry theories. This enormously difficult problem will only be solved by joint attacks on the issue; in isolation, none can get much further.)

Once S–F theory is regarded as a program designed *inter alia* to provide the framework within which cognitive psychology, neuropsychology, neurophysiology and biochemistry should proceed, then a number of traditional problems seem to disappear—or at least prove not to be stable within the model. Take, for example, the mental–physical split. Since Descartes philosophers have agreed that the mental is very special and very puzzling; they have tried to pick out the mental either by the epistemological criteria of incorrigibility, immediacy, privileged or asymmetrical access, and privacy—criteria alleged to single out at least *conscious* mental events, though they leave the rest in limbo—or by the logical criterion of intentionality, or by a combination of the two. Given the presupposition that the mental constitutes a very special category, philosophical functionalists have sought to identify the mental–physical distinction with the structure–function distinction. Such an enterprise can now be shown to be seriously mistaken. First, S–F theory has no bearing upon the everyday mental terms in common use; second, the function–structure distinction is flexible and theory–relative, shifting according to the purposes of the analysis. Then third, there will be and are countless functions ascribed to cerebral structures that can by no stretch of the imagination be termed 'mental', for even single cells can often be assigned functions. And fourth, most fundamentally, the science of cognitive psychology need have no truck with the criteria employed in philosophy to pick out the mental. It is rightly uninterested in epistemology; and although it acknowledges the need to employ intentional terms, it need not regard this as a particularly distinctive feature, for so too will the neurosciences to some extent. Thus the only distinctions that are even roughly analogous to the mental-physical split will be those that it seems useful or appropriate to draw within the broad spectrum of analysis that stretches from the abstract studies of the cognitive psychologist at the one extreme to the nitty–gritty examination of cellular chemistry and structure at the other. So there will of course be a distinction (albeit a thoroughly pedestrian and unexciting distinction) between 'psychological' and 'neurophysiological' terms; the first label can be applied to the terms used by psychologists and the second to those used by neurophysiologists. But such a distinction will have little if anything to do with the traditional mental–physical split ('information' or 'stimulus analysis' are hardly paradigm mental concepts). Moreover, there will be an extensive range of terms used in the middle of the spectrum of inquiry, terms used to describe the structure and functioning of complex subsystems of the brain ('parallel processing', 'arousal levels', 'stimulus readiness' 'columnar representation') and of these the question, 'psychological or physical?', simply refuses to arise; they transcend or ignore the Cartesian dichotomy. They range from terms shared with cognitive psychology to those shared with neurophysiology, and for the sake of a label they could be termed 'neuropsychological'. All such labels, though, are completely unimportant; they simply serve to pick out terms typically useful at distinguishable levels of a single framework of analysis, the S–F framework. So it cannot be the task of S–F theory to tell us anything about 'what mental states are', for S–F theory denies that there is anything special about the mental by denying that the mental–physical distinction is special.

As soon as we realize that we have a continuum rather than a yawning chasm between molar and micro, then even intentionality presents no problem. As we proceed with the analysis into greater and greater detail intentionality fades out (in other words, the functions postulated or discovered become increasingly limited and inflexible; put another way, the homunculi of the brain get stupider and stupider) until it has vanished. The primary fact is that S–F theory reveals that we do not have an either/or choice between molar and micro, but rather that *via* several intermediate stages of analysis, molar and micro are engaged in a continuous process of fit and mutual adjustment; and the only constraint upon this process is the fact that psychology must also suffice to explain the actual behavior of purposive creatures (under some description and in some taxonomy) while neurophysiology must be adequate to describe the actual behavior of nerve cells (under some description and in some taxonomy).

IV

I conclude this paper with some very brief remarks about one or two of the most familiar criticisms of S–F theory. The first and best-known is the "multiple realizability" objection: not only does the lability of the CNS—the fact that for many functions there is neurological equipotentiality in the brain—show that the function–structure relation might be irreducibly and unhelpfully one–many, but also, a functional map of a human brain could be realized in quite other stuffs: by a computer, or by the population of China (one man per nerve cell). The point about the lability of the CNS purports to show that S–F theory cannot come up with truly interesting or adequately general statements about the organization of the human brain, and the "Great Brain of China" point has been used to suggest that S–F theory is simply false, inasmuch as we do not want to say that a system constructed of 10^{10} Chinese could 'believe that it is English', 'want a banana' or 'feel a pain in its toe'.

It is true that the CNS is immensely labile, especially in the very young. The impact of much brain damage can often be circumvented in time by the development of alternative structures or indeed by a change in the functional map, i.e., by the development of alternative strategies[13]. The S–F organization of the brain, even in those with intact brains, does vary: for example, about 10% of the population has no left–hemisphere dominance for language. However, the force of this objection is much weakened if we abandon the assumption that the functions postulated by cognitive psychology have to be realized *instanter* by micro-structures; i.e., that we have to jump straight from the global to the micro. Given that we proceed down a whole hierarchy of functions and structures, we find in fact—as indeed we might expect—that not only functional but also structural isomorphism holds in the human brain for a long way down the increasingly detailed analysis. Second, we should remember the *explananda* with which we are concerned: these are *not* individual propositional attitudes but are basic capacities. We are asking how information (of classified kinds) is stored, by what sorts of processes it can be retrieved, how we recognize objects of various types, and so forth; and there is little evidence to suggest that at this level of investigation there is much unpredictable lability. It is of course true that if we *were* to try to pin down an individual occurrent thought to a specific complex of neural activity, we would find that the same thought in X and in Y had different neurological realizations—as indeed it would have in X alone on two separate occasions. But analogously, two copies of *Hamlet* may have grossly different microphysical descriptions: the behavioral and brain sciences are no more concerned with individual thoughts than atomic physics is with copies of *Hamlet*. Psychophysiology may indeed hope to tell us how it is that *any* occurrent thought can come about; and (as lesion studies suggest) may need to provide different accounts for thoughts that occur in verbal form and thoughts that occur in visual form. But individual propositional attitudes do not feature in the taxonomies either of cognitive psychology or of the neurosciences; if they did, then we would indeed have for them nothing but unworkable and profitless token–token statements at best. However, granted the actual domain of *analysanda* of the sciences concerned, the residual multiplicity of realizations looks to be reasonably tolerable and manageable, allowing for substantial general statements.

That robots or, more absurdly, the Great Brain of China might be made to model my functional organization (and, of course, much of my cerebral structural organization as well) should, with certain reservations, be accepted. We can and should ascribe to such systems capacities to store and retrieve information, recognize patterns etc.; we could not work out merely by scrutiny of the functional–structural transactions *what* information they are storing (if God could look into our brains, he would not know what we were thinking, since individual information–bits would have only token–token relations with neural activity), for to discover that we have to examine the output of the system. Once we try to ascribe a specific belief or desire, we are in the domain of everyday psychology; and then it is up to our linguistic intuitions to work out whether the fact that the Great Brain of China "says" that it thinks there are tigers in India implies that it does indeed think that. Here common sense determines the answer; and common sense, of course, will require more than verbal output in disputed cases. But as far as psychology is concerned, if the behavior of the system fits, it can be ascribed the capacities of manipulating information.

Ascriptions of desires or of pains, however, may be much harder to model than the objection suggests. Not all structures can fulfil functions postulated by the model (meringues can't carve joints) and some of the functions postulated by a S–F description of pain, for example, may simply be things that silicon chips or Chinamen cannot perform. Functional–structural isomorphism must stop somewhere in every model; if the Chinamen or the chips are to model individual cells, then they cannot model the chemical transactions *within* those cells, which may be critical for the ability to model more global functions. Extensive functional isomorphism may be required before the behavioral output is appropriately analogous, and both output and isomorphism are required for ascriptions of psychological terms.

This question can be taken further by considering another related and rather messy objection: namely, that S–F analysis cannot cope with consciousness, sensation, experience, the phenomenal qualities of human experience. It has been argued,[14] for example, that the hypothesis of the inverted spectrum is perfectly coherent but would be ruled out by a S–F analysis; and, more generally, that not all psychological phenomena are exclusively functional. However, once it is acknowledged that the inverted spectrum is a thought–experiment, it can surely be countered by another, and there are readily–imaginable situations in which an inverted spectrum would make a difference: if, for example, the inversion of the spectrum took place in the retina, and if the right eye only of X (who has an inverted spectrum) were transplanted into the head of Y, who does not. Even if Y would eventually settle down, at least at first he would react to colors differently with each eye separately. Alternatively, we could imagine the less plausible operation of a partial transplant of the visual cortex, with the same effects.

The inverted–spectrum objection focusses the more obscure, but intuitively powerful, objection that S–F analysis leaves out phenomenal properties, sensations, subjective experiences. This objection is hard to counter because of its vagueness about what precisely is getting ignored; if one does not share the intuition that subjective sensations are left out, then it is unclear what is left to argue. The popular response to this is to say that such scepticism about the reality of experiences and sensations is simply disingenuous or dishonest: such phenomena obviously exist and have to be acknowledged. This is too quick, however. That it is too quick can be seen by reflecting that the ancient Greeks, for all their subtle and immensely flexible vocabulary, seemed not to need, nor to have, any readily-available means of picking out qualia, sensations, or experiences, and had no word that translates as 'consciousness'; yet nevertheless found no difficulty in talking about all kinds of psychological phenomena.

Let us consider the most intuitively obvious of all, the sensation of pain. Intuition seems to tell us (although it is not apparent that intuition is coherent here[15]) that the *esse* of pain is *percipere*, and *percipere* is *esse*. Hence, if you are in pain, you typically believe that you are, and if you believe that you are, you are right. Intuitively again, to feel pain *is* to be in pain; and the sensation of pain is the feeling of pain. Now a suitably-constructed robot (which might have to be made out of soft protoplasm-like stuff, if the necessary isomorphisms are to go deep enough) might model the CNS transactions whereby we feel a prick in the finger; because of appropriate self-scanning mechanisms, it could store and report the information that it was in pain. If, then, pain played an analogous role in its life to the part it plays in ours—so that the behavioral output was relevantly parallel—it becomes highly obscure what, if anything, has been left out: *not* 'the sensation', because the sensation is the *esse* of pain and the *esse* (according to intuition) is *percipere*. The onus is surely upon the objector to try to spell out more precisely just what he feels has been left out; until he does, the objection cannot be decisive.

Dennett has argued persuasively that the everyday concept of pain is internally inconsistent and that therefore pain perception could not be modeled as such by any theory.[16] So perhaps discussion of S–F theory's ability to cope with pain should await the day that a coherent notion can be provided. However, if this is indeed true of pain, it is much more so with 'consciousness'; of all the messy and unclear notions in ordinary language, this must take the prize. The heterogeneous phenomena that fall under this umbrella term need to be split up and classified before they are tractable for any sensible discussion; and once split up, they seem amenable enough. For example, what is special about conscious perception is surely captured by an analysis that distinguishes perception simpliciter from subliminal perception; conscious thoughts differ from nonconscious ones, but a postulate of a self-scanning device seems to capture reasonably well what is special about them: they can be reported, expressed, assessed and the like. Above all, consciousness *per se* is not a single phenomenon which as such provides a manifestly self–evident *explanandum* for any adequate psychology. It may even prove to be best understood as a second-order property, like intelligence: i.e., a property that becomes ascribable once a sufficient subset of first–order psychological predicates can be ascribed.[17] If so, it would be a function of the complexity and flexibility of the system in question.

The most powerful current attempt to pick out what is special about the phenomenal is the use of Nagel's question, "What is it like to be an X?" The suggestion is that there is nothing that it is like to be a robot—*whatever* its S–F design—whereas there is something that it is like to be a bat or a human. Insofar as I follow this objection, it seems to me to beg the question in advance: certainly there is nothing that it is like to be any contemporary IBM computer, but all computers so far devised are relatively incredibly simple (a recent notional IQ test on the most sophisticated computers brought them out on a level with the earwig). What we would say if a system was constructed which had, throughout the range of human capacity, substantial functional and structural isomorphism with a human agent is surely a question that nobody could possibly answer a priori at this stage.

NOTES

1. A recent survey of such objections can be found in N. J. Block, "Troubles with Functionalism," in C. Wade Savage (ed.) *Perception and Cognition: Issues in the Foundations of Psychology* (Minnesota Studies in the Philosophy of Science, vol. IX (Minneapolis: University of Minnesota Press, 1978)), pp. 261–325.

2. K. Gunderson, "Robots, Consciousness and Programmed Behavior," in Gunderson, *Mentality and Machines* (New York: Doubleday, 1971), pp. 66–67.

3. For example Armstrong, Smart, Shoemaker, Lewis.

4. J. Kim is a good example; see his "Physicalism and the Multiple Realizability of Mental States," *Monist* 56 (1972), pp. 177–92.

5. A. Morton, in a recent book *Frames of Mind* (Oxford: Clarendon Press, 1980) also argues that common–sense explanation is not to be seen in terms of a theory, but suggests and develops the idea that it is backed by what he calls a 'schema'.

6. I owe this example to P. Alexander.

7. D. C. Dennett, "Artificial Intelligence as Philosophy and as Psychology," in Dennett, *Brainstorms* (Hassocks: Harvester Press, 1978), pp. 109–26.

8. There are good reasons for distrusting the theoretical integrity of the notion of belief, however. See *inter alia* Dennett, "Brain Writing and Mind Reading," in *op. cit.*

9. Everyday psychology is, of course, several thousand years old, and scientific psychology is scarcely a hundred. Moreover, we need to explain and predict the behavior of other people as we do not, usually, need to explain and predict (say) biochemical changes. Hence we are more inclined to interfere with psychology than with biochemistry.

10. This example is borrowed from W. Kalke, "What is Wrong with Fodor and Putnam's Functionalism," *Nous* III (1969), pp. 83–94.

11. For the evidence cited or mentioned here, see: J. Hinshelwood, *Letter–, Word–, and Mind–Blindness* (London: H. K. Lewis, 1900); H. Gardner, *The Shattered Mind* (London: Routledge & Kegan Paul, 1977); A. R. Luria, *The Working Brain* (Harmondsworth: Penguin, 1973) and *Restoration of Function after Brain Injury* (New York: Macmillan, 1963); J. Gerstmann, 'Zur Symptomatologie der Hirnläsionem im Ubergangsgebiet der unteren Parietal und mittleren Occipital wendung," *Nervenarzt* III (1930), pp. 691–95; and especially N. Geschwind, *Selected Papers on Language and the Brain*, (Boston Studies in the Philosophy of Science vol. XVI (Dordrecht: D. Reidel, 1974)).

12. See N. A. Lassen, D. H. Ingvar, and E. Skinhøj, "Brain Function and Blood Flow," in *Scientific American* vol. 239 no. 4 (October 1978), pp. 62–71.

13. An illustration of a completely new strategy for visual recognition is given by Luria in *The Working Brain*. A patient with a lesion in the prestriate cortex could no longer recognize *Gestalts*, only the discrete details of a visual presentation; consequently he had to work out by conscious inference what those details *should* add up to.

14. See for example N. J. Block and J. A. Fodor, "What Psychological States are Not," *Philosophical Review* 81 (1972), pp. 159–81.

15. As D. C. Dennett argues in "Why You Can't Make a Computer that Feels Pain," in *op. cit.* pp. 190–229.

16. See n. 15.

17. I have argued for this at greater length in *Physicalism* (London: Routledge & Kegan Paul, 1978), pp. 103–12.

A Note on Functionalism and Function

COLIN MCGINN
University College London

I suspect that the functionalist theory of conscious states is nourished by the thought that conscious states have a function. One may be tempted to reason thus: since consciousness is an evolved characteristic of organisms, it must have a biological function; but then it seems that conscious states should be capturable in functional terms. That is, it can seem that either a functionalist theory is available or conscious states are biologically epiphenomenal, contributing nothing to the functional adaptiveness of an organism. Encouraged by this apparent dilemma, the functionalist might feel that a motivated dismissal of cases of absent and inverted qualia is available to him: for to take such possibilities seriously would be to make conscious states epiphenomenal. Thus the anti–functionalist invites us to consider such cases as this: one type of creature has an achromatic visual field of the standard sort, while another has a visual field that is the negative (in the photographic sense) of that of the first. Here it seems that both types of creature could instantiate a single functional description, presumably because the same information about the environment can be encoded in these phenomenologically distinct ways. Or again, it might be claimed that two sense–modalities, say vision and echolocation, could be functionally equivalent with respect to a pair of creatures, though differing in their phenomenology. But now the functionalist will protest that there must be something amiss with such cases, since they imply that conscious states are biologically epiphenomenal—distinctions among conscious states are not reflected in distinctions of function. So we should dismiss them and accept the first limb of the dilemma.

I think this line of reasoning rests upon a mistaken assumption about the relation between a biological function and its basis in the intrinsic traits of an organism. The central point to appreciate is this: the function of an evolved organ or characteristic underdetermines the mechanism or realization of that organ or characteristic. That is to say, you cannot *in general* recover from a functional ascription to an organism the specific means of discharging that function in the organism in question. You may know, for example, of some characteristic that it has the function of maintaining the body temperature of an organism but be ignorant of the mechanism or property whereby this is achieved; it might be by way of a thick skin or a furry coat or whatever. The point is simply that a single function may be severally discharged in the intrinsic traits of organisms. Once this general principle is accepted, it appears open to the anti-functionalist to invoke it in his defence: the fact that the intrinsic nature of conscious states is not fixed by their functional description is just a special case of the general truth that the function of an evolved characteristic does not determine the specific intrinsic nature of the characteristic. (How it comes about that a given function is discharged as it is in an organism is a matter, presumably, of the particular evolutionary history of the organism, specifically of the resources or "raw materials" with which natural selection had to work in promoting adaptiveness.) If this is right, then there should be nothing especially untoward, biologically, about our being able to envisage different ways in which information about the internal and external environment might be represented in states of consciousness. A functionalist wishing to enlist evolutionary biology in his support would need to show that consciousness cannot be correctly conceived as an organ whose intrinsic nature is underdetermined by its biological function. Since I know of no way of showing that, I conclude that no support accrues to functionalism, taken as a reductive or definitional thesis, from the observation that conscious states have a function.[1]

NOTE

1. The point I am making in this note can be seen as closing a gap in my "Functionalism and Phenomenalism: a Critical Note," *Australasian Journal of Philosophy*, March 1980. There I argued that causal–role functionalism is no more plausible than an analogous phenomenalist thesis about material objects. Someone might hope to introduce an asymmetry between the cases, favorable to functionalism, by claiming that mental states have a biological function whereas material objects (in general) do not. Certainly there is such an asymmetry, but it does not seem to me that this gets the functionalist to his destination. Conscious states have a function, but this does not exhaust their nature; I am saying that this is *typical* of evolved characteristics.

Internal Representation: Prologue to a Theory of Intentionality[†]

ROBERT C. RICHARDSON
University of Cincinnati

The ideas of which psychology seeks to investigate the attributes, are identical with those upon which natural science is based; while the subjective activities of feeling, emotion, and volition, which are neglected in natural science, are not known through special organs, but are directly and inseparably connected with the ideas referred to external objects.

—Wilhelm Wundt

Synopsis

A series of desiderata are elaborated which any explanation of mental representation must satisfy, and it is shown that no functionalist theory has the capacity to do so. The argument divides into five stages.

I. *Cognition and Function*. A conception of functionalism is sketched that is both sufficiently restrictive to distinguish cognitive theories from behavioristic and neo–behavioristic competitors, and sufficiently powerful to promise a practicable functional analysis.

II. *The Problem of Intentionality*. The leading assumption of the argument is elaborated and defended:

(D1) Intentionality is sufficiently distinctive to differentiate, at least *prima facie*, the mental from the merely physical.

This alone is shown to be sufficient to drive us toward a 'realist' theory which takes Intentionality as an attribute of mental acts and away from 'linguistic' theories which attempt to explain Intentionality in terms of intensionality.

III. *Intentionality: The Object as Extrinsic*. There are two species of relational theories; theories, that is, which take Intentionality as a relation between subject and object.

[†] I am indebted to a number of people for comments and criticism on earlier versions. In particular: P. William Bechtel, J. I. Biro, Alan Donagan, Kathleen Emmett, Donald Gustafson, William G. Lycan, John Martin, W. E. Morris, Manley Thompson, and William Wimsatt.

The work began under successive grants from the University of Chicago and the Ford Foundation. It was completed under support from the National Endowment for the Humanities.

(1) Causal theories take the object as concrete, external, and independent of the subject and the subject's thought. The relation between subject and object is a species of causal relation. Causal theories violate the demand:

> (D2) Mental representation must be such that it allows for the possibility of representation of what does not exist.

Without satisfying this demand, a theory of mental representation cannot do the work necessary for cognitive psychology.

(2) Representative theories take mental reference to be a relation between a subject and a surrogate object which mediates between subject and (external) object. Such theories fail in ways that warrant adopting the requirement:

> (D3) Mental representation must be such that the act represents external objects directly and without epistemic intermediaries.

IV. *Intentionality: The Object as Intrinsic.* An outline of a theory which treats Intentionality as non-relational is provided; a theory, that is, which takes the (type of) object as definitive of the act. It is demonstrated that no theory which takes the peculiarity of Intentionality to lie in the existential status of the object is able to satisfy (D1). A non-relational theory can satisfy (D1) by embracing the desideratum:

> (D4) A mental act which represents an object of a specified type necessarily, or essentially, represents an object of that type.

It is contended that such a theory is tenable if the type of object intended by the mental act is determined by the concepts mobilized in the judgments in question. It is also shown how such a theory simultaneously satisfies (D2) and (D3).

V. *The Explanation of Representation.* It is shown, in conclusion, that no explanation of Intentionality in terms of function can satisfy (D4) or, therefore, is likely to satisfy (D1). It is possible to satisfy (D4), and thereby (D1), (D2), and (D3), either by taking an emergentist approach which assumes Intentionality as a primitive or by embracing a reductionist program of research.

I. *Cognition and Function*

It was once unfashionable to think we can think. Fortunately, fashions change. Among philosophers and psychologists alike, it has once again become common to speak and think in terms of internal representations, cognitive processes, mental acts, information, interpretations, or any of a host of related conceptions when attempting to explain or understand human behavior. For example, in *The Language of Thought,* Jerry Fodor asserts with little or no compunction:

> To have a certain propositional attitude is to be in a certain relation to an internal representation.... More exactly: Mental states are relations between organisms and internal representations, and causally interrelated mental states succeed one another according to computational principles which apply formally *to the representations*. [1975, p. 178]

Indeed, the idea that we not only may, but must, employ such conceptions is taken as obvious. Ulric Neisser asserts in his influential *Cognitive Psychology*: "The basic reason for studying cognitive processes has become as clear as the reason for studying anything else: they are there.... Cognitive processes exist, so it can hardly be unscientific to study them" (1967, p. 2).

Cognitive theories are commonly coupled to a functionalist interpretation of mental states and psychological explanations. Fodor tells us that psychological theories involve two phases, the first of which he describes as follows:

> Phase one psychological theories characterize the internal states of organisms only in respect of the way they function in the production of behavior.... A phase one psychological explanation attempts to determine the states through which a device must pass if it is to produce the behavior the organism produces on the occasions when the organism produces it. [1965, p. 173]

In a similar mood, Hilary Putnam writes in "The Nature of Mental States,"

> ... pain is not a brain state, in the sense of a physical–chemical state of the brain (or even the whole nervous system), but another *kind* of state entirely. I propose the hypothesis that pain, or the state of being in pain, is a functional state of the whole organism. [1967, p. 433]

Or, again, we hear from Neisser: "Psychology ... is a science concerned with the interdependence among certain events rather than with their physical nature" (1967, p. 7).

A functional explanation of a capacity or a piece of behavior will be in terms of the transformations on incoming information and the impact of that information on the internal state. To use a starkly simplistic case, an animal conditioned in a "go—no-go" situation is rewarded only in the presence of a cue (e.g., a tone or light). The resulting story designed to explain the behavior of an appropriately conditioned animal would represent the appropriate drive state as involving a single choice–point: the organism need only discriminate between the presence or absence of an appropriate stimulus, emitting the response only in its presence. The drive state would be identified as that state in which the discrimination is or would be made, with the appropriate response.

In a functional analysis, all the relevant states are to be identified in terms of their causal relations (whether deterministic or probabilistic) to other internal states of the entity and/or to external states including bits of behavior and stimuli, but subject to the condition that this identification leaves no bias concerning the particular structural, or physical, realization of that state (indeed, so far as its functional traits are concerned, the state need not be physical at all). There will be *some* constraints on structural properties, since a functional characterization may be sufficiently complex to rule out some sorts of physical realizations. There will, however, typically be alternative physical systems capable of manifesting the functional traits; when there are, the functional characterization alone will not give us grounds for deciding what the physical state of the system is. The functional characterization of a state is, in short, *relational* and *abstract* in that it describes the state extrinsically—in terms of its relations to other states—rather than intrinsically—in terms of, say, its physical make–up.

Maintaining that psychological characterizations are in this way relational and abstract has striking consequences. It can be shown, for example, that if functionalism is right, psychological descriptions cannot allow any "intrinsic" component: psychological characterizations can allow only "formal" dimensions, reflecting organization rather than structure. The basis for this is quite simple. If some psychological characterization incorporates an intrinsic component, then that component will, in turn, determine a type of state which is not functional. If that intrinsically characterized type is psychological, then psychological characterizations are not all relational and therefore not all functional. If that type is not psychological but, say, physiological, then the original characterization is not sufficiently abstract to acknowledge psychology as a distinct science. (Cf. Richardson, 1979, §§1–3 for a detailed development of this argument.) Functional theories must, thus, be computational.

This holds for the identification of 'stimulus' (or 'response') classes no less than for internal states. Early pattern–recognition programs ran afoul of the abstract nature of the stimulus class: the attempt to produce an algorithm for 'recognizing', e.g., instances of the letter "A" independently of changes in orientation and distortion failed simply because there is no significant topological invariance to be recognized. Since there is only marginally more invariance to instances of the letter "A" than to, say, threatening gestures, what we need to accept is that an instance of "A" is whatever is recognized and treated as such by the appropriate organisms, just as a gesture is threatening if it generally is or would be taken to be so.

This provides a basis for maintaining a principled distinction between behavioristic and cognitive theories[1]; indeed, it is the only basis I know of for grounding a firm distinction. Skinner requires that the defining properties for stimulus and response classes be definable in simple descriptive—non–functional—terms. (This, he claims, is a condition on gaining non–vacuous laws.) Cognitive theorists have not unanimously embraced the constraint. Garrett, Bever, and Fodor, in particular, have conducted experiments indicating that segmentation of speech units corresponds *not* to actual rises and falls in acoustic patterns but to semantic interpretation: the content determines the structure. (See: Garrett, Bever, and Fodor, 1966; Fodor and Bever, 1965; Fodor, 1968, pp. 79–86.) This is experimental warrant for departing from the Skinnerian standard.

The impact of requiring a computational theory has not been appreciated, and as a result there is a tendency to doubt the existence of a real distinction between functionalist (or cognitive) theories and behaviorist theories. Thus, George Bealer (1978) has offered an elegant, formally oriented, demonstration that functional definitions will be possible only if explicit definitions are possible (though he expresses some skepticism as to the adequacy of functional definitions). The argument founders on the assumption (Bealer 1978, p. 340) that there is a categorial definition base for "functional definitions" as there supposedly is for "explicit definitions": neo–behaviorists, to be sure, make such an assumption, but the assumption is anything but universal and in fact is one of the crucial points of contention. Bealer shows no more than that if you start with behavioristic assumptions, it's behaviorism you get. If you forego the assumptions, so, too, you can forego the behaviorism.

The explanation of functionalism above is liberal in another dimension: it allows functional definition bases to incorporate relations to states (and objects) external to the system, while some—especially Fodor—would restrict the base to internal (or peripheral) states. The latter view, which Fodor (1980) dubs "methodological solipsism," leaves everything external to the system under consideration undifferentiated as to structure or function. One ought to be reluctant to embrace a "methodological solipsism." It would, in particular, deprive us of much interesting and promising work in the cognitive sciences. For example, Ulric Neisser's more recent (1976, 1978) models of perception as well as Reitman, Nado, and Wilcox's (1978) work on machine perception in the game of Go critically require appeal to the environment functioning as a kind of externalized memory. Solipsism, whether methodological or principled, is inimical to such theories.

Nothing would be lost in *our* conclusions if we were forced to adopt a methodological solipsism, but it can be shown on other grounds to be unwarranted. Any determination of the functions of units—or, for that matter, the units of function—must discriminate between functional and incidental effects of system action. (See, e.g., Hempel 1965, pp. 297–300.) The problem is one that has defied any superficial solution. In defending teleology and function largely with reference to this problem, William Wimsatt has proposed a "normal form" for function statements which demands that the function of a sub–system must be defined relative to (a) the behavior of that sub–system, (b) the system of which it is a part, (c) the (normal) environment of the system, (d) the function or purpose[2] of the system of which the sub–system is a sub–system, and (e) a theory concerning the operation of the system.[3] The third and fourth dimensions are most important for our purposes. As Wimsatt explains (1972, p. 20), the function of the swim bladder in lungfish varies with the environment: in an aqueous environment, it facilitates hearing and serves to indicate rate of climb or dive; in times of drought when the swamps in which they live dry out, it serves as a lung.[4] The function of a sub–system is, in part, determined by the relation of the system (and therefore of the sub–systems) to external items. The fourth dimension incorporates more general plans. For example, a device may be taken as poorly designed or as designed to fail, depending on whether we take the designer's goal to be the production of good material or the maximization of profit through planned obsolesence. Thus, even what states are taken to be functional or dysfunctional depends upon the use of the system. The same point holds for considering what effects are, or are not, part of the function. This fourth dimension is a special case of interaction with extra–systemic entities: if the function of s in S is f, and this function is relative to the function F (or purpose) of S, F will (at least generally) be a goal state external to S and neither input nor output of s; yet, that f is a function of s is partly determined by the fact that S produces F. To embrace methodological solipsism is, hence, to embrace a view that leaves us unable to discriminate the function of systems or sub-systems from among the various effects. Once we allow a consideration of relations to external systems, there is some hope of resolution.[5] Without it, there is none.

The conclusion I shall finally press for is that mental representation is recalcitrant to a functionalist explication: functionalist theories, though utilizing a rich notion of representation, are impotent when it comes to explaining mental representation or our capacity for it; if any explanation of mental representation is possible, it will only be by appealing to the more basic brain sciences.[6] The argument will be strong enough to embrace the internalist focus of methodological solipsism no less than a more robust treatment of functions which acknowledges and employs extra-systemic relations. Some reasons have been advanced for preferring the robust treatment, but it should be obvious that to allow a robust analysis of function can only increase the functionalist's resources. If anything, it makes it easier to weld together the functionalist program with cognitive theories powerful enough not only to employ representations but to explain how a system gains representational capacities. The first order of business, however, is to elaborate on what needs to be explained: mental representation, or what is classically known as Intentionality.

II. *The Problem of Intentionality*

The dilemma philosophers have traditionally faced in attempting to explicate the notion of Intentionality—or, equivalently, of explaining what it is to be a mental representation—is as simple to state as it is difficult to resolve. We begin with but two basic, quite intuitive, principles: first, that mental acts are Intentional in virtue of the fact that they somehow relate the thinking (feeling) subject to external objects; and, second, that it can happen that the supposed object of the Intentional act does not exist. Once it is asked how *anything* could serve to relate an existing thing (the subject of the mental state) to a non-existent 'object', we must seemingly reject at least one of the two above claims; yet, if we reject either of these, we lose the appeal of the notion of Intentionality altogether. On the one hand, if we maintain that there are non-existent but real objects which are the objects of our thought, we are compelled to admit that none of our objects of thought are in the real world. We are barred from thinking of the concrete. On the other hand, if we admit that mental acts are not really relational, we are led to the conclusion that mental acts cannot really direct us to objects in the world (or out of it either). Our thinking does not relate us to the world. In either event, such acts can hardly be viewed as Intentional.

I shall approach the traditional options obliquely by asking what, if anything, could lead us to accept Intentionality as distinctive of the mental. This will be expressed, in what is the leading assumption in the argument to follow, as the view that Intentionality is paradigmatically a characteristic of the mental and *not* of the *merely* physical; that is, Intentionality will, at least *prima facie* differentiate the mental from the merely physical. What I shall develop is *not* an explanation of Intentionality, but a series of *desiderata* which an explanation of Intentionality must satisfy. In this sense we will have a *prologue* to a theory of Intentionality, and not a theory of Intentionality. In part V, we will conclude by measuring some of the proposed options for a theory of Intentionality against these desiderata.

The assumption is subject to several caveats. *First*, the assumption creates no bias on the question of whether the mental is also physical. The distinction to be acknowledged is between mental events, whether or not these are also physical, and those physical events that are not also mental. The *desiderata* derived are consistent with both materialism and its denial.

Second, this assumption is made quite independently of, and without prejudice to, the possibility that something other than mental states might be Intentional states. No *principled* distinction is assumed, though the *appearance* of a principled distinction must be acknowledged. Whatever resolution we finally reach concerning the existence of a principled distinction, this should be the conclusion rather than the premise of an argument. All one need grant is that mental states, as representations, are representations of a sort sufficiently unique to allow for the *plausibility* of the claim that this representational character—Intentionality—is a definitive mark of the mental. Many of the theories that have been proposed cannot warrant even a *prima facie* distinction: they lead *trivially* either to the conclusion that no mental states are Intentional or to the conclusion that all physical states are Intentional. The assumption rules against any such theory.

Third, the category of mental events should not be taken to encompass the 'raw sensory data' of our judgments or the synthetic, integrative, processes that transform such 'data' into perceptual judgments. Whether or not there are *un*conscious representations (Mullane, 1977) or "subdoxastic" states (Stich, 1978), it is only post-synthesis that we have full-blooded internal, mental, representations: like consciousness, Intentionality and the internal representations which manifest it are largely the result of synthetic operations, or, in Kantian terms, the application of schemata to the (*pre*conscious) sensory manifold. (See Richardson, 1981, Part III.)

Nothing more is asked than that the assumption be adopted in a critical spirit, and that we proceed to see what can be done with it. The consequences, as we shall see, are surprising and significant. Since the only plausible psychological theories now available—those covered rather vaguely by the title "cognitive psychology"—appeal in an ineliminable way to internal representations—representations which do manifest Intentionality—I find the assumption untroubling and am prepared to accept the consequences. Others may find the consequences more unsettling and turn an argument by *modus ponens* into one by *modus tollens*. Any argument whatsoever is subject to such a transformation, but those who do so should be willing to accept the consequences of *that* maneuver; *viz.*, that nothing remotely akin to the best psychological theories to date is even approximately true.

The assumption, and the resulting *desiderata*, are unabashedly realistic in tenor. The problem it poses is to provide a theory capable of distinguishing the class of mental events from the class of (merely) physical events. If we are to confront this problem, it is necessary to depart from the more recent fashion of explaining Intentionality by deploying a linguistic regress. Attempts to analyze Intentionality by means of a linguistic regress have shown themselves to be wholly unacceptable. The problem, however, is *not* that we have failed to find an acceptable characterization of our psychological vocabulary.[7] The difficulty lies in returning to the phenomena once the regress is made. Once we settle on criteria demarcating the relevant subset of intensional idioms, we must apply them in picking out Intentional events. Only three options are available: first, we might contend, with Donald Davidson (1970) and (occasionally) D. C. Dennett (1971), that mental events are those events that *can* be described in an intensional idiom of the appropriate sort; second, mental events might be taken, with R. M. Chisholm (1956 and 1959), to be those which *must* be described in an appropriate intensional idiom; or, third, mental events might be taken, with Dennett (1971) in his better moments, to be those which for pragmatic reasons *should* be described in appropriate intensional idioms. For something to be a representation then is for it to be possible, necessary, or useful for it to be described in terms the linguistic criteria provide.

Consider the Davidson criterion: an event is mental if it *can* be described in mental terminology. It is easy to see that given enough ingenuity we can describe virtually anything in virtually any terms we like. Consider the following argument employed in "Mental Events":

> Take some event one would intuitively accept as physical, let's say the collision of two stars in distant space. There must be a purely physical predicate "Px" true of this collision, and of others, but true of only this one at the time it occurred. This particular time, though, may be pinpointed as the same time that Jones notices that a pencil starts to roll across his desk. The distant stellar collision is thus *the* event x such that Px and x is simultaneous with Jones' noticing that a pencil starts to roll across his desk. [Davidson 1970, p. 84]

The argument is easily generalized. Consider any other event satisfying some open sentence "Qx", but satisfying "Qx" uniquely only at some time t; then there will be some n such that the event under consideration is uniquely described by "the event which is Q and happened some time span n after [or before] Jones' noticing his pencil start to roll across his desk." Since it makes no difference whether the predicate "Qx" is given in mental or physical terms, we can always produce such an open sentence; so, any event whatsoever *can* be described in mental terms.

It is equally easy to show, though I will not dwell on it here, that any mental event *can* be described in *physical* terms. Causal relations could, e.g., provide the foundation of a vocabulary enabling us to identify mental events in terms of causes and effects. The Dennett standard fares no better either, since it can be useful to describe virtually anything in mental terms and it *is* useful to describe many patently non–mental items in mental terms (see Richardson 1980 for a critique of Dennett). Of course, sometimes it is *correct* to describe things in mental terms and, to get them right, we need to do so. This requires, though, that we take Intentionality as a trait of the events. It will then follow that an adequate characterization of a mental state—a characterization, that is, which reflects its mental character—must treat that state as a representation. The critical point in the understanding of Intentionality, therefore, is not that our talk of the mental has certain logical or quasi–logical features; even less is it to the point that all or only our talk of the mental has these characteristics. Intentionality should, rather, be taken as a characteristic of psychological states and, at least in the first instance, as a characteristic of mental acts.

It is incontestable that philosophers have traditionally viewed Intentionality as a characteristic, or property, of psychological *states*; the notion that Intentionality should or even could be understood as a characteristic of psychological *sentences* is only of rather recent vintage and dubious heritage. To cite a premier instance, Brentano states clearly in *The Origin of Our Knowledge of Right and Wrong*:

> The common feature of everything psychological . . . consists in a relation we bear to an object. The relation has been called *intentional*; it is a relation to something which may not be actual but which is presented as an object. There is no hearing unless something is heard, no believing unless something is believed; there is no hoping unless something is hoped for, no striving unless something is striven for; one cannot be pleased unless there is something that one is pleased about; and so on, for all other psychological phenomena. [1889, section 19]

In more modern dress, Husserl wrote in his *Cartesian Meditations*: "without exception, every conscious process is, in itself, consciousness *of* such and such, regardless of what the rightful actuality-status of this objective such–and–such might be." He continues to say the "word intentionality signifies this universal fundamental property of consciousness; to be conscious *of* something; as a *cogito*, to bear within itself its *cogitatum*" (1929, §14). This same general thesis can be found in the Anglo–American tradition by turning to the writings of Wilfrid Sellars. Although Sellars claims "the aboutness of thoughts is to be *explained* or *understood* by reference to the categories of semantical discourse," he is nevertheless quite explicit in his recognition that "thought *episodes* are essentially characterized by the categories of Intentionality" (Sellars and Chisholm, 1958, p. 522; my emphasis).

I said above that Intentionality should be viewed as a characteristic of psychological states and, at least in the first instance, as a characteristic of mental acts. I said Intentionality is *in the first instance* a characteristic of mental *acts* simply because, when confronted with *The Concept of Mind*, it is beyond all dispute that not all psychological verbs signify mental acts. But while many psychological states are 'dispositional', we need not restrict ourselves to the view that the dispositions in question are merely behavioral dispositions. Brentano observed rather casually in his *Psychology from an Empirical Standpoint*:

> Naturally philosophers were well familiar with the fact that we can possess a store of acquired knowledge without thinking about

it. But they rightly conceived of this knowledge as a disposition toward certain emotions and volitions, but not as cognition and consciousness. [1874, § 2]

Whether or not philosophers—including Brentano—recognized clearly the extent to which many psychological states are 'dispositional', and whether or not this insight was followed through consistently, it is now clear that an adequate account of mind must carefully distinguish acts from dispositions. I shall take it that psychological dispositions (capacities, inclinations, etc.) are Intentional only in a secondary sense: psychological dispositions are Intentional insofar as they are dispositions toward certain mental acts; these mental acts are themselves Intentional in a non-derivative sense.[8] Mental acts are the principal vehicles for representation.

The needed distinction can be illuminated using a programming analogue. Beliefs correspond to the software of the computer: they are relatively long-term configurations which regulate inference patterns, or the flow of information. On the other hand, thoughts correspond to a temporary cross-sectional state of the machine: at an extreme limit, we might identify the 'thought' occurring at a moment with the total state of the machine at that moment, excluding those configurations identified as 'beliefs' (i.e., those configurations enduring beyond the limits of our temporal cross-section). Thoughts then correspond to the results of processing, and inference, of course, to the processing. Beliefs correspond to the program regulating the processing. So understood, the distinction between dispositional states and acts (occurrences) is bound to be rather ill-defined: what counts as a 'thought' and what counts as a 'belief' depends upon the width of our temporal slice. If we take a slice too thin, then we will be left with only 'beliefs'; too thick, and we will have only 'thoughts'. Where the line is to be drawn must be decided largely on holistic grounds: theoretical fruitfulness will serve to determine where the distinction should be drawn for the greatest benefit.

At least two advantages would accrue to such an analysis which grants primacy to the act. *First*, we could explain why certain psychological states (e.g., dread, depression, lightheartedness) either have no object at all or have an object that is 'diffuse' or 'general': if such states of mind are thought of as dispositions manifested in mental acts (occurrences), then, in those cases in which the various acts have sufficiently different objects, the disposition to have those sorts of mental acts will have no one clear object or type of object. To consider an example, J. C. Gosling (1965) asks us to consider the case of a person "who simply has bouts of depression," and suggests that such "pointless depression" actually lacks an object: "a man who is depressed for no reason is the person to whom things just look black" (1965, p. 494). To have such a bout of depression seems to be to be disposed to have bleak thoughts and to view situations from a particularly pessimistic perspective. *Anything* is depressing. That is part of what makes depression what it is. So understood, as Gosling himself remarks, in "type it is closer to explanations by reference to lethargy, apathy, cheerfulness, good humor, elation" (loc. cit.). Such depression, from our point of view, is 'objectless' just because the objects whose perception it colors and the acts in which it is manifested are so diverse. *Second*, if we bifurcate the mental realm into acts and dispositions and make the Intentionality of the psychological dispositions parasitic on the Intentionality of acts, we will be able to incorporate the point (which lends much to the credibility of logical behaviorism) that it is a conceptual truth that if we have certain beliefs (and/or certain desires), we will tend to act in certain ways. If mental acts have a 'natural expression' in overt behavior, then the disposition which is manifested in those acts will also have a 'natural expression' in overt behavior; and the variety of the mental acts will in turn account for the varieties of overt behavior that count as the manifestations of, say, a belief.

Again, we may turn to a programming analogy. Some software—some routines—will be quite general, and some quite specific. The more general the routine, the more constraints there will be in describing that software insofar as there will be more 'thoughts' and 'inferences' which are the outcome of the influences of that portion of the software. The more general routine will apply in more cases. Suppose we can isolate the 'objects' the specific 'thoughts' 'represent' and take the 'object' of the 'belief' to be a sum of the 'objects' of the 'thoughts' that that 'belief' places constraints on; then the more general a routine—a 'belief'—is, the less likely it will be to have a unique object. Depending on *how* general the routine is, it will have either a specific 'object', or a diffuse 'object', or no 'object' at all. Furthermore, and this corresponds to the second advantage, if it is the occurrent states (the 'thoughts') which are the proximate causes of output, then the dispositional states (the 'beliefs') will be manifested in behavior insofar as they constrain the occurrent states. The more general the routine the more diverse the behavioral manifestations.

It is, hence, reasonable to assume that if an acceptable account of the Intentionality of mental acts can be worked out, then the Intentionality of psychological dispositions will follow on its heels. If it should, contrary to appearances, turn out that *some* psychological states are non–Intentional, this is not of great concern for the present enterprise. The greatest sacrifice would be for the unity of the psychological enterprise. We would still have made progress in a major domain of the mental.

One final qualification is in order. I shall concern myself primarily with what could be termed "objectual acts"; that is, acts which would be properly described using a singular term to specify the object of the act. I shall speak as if the paradigm of the mental is the objectual "S thinks of O" or "S thinks of an A" (with "O" going proxy for singular terms and "A" for common nouns), and shall speak freely of the "object of the act" or the "relation between act and object." This would not be possible for one emphasizing the intensional in explaining the Intentional. I use it, in part, to emphasize my departure from this tradition. It should be acknowledged, though, that a return to propositional attitudes *is* needed. Some hints will later be offered in this direction. I accord no primacy to objectual states. The basic vehicle of thought is a judgment. The use of objectual ascriptions, like the use of *de re* attributions, is pragmatically motivated. It would only complicate matters, and change nothing of substance, to move to a "propositional" format: we could as well take the paradigm of the mental to be "S thinks that O is P," "S thinks that an A is P," or, generally, "S thinks that p," and make the necessary discrimination between the objectual and the propositional content of thought.

III. *Intentionality: The Object as Extrinsic*

Within the framework provided above, then, the best way to begin is to recall the platitude that when we describe, say, a thought, we generally specify the object or content of that thought. Thus, a thought is a thought of O or a thought that p. It is in all likelihood the grammatical form of such attributions that led Brentano, in the passage cited above, to describe Intentionality as a "relation we bear to an object."

If we take Intentionality seriously as a *relation*, current fashions are bound to lead us to a "causal" theory of representation. As Jaegwon Kim remarks,

... knowing, perceiving, and referring are among those Brentano and others have called "intentional relations" and . . . the causal theories of these topics can plausibly be viewed as attempts to explain intentionality via causality. The principal feature of an intentional relation is its "aboutness" or "ofness," and these causal theories share this common theme: for a thought, name, perception, or emotion to be *of* an object is for it to stand in an appropriate causal relation to the object. [1977, p. 606]

The so-called "causal theories" are not—and Kim is under no illusion on this point—quite that strong: the most that is normally claimed is that a causal relation between act and object is a *necessary* condition for there being an Intentional relation between act and object. It is not misleading to treat such theories, when applied to states such as perception, as causal in a relatively straightforward sense; but when the account is generalized to cover all Intentional states, the appeal to a causal connection becomes strained. Thus, if you are informed that Genevieve is my daughter, you are said to be put in a causal relation to her; it matters not that the only reference you have heard is the one immediately above. To say there is a causal connection in this broad sense seems only to say there *is* a connection and says nothing about the *kind* of connection it is. Surely, there is some sense in which such relations are causal, but we should not let the appeal to causality supplant the demand for an explanation.

Among such causal theories, there is an ambiguity which determines the scope of the theory. It is by now commonplace to point out that singular terms embedded in intensional contexts can occur either referentially (*de re*) or non-referentially (*de dicto*). The cognitive verb might correspondingly be said to be relational or non-relational. Causal theories, accordingly, may be taken to provide accounts of 'Intentional objects' and 'Intentional relations' in either a referential or a non-referential sense, or both; that is, causal theories may specify the thing which is related to our cognitive state or they may specify the content of the representation. In either case, causal theories cannot do the required job.

If causal theories are meant to provide only conditions for the specification of the objects of Intentional attitudes in the purely referential sense, there is no reason to think they can do anything to illuminate the problems connected with Intentionality. Avoiding the propositional format, "*S* sees *O*" can and often is taken to be purely relational, or *de re*. Thus, although Harry may have taken what he saw to be a bear, what he saw was a bush. Once we adopt this paradigm, we have simply abandoned the hope of explaining an Intentional relation; for in this *de re* sense, we can see something without ever thinking, noticing, or entertaining anything whatsoever about that object under that description. The relation is not a cognitive relation, nor is it essentially a relation to a cognitive item. In short, we may stand in such a relation without having any internal representation of the object at all. And when it is a representation standing in such a relation, it is not the causal relation which makes it a representation; indeed, the fact that it is a representation, if it is, is wholly incidental. Thus, though there may be some purely relational sense of, e.g., perceiving, and though a causal account may be adequate for such cases, it will *not* do as an explanation of what it is to be a representation.

We want more than so limited an account. In "Charity, Interpretation, and Belief," Colin McGinn lays down the following *causal condition*: "it is a *necessary* (but not sufficient) condition of an object's being referred to in correctly specifying the intentional content of a relational mental state that it—that object—figure suitably in the *causal* genesis of that state" (1977, p. 527). McGinn is unclear as to the exact scope of his thesis, but if his argument does not constitute a patent *ignoratio* against his intended target (Donald Davidson), it cannot rest on only the claim that purely relational states in our sense require a causal genesis. In our terminology, Davidson's concern is with the conditions for the attribution of some representation (e.g., a belief) to a subject. What McGinn appears to mean, thus, in speaking of a "relational mental state" is a mental state whose propositional content is not merely general. To think that all politicians are corrupt is not "relational," though to think that *Nixon* is a politician, or that *the junior Senator from Ohio* is a politician, is. "Relational" states in this sense include states whose propositional content is specified by using a singular term. McGinn may also intend his "relational mental states" to be relational in the sense of being *de re* (although this has no clear meaning when applied to states as opposed to descriptions or sentences); however, if this is relevant to problems of translation and indeterminacy, any *de re* attributions of mental states must admit of importation, and thus carry implications for the (*de dicto*) propositional content.

In the course of developing his argument against Davidson, McGinn claims that "if a mental state is correctly described in respect of its intentional content by reference to an object as comprising its subject matter, then the identity and existence conditions of that state are dependent upon and fixed by those of that object." He draws out the following consequence:

Suppose you are undergoing a perceptual experience as of seeing an F. And suppose that the content of your experience—what you are perceiving—is correctly specified by mentioning an object a. Let a be uniquely F. Now suppose yourself in a world in which again you have an experience as of perceiving an F; but now your perceptual state is correctly specified by reference to an object b, where $a \neq b$ though b is uniquely F in *that* world. Then plainly you are in different perceptual states in these two worlds, since perceiving a is not the same state as perceiving b—no matter how it may *seem* to you.

McGinn has committed a double error: one of omission and one of commission. First the omission: a causal relation has not been shown to correctly capture the notion of an Intentional object. We need only note a consequence which McGinn acknowledges to be a result of his position: "Again, suppose you are in a world in which a does not exist; then you cannot be in that world in the very same mental state as you instantiate in this world when you perceive a" (McGinn, 1977, pp. 527, 528). Causal relations, on such a view, must be necessary: if causal relations serve to *individuate* events then, on McGinn's principles, the causal genesis of any arbitrary event—and, indeed, all of its causal relations—must be essential to that event. Surely, and here we have the omission, more than a bare assumption is needed to warrant such a contention. This is closely related to the error of commission. Consider the following argument: "The spatio–temporal relations of an object can be used to individuate the object. Then the identity and existence conditions of that object are dependent upon and fixed by its spatio–temporal relations. So if a stands in the spatio–temporal relation R to b; then in any possible world in which b does not exist, a does not exist, since there is nothing standing in the relation R to b in that possible world." Spatio–temporal relations become essential to the objects which occupy them. It is clear in this case that 'epistemological' and 'metaphysical' issues have been conflated. Even if the relations to b are used to individuate a—to tell a apart from other objects—this by no means implies that a could not have stood in some other relation to b and stood in the relation R to a third object c. Similarly, the object a is not necessarily the cause of the subject's seeing an F; for the object of the seeing, a, is only used here to pick out the act under consideration.[9]

The most any of this shows, obviously, is that McGinn has not produced a compelling case for his position. But there is also reason to think a causal account such as this *cannot* give a proper account of

Intentionality. If a causal condition obtains, then if *S* is thinking of *O*, there must be an object *O* in a suitable causal relation to *S*, or *S*'s thought. But this involves an unacceptable condition on the attribution of Intentional objects. As Brentano is known to have stressed, an Intentional relation is a peculiar sort of relation indeed: unlike relations normally conceived, the terminus of an Intentional relation need not exist. In the appendix to "The Classification of Mental Phenomena" (1911), Brentano wrote:

> If someone thinks of something, the one who is thinking must certainly exist, but the object of his thinking need not exist at all. In fact, if he is denying something, the existence of the object is precisely what is excluded whenever his denial is correct. So the only thing which is required by mental reference is the person thinking. [1874, p. 272]

Due to the odd nature of the relation in question, Brentano was led to suggest we might better speak of Intentional relations as something relationlike (*etwas relativliches*) than of a relation *simpliciter*.

This is hardly an arbitrary restriction, nor is it one we can easily do without. An explanation of Intentionality which demands the existence of the object represented cannot fulfill the demands of an adequate psychological theory. Take a simple process such as perception. In the process of scanning an area, the human eye makes a series of fixations; yet this is not reflected in the way a scene appears. Neisser presents the following scenario:

> ... if we see moving objects as unified things, it must be because perception results from an integrative process over time. The same process is surely responsible for the construction of visual objects from the successive "snapshots" taken by the moving eye .... Such a process requires a kind of memory .... The individual "snapshots" are remembered only in the way that the words of a sentence are remembered when you can recollect nothing but its meaning: they have contributed something which endures. [1967, p. 140]

Neisser concludes: "a residue of information extracted from earlier fixations remains available" (1967, p. 134). The encoding of the required information, to be sure, is subject to stimulus conditions of the sort envisioned by causal theories. Such encoding, however, will be possible only if the system is capable of representing what is not present; and if there is a representational system sufficiently powerful to do this, it should be capable of representing what does not exist. This shows only that current action is not needed. What is used may, of course, have been stored. Even such a storage system, though, has a representational capacity whose representational powers are substantially independent—save in etiology—of actual objects.

A second example may be even more probative. In considering an account of choice and decision in the explanation of human behavior, Fodor points out that "it is often part of the explanation of the way that an organism behaves to advert to the beliefs it has about the kind of behavior it produces" (1965, p. 28). Fodor suggests a classical schema for explanation according to which the agent represents a series of behavioral options believed to be available, and assigns a preference–ordering based on the estimation of probable consequences and the evaluation of those consequences. Behavior is then treated as a function of the preference–ranking together with the anticipated probabilities of success.

One immediate upshot of such a model (or variants on it) is this: not only is it necessary to attribute a representational capacity of considerable complexity to the subject, that representational system must be capable of representing mere possibilia. Decisions are made, after all, on the basis of a consideration of a series of possible outcomes at most one of which is generally realized.

A causal condition is not and cannot be required. We can correctly make attributions of Intentional attitudes—even objectual attributions—without conforming to a causal condition. It is possible to elaborate causal theories in a more subtle way that can handle non–existent objects. D. M. Armstrong tells us in *A Materialist Theory of the Mind*:

> According to our general formula, the concept of a mental state is the concept of a state of the person apt for bringing about certain physical behavior . . . in the case of certain concepts, notably perception, the state involved is also to be conceived as a state apt for being brought about by certain physical causes.

In the final theory, the specification of the Intentional object of a state of perception is to be given by isolating a full "causal circuit":

> . . . the criterion by which we pick out the *blue surface of the block* as the intentional object of the perception, and the *putting of the block into the box* as the objective, is that, by taking these, and only these, as object and objective we can close the causal circuit, and close it without bringing in anything causally irrelevant.

The Intentional object is, as it were, the causally most distant thing which closes the causal circuit. So far, the account Armstrong develops may appear to conform to the causal paradigm; however, he goes on to explain more fully:

> If it was clear that processes were going on in the perceiver's brain that were associated with correctly selecting red objects in the limited context where the perceiver was regularly successful, we might have good reason to think that the perceiver 'seemed to see something red.' . . .
>
> In the same way, we can even imagine evidence that would show that a perceiver who never in fact had a veridical perception of something red, nevertheless did have perceptual illusions as of red objects. [1968, pp. 231, 265, 267]

Hence, according to Armstrong, a mental state m will have O as an Intentional object if m is an instance of a type of state apt to be brought about, in suitable circumstances, by objects of the O-type. In some cases, m might satisfy such a condition without satisfying a strict causal theory. We shall, in the concluding section of the present paper, return to evaluate the potential of this sort of view; while it does allow for the possibility that the purported object not exist, we shall see there are others it fails to meet.

There are yet other, less popular but more traditional, approaches toward defending a theory which takes the object to be extrinsic. For example, it has been held that Brentano (in an early phase of his career) maintained the view that "mental reference" is on a par with other relations, thus requiring the 'existence' of both relata. Roderick M. Chisholm writes:

> According to Brentano's early doctrine . . . , as soon as a man starts to think about a unicorn there comes into being an actual contemplated unicorn. This actual contemplated unicorn is an *ens rationis* that depends upon the thinker for its existence and that ceases to be as soon as the man ceases to think about a unicorn. [Chisholm, 1970, p. 137; cf. Srzednicki, 1975 and Kamitz, 1962]

If I think of O and O exists, then even if I cease to think of O, O may continue to exist; and, vice versa, even if O ceases to exist, I may continue to think of O. If when I think of O, O "exists" as the object of my thought, then the "existence" of O as an object of my thought is independent of the existence of O in the world (Brentano, 1930, §27). Thus, it is alleged, the well-known passage in the *Psychology* has two faces:

> Every mental phenomenon is characterized by what the Scholastics of the Middle Ages called the intentional (or mental) inexistence of an object, and what we might call, though not wholly unambiguously, reference to a content, direction toward an object (which is not to be understood here as meaning a thing), or immanent objectivity. Every mental phenomenon includes something as an object within itself, although they do not all do so in the same way. [Brentano, 1874, p. 88]

The psychological thesis is that mental phenomena have a peculiar "reference to a content" or "direction toward an object" which distinguishes them from physical phenomena; the ontological thesis is supposed to be that the objects (or contents) have a mental or intentional inexistence (cf. Chisholm, 1967, p. 201; Bergmann, 1967, p. 269 n. 11).

It is not true that Brentano endorsed this ontological thesis: Intentional inexistence is to be equated with "reference to a content," and is attributed not to the object or content of thought but to the actual mental phenomenon (or psychological state). Intentional inexistence is nothing but Intentionality and is a trait of the mental act. The evidence favoring the contrary rendering is thin enough once we accept the fact that—even on the "earlier view"—Intentional inexistence is a characteristic of mental phenomena and not of the "objects" of such phenomena; the evidence in fact pales before Brentano's own denial that he ever held such a view. We shall subsequently provide an interpretation of Intentionality (Intentional inexistence) that denies there are any *entia rationis* and is consistent with even the 1874 edition of the *Psychology*.

But whether or not Brentano ever held such a view, it is obvious that similar claims have been advanced by others. It will be necessary to highlight only one of the problems confronting this sort of 'realist' theory when conceived of as an account of Intentionality. Assume for the moment that Intentional relations are akin to relations proper and, hence, require that the objects of Intentional acts have some kind of Being or some sort of existence in or for the mind. Suppose, further, that I am thinking of Pegasus. Then there is something which is non-actual and yet is the object of my thought. The object of thought is, thus, not something that exists, although it has some kind of Being. Similarly, if we accept such a view, we should say that if I am thinking of War Admiral, I am thinking not of the actual winner of the 1937 Triple Crown, but of a Being on an ontological par with Pegasus. Once the object term in expressions such as "I am thinking of Pegasus" is given a referential role, then the object term in, e.g., "I am thinking of War Admiral" is subject to a parallel accounting. This, however, is a desperate view; for in thinking of War Admiral, I am thinking of a real horse sired by Man o' War. As Brentano remarked:

> What we think about is the *object* or *thing* and not the 'object of thought'. If, in our thought, we contemplate a horse, our thought has as its immanent object—not a 'contemplated horse' but a horse. [1905, p. 77]

Since one—now the principal—drive behind 'realistic' theories is the desire to deal with Intentional relations, the fact that just these relations are not handled cogently poses a serious difficulty. The point here to be stressed is this: *just as an adequate account of Intentionality must allow that the object of a thought need not exist, so it should also allow that one can think of objects which do exist.*

This can be underscored again by a consideration of the work representational states are to perform within a cognitive theory. One of those tasks is to provide an account of perception. Fodor tells us:

> . . . models of perception have the same general structure as models of concept learning: One needs a canonical form for the representation of the data, and one needs a confirmation metric to select among the hypotheses. [1975, p. 42]

Even though the formation of perceptual judgments is not a passive process, but one involving both an integration of the perceptual data and a projection on the basis of the derived representations, there is no question but that the resulting representation must be a representation of environmental items. The perceptual judgment may in fact be a *mis*representation, but if we do have a case of perception at all—or even of misperception—it must be a representation of an actual object. Hence, any account of Intentionality, or representational states, which precludes the possibility that an internal representation should represent an actual object must certainly be deemed inadequate.

One could attempt to retain the relational analysis and incorporate this insight by making the object of thought itself mediate between the act and the world. We could try to maintain, that is, that the mental act is indeed relational; that the immediate terminus of this relation (the 'object of thought') is an object having what Meinong called *aussersein*; and that this in turn represents an object in the world. On such a theory, the object in the world would be mediately the object of thought. Whatever the merits of such a view, it is evident that there cannot be any substantial gains. The immediate object of thought (the "pure object") in some way represents the world or an object in the world; this mode of representation cannot be a straightforward relation (e.g., resemblance, satisfaction, or causation) since the object in the world may not exist. We are again confronted with the initial choice: either this representation is indeed a real relation, but the terminus is not in the world; or this mode of representation is non–relational. On the first option, we are back where we began: the terminus of this relation of representation (i.e., the object represented by the object of thought) either is itself the object of thought (in which case we do not think of existing things), or represents the ultimate, external, object of thought (and again we face the need to give an explanation of the form of representation). So it is clear that we must at some point have recourse to the second option and allow for a non–relational mode of representation. But since our only motivation for introducing non–existent but real objects (or what Meinong calls the "*aussersein* of the pure object") is to avoid non–relational modes of representation, we can just as well dispense with such objects at the outset and hold that the act itself is a non–relational representation. Theories which take the immediate object as extrinsic to the act, and as mediate between the act and the world, can explain Intentionality only by finally invoking items which represent directly. To admit such direct representation makes such theories of Intentionality superfluous.

The problems are most evident in the Meinongian theory, but confront contemporary theories to no less an extent. We can relieve ourselves of the puzzling aspects of mental representations, or propositional attitudes, by taking these mental representations to be relations to guises (with H. N. Castañeda), or to some form of internal representation (with Jerry Fodor [1978]), or to other linguistic objects (with Stephen Stitch[10]). This only puts the problem at one remove beyond its initial place and thereby makes it less prominent. We still lack, and need, an account of how these immediate objects represent, and how we finally come to be related to the world.

IV. *Intentionality: The Object as Intrinsic*

We are obliged, then, to adopt the second of the traditional options and admit that Intentional relations are really only "relationlike."

Unfortunately, if we look to Brentano with the hope of some further explanation either of this "relationlike" characteristic or of how this characteristic can serve to differentiate the mental from the physical—beyond the mere assertion that the terminus of an Intentional relation need not exist—we look in vain. While Brentano does give examples of Intentional relations and attempts to produce a taxonomy of the different species of mental phenomena in terms of the kind of Intentional relations involved, in the *Psychology* he prudently foregoes the attempt to explain just what it is that is peculiar about Intentional relations and how this peculiarity is to be understood.

Some light on the problem can be gained from one of Brentano's scholastic precursors. St. Thomas Aquinas says in *Summa Theologica* that acts are to be "diversified according to the various natures of the objects" (I, q. 77, a. 3, 2). Just as an act of heating differs from an act of cooling in that the 'objects' differ, so my thinking of Pegasus differs from my thinking of War Admiral in that these two 'objects' differ. This much—a relation to, or direction upon, an object—is held by Aquinas (as later by Kant and more recently by Donald Davidson) to be common to acts of all sorts. It thus will not serve to differentiate the mental and the physical.

We may distinguish between two species of acts by appealing to a difference in their relation to their 'objects'.[11] Actions of one sort, Aquinas says, "pass out to external matter," while others "remain in the agent" (I, q. 18, a. 3, ad 1). We can take this to mean, as a first approximation, that acts of the first sort effect some change in the object of the act, whereas the latter sort of act need not. Thus, Anthony Kenny says "the scholastics placed the intensionality [sic!] of psychological actions precisely in the fact that they did not change their objects." He continues: "where a nonpsychological action brings about a change, the change is in the object and not, save *per accidens*, in the subject; where a psychological action brings about a change, the change is in the subject and not, save *per accidens*, in the object" (1963, p. 196). This is the parallel to Brentano's claim that the object of a mental act need not exist and, at least when this object is a physical phenomenon, may enjoy only Intentional existence: just as a mental act or mental phenomenon can occur without inducing any change in the object of the act, so could that act occur even if the object of the act did not exist.

The natural query, however, is this: "Is it not the case that, e.g., willing that something should happen often does 'pass out to external matter'? If I will to raise my arm, I raise it. Should not willing, then, be included in the former category of acts?" Aquinas, of course, explicitly places willing in the category of acts which "remain in the agent," and his motives for doing so seem reasonably clear. Those actions which remain in the agent are acts which, even if they do not, could occur without any change in the object of the act. I could will to raise my arm and not raise it, just as it can rise without my so willing. Thus, it might be said, in the case of cutting but not of willing, the object of the act *must* change or the act would not have occurred (cf. I, q. 23, a. 3, ad 1; and I, q. 34, a. 3, ad 2).

It takes only a little reflection to see that this interpretation, if viewed as an approach to distinguishing the mental from the physical, is inadequate. We will return to the Thomistic distinction. For simplicity, let us first backtrack to consider what has been thought to be Brentano's distinction; namely, that all and only mental phenomena are such that the object of that act need not exist. Since it should be allowed that in some cases the object of the mental act does exist, the important point must be that the object of the act *might not have existed even if it does in fact exist and its non–existence would not have compromised the existence of the act*. If we use "S's ϕ–ing of O" or, alternatively, "the ϕ–ing of O by S" to represent in a schematic way an act which is 'directed upon' an object O (whether the act be mental or physical), then what some have thought to be the criterion Brentano deploys to distinguish mental phenomena from physical phenomena can be schematically presented as follows:

(P1) S's ϕ–ing of O is a physical phenomenon if and only if it is necessary that if S's ϕ–ing of O occurs, then O exists;

and

(M1) S's ϕ–ing of O is a mental phenomenon if and only if it is possible that S's ϕ–ing of O occur and O not exist.

We might note that while all mental phenomena will be 'directed upon' an object and, consequently, will be covered by this pair, not all physical phenomena are thus directed upon an object and, perhaps, not even all physical acts have this characteristic. Thus, we could add: "If any phenomenon is not 'directed upon' an object, then it is a physical phenomenon." (M1) and (P1) constitute a mutually exclusive and exhaustive classification of all acts which are directed upon objects.

It was only said that some have thought Brentano's distinction to be of this sort. This is in fact not what Brentano intended. Brentano held that all judgments of inner perception are evident (i.e., infallible), and any contingent evident judgments would satisfy not (M1) but (P1): if there is even one such case of an evident judgment (e.g., my judging that I am in severe pain) then that judgment satisfies (P1); consequently, such acts would be counted as physical phenomena. The presence of such an obvious inconsistency should lead anyone to doubt that what Brentano advocated was a distinction of this sort.

It could nonetheless be asked if this is not just the sort of distinction which is needed. In order to see that it is not, let us turn to a second, somewhat more elusive point. Consider a particular mental act, say, my thinking of War Admiral. What would we be able to say about that act using the resources of (M1)? In full:

(1) My thinking of War Admiral is directed upon an object and it is logically possible that my thinking of War Admiral occur and War Admiral not exist;

that is,

(1') My thinking of War Admiral is directed upon an object and it is logically possible that I think of War Admiral and War Admiral not exist.

We are to conclude from this:

(2) My thinking of War Admiral is directed upon an object and it is a mental phenomenon.

While there is no doubt as to the truth of (1), (1'), or (2), the *inference* from (1) to (2) is invalid. In (1), the only thing said about the particular mental act which is my thinking of War Admiral is that it is directed upon an object. The second conjunct of (1), that is,

(1*) It is logically possible that my thinking of War Admiral occur and War Admiral not exist,

says nothing, save *per accidens*, about *my now thinking of War Admiral* except that an act similar to it might occur and War Admiral not exist.[12]

We will do well to use a slightly different case. The following statement is true:

(3) It is logically possible that the 39th President of the United States is not from the state of Georgia.

(That is, it might have been the case that the 39th President was not from Georgia. This is not to be confused with the [epistemic] assertion, made any time prior to the proper election, "It might not *be* the case that the 49th President will be from Georgia." We do know that the 39th is from Georgia; we do not (yet) know whether the 49th will be from Georgia.) Statement (3) says nothing particularly about Jimmy Carter: it would still be true if being from Georgia were an essential property of Jimmy Carter (though of course it is not); for Carter might not ever have been President. In an even clearer case, the expression "the 39th President of the United States" is not naturally taken to refer to Jimmy Carter as used in:

(4) It is logically possible that Jimmy Carter is not identical with the 39th President of the United States.

If it did, this would be taken to assert the logical possibility that Jimmy Carter not be Jimmy Carter, and of course that is not possible. Just as with (4) under the construal which renders it true, when we turn our attention to (3), the expression "the 39th President of the United States" as used there does not refer to Jimmy Carter and, consequently, the statement as a whole says nothing about the man who in fact occupied the White House for the last half of the 1970s. It may betaken to have its indirect reference, or, in the style of possible–world semantics, to have in its extension classes of objects in possible worlds. The point, in any case, is that it lacks its normal, or direct, reference. Therefore, it would be an error to *infer from* (3) that Jimmy Carter might not have been from Georgia. Yet this is the parallel to the inference from (1) to (2). Both are invalid.

The temptation to think that "the 39th President of the United States" does refer to Carter in (3) is almost an overwhelming one. This temptation can be accounted for once we recognize that the *de re* counterpart of (3), namely,

(5) There is exactly one man who is the 39th President of the United States and it is possible that he not be from Georgia,

that is,

(5′) The 39th President of the United States is not necessarily (essentially) from Georgia

is also true. There will be a possible world in which the individual satisfying the conditions of (3) is Jimmy Carter. The important point to appreciate, however, is that there will be other possible worlds (e.g., one in which Ford won the election and was succeeded by his Vice President) in which the individual satisfying (3) is not Carter.[13]

Scope distinctions in modal contexts cut both ways: in general when a singular term is used within the scope of a modal operator, that singular term does not have its standard reference; the exception to this is when the singular term in question is what Kaplan has termed a "standard name" or what Kripke has called a "rigid designator."

As a result, unless "my thinking of War Admiral" is a rigid designator (and it is not), the statement

(1*) It is logically possible that my now thinking of War Admiral occur and War Admiral not exist

says nothing, save *per accidens*, about that very mental act which is my (now) thinking of War Admiral. Yet in saying that my thinking of War Admiral is an Intentional act, we *do* want to be saying something about that very act which makes that act different from acts which are (merely) physical.

Let us, then, follow the lead provided by the above discussion and reformulate (P1) and (M1) in such a way as to circumvent this sort of problem. The only approach which presents itself as a reformulation proceeds thus:

(P2) S's ϕ–ing of O is a physical phenomenon if and only if the event which is S's ϕ–ing of O is such that it is necessary that if that event occurs then O exists;

and

(M2) S's ϕ–ing of O is a mental phenomenon if and only if the event which is S's ϕ–ing of O is such that it is possible for that event to occur and for O not to exist.

Notice that, by way of contrast with the first distinction, there is here no commitment to counting evident judgments as physical phenomena; and, in addition, since the occurrence of "S's ϕ–ing of O" is *de re* rather than *de dicto*, the individual referred to is S's ϕ–ing of O. Returning to our previous example, even in the consequent of

(6) Given an event which is my now thinking of War Admiral, that event could have occurred even if War Admiral had not existed,

we are asserting something concerning my now thinking of War Admiral; namely, that that very act could have occurred even if War Admiral had not existed.[14]

Despite the initial promise of the second distinction, it also will not do: while it avoids the problems which confront (P1) and (M1), it is subject to difficulties of a quite different sort. Let us consider a patently physical act—say, Harold's shooting of Man o' War. We can say:

(7) Given an event that is Harold's shooting of Man o' War, that event could have occurred even if Man o' War had not existed,

and this is true, though, of course, the act wouldn't then be a shooting of Man o' War. Harold might have done exactly what he did do—raising his arm and moving his hand just as he did—and that act might even have had some of the consequences it did—for example, the firing of the gun—and yet Harold's act might not have resulted in Man o' War's being shot.[15] That very act of Harold's might have resulted in, say, the death of Seabiscuit. If this is so, then Man o' War might also not have existed without prejudice to the occurrence of Harold's action. It may be pointed out that the particular description used is irrelevant since the occurrence of "Harold's shooting of Man o' War" is *de re*: the description we hit upon is irrelevant to the truth of (7). If physical acts have objects, the relation to those objects will be causal—thus, Harold's act causes the death of Man o'War—and surely the effects of at least some physical acts might have been different from what they in fact are. Hence, if the (P2)/(M2) distinction is adopted, we would class as mental phenomena much that is physical.

If we attempt to express Aquinas' distinction between acts which "pass out to external matter" and acts which "remain in the agent" by a similar appeal to the status of the objects involved, parallel sorts of difficulties ensue. In lieu of (P1) and (M1) we would have:

(P3) S's ϕ–ing of O is a physical act if and only if it is necessary that if S's ϕ–ing of O occurs, then S's ϕ–ing of O causes some change in O;

and

(M3) S's ϕ–ing of O is a mental act if and only if it is possible that S's ϕ–ing of O occurs and S's ϕ–ing of O does not cause any change in O.

While in this form there is no problem with infallible or evident judgments being counted as physical, we are still clearly faced with problems of scope. Corresponding to (P2) and (M2), we have:

(P4) S's ϕ–ing of O is a physical act if and only if the event which is S's ϕ–ing of O is such that it is necessary that if that event occurs then it causes some change in O;

and

(M4) S's ɸ–ing of O is a mental act if and only if the event which is S's ɸ–ing of O is such that it is possible that that event occur and not cause any change in O.

While mental acts generally will satisfy (M4) rather than (P4), there will as well be physical acts satisfying (M4) and not (P4): we are again confronted with the contingency of causal relations.

We conclude: *it is a mistake to interpret the thesis of Intentionality in such a way that it hinges on the existential status of the objects of the acts in question; what is crucial to the thesis of Intentionality is the way the acts are related to the objects rather than some peculiarity concerning the objects themselves.* Furthermore, we would be justified in claiming that neither Brentano nor Aquinas intended his views to be taken in any of the ways proposed above if only we can find another way of understanding what they do in fact say.

An alternative rendering is available. Aquinas said, regarding the difference between the two categories of acts:

> Action which is transient, passing to some extrinsic thing, is really mediate between the agent and the subject receiving the action. The action which remains in the agent is not really a medium between the agent and its object, but only according to the manner of signification (I, q. 54, a. 2, ad 3).

Again echoing Brentano, acts which are transient *are* relations, but nontransient acts are only "relation–like." In Aquinas' hands, the claim that Intentional relations are only relation–like becomes the much richer idea that Intentional acts are those acts that are *mediate according the manner of signification.*

Aquinas' position, like that of Aristotle, is that what makes, say, a thought of an *A* a thought *of an A* is that the thought is itself an occurrence of the form of A in the subject. For a person to be thinking of an *A* is not for that person to stand in any relation at all to an *A*, but for a certain *sort* of act to occur in the person, this act being an informing of the intellect in a determinate way. (Aquinas is evidently committed to alternative forms of *exemplification.* Informing the intellect is one form of exemplification. As it stands, it is a primitive.) In Aquinas' words: "although in operations which pass to an external effect, the object of the operation, which is taken as the term, exists outside the operator, nevertheless, in operations that remain in the operator, the object signified as the term of the operation resides in the operator; and according as it is in the operator is the operation actual" (I, q. 14, a. 2, 2). In our terms, physical acts take extrinsic objects and mental acts take intrinsic objects. In the case of nontransient acts, the object "resides in the operator" and only insofar as it does, does the act occur. But this does not mean that the object has a peculiar mode of existence in or for the mind, save in the sense that the intellect is in act; that is, it is informed by the sensible or intelligible species. (Intelligible species are those traits able to be grasped by the intellect [e.g., extension] and sensible species those traits able to be grasped only through or by the senses. [e.g., redness].) This informing of the intellect, as Aquinas understands it, is the occurrence of a thought. Just as the intellect cannot be 'informed' without being 'informed' in some determinate way, so we cannot have a thought without thinking of something.[16] In non-Thomistic terms we can say: (1) to specify the object of thought is to specify the *type* to which a particular thought, as *token*, belongs; (2) the specification of the type involves a specification of the intrinsic, rather than the extrinsic, properties of the act; (3) just as any token is a token of a type, every thought, as a token, has an object; and (4) indeterminancy in the object is allowed insofar as the type in question is more abstract.

Wresting this account from its ties to passivity which lead the Thomist to view the mind as receptive to 'forms' inhering in external things, we may bring it into line with a Kantian slant that is more amenable to contemporary cognitive psychology. A judgment would then be taken to involve the exercise of concepts or conceptual capacities. The concept determines the type of object to which the thought is directed and the exercise of the concept is a thought. To specify the concept is not to give the object, but to fix the type of thought; in this sense, it provides an intrinsic characterization of the thought. Of course, every thought will have an object, since every thought is an exercise of a concept. Indeterminacy in the object is allowed because the concept may be more or less abstract.

Whatever problems may face this view—especially its need for systematic elaboration—there are at least two clear advantages. First, it does not require that we posit non-existent Beings to serve as the mediate or immediate 'objects' of thought and judgment: the type-specification is not a relational one. Consequently, it can be allowed that, e.g., in thinking of War Admiral I am thinking of an existing horse. Aquinas says:

. . . what is understood is in the intellect not in itself, but according to its likeness; for *the stone is not in the soul but its likeness is* . . . . Yet it is the stone which is understood, not the likeness of the stone, except by a reflection of the intellect upon itself. [I, q. 76, a. 2, ad 4]

Second, this account attempts to make it clear exactly what the relation is that obtains between act and object in virtue of which an act is deemed an Intentional act, and in what sense the "immanent object" is essential to the act. Every Intentional act is an act of a determinate sort, and the determinate in question is specified by specifying the object of that act. Hence if the object of the act were to differ, we would have a different act, though, perhaps, an act of the same general kind. For example, while my thinking of Pegasus would not be the same act if I were thinking of something other than Pegasus, it could yet be true that the acts are both acts of thinking (rather than, say, entertaining or desiring something). In short, it is essential to my thinking of X that it be *of* X; for it is essential to my thinking of X that it be an exercise of the concept of X.

This does not mean, e.g., that it is necessary that if I am thinking of a book then that thinking is of a book, although, of course, this is true. The same could be said here of physical acts: it is necessary that if I hit a book then that hitting is of a book. The point to be made, rather, is that it is an essential property of that very act which is my thinking of a book that it is of that book rather than, e.g., of a cat or of a different book. It is not essential to my hitting the book that it is of that book rather than, e.g., of the cat or, for that matter, of nothing at all. Perhaps this is best expressed again as a matter of scope. While it is true that it is necessary that if I am thinking of a book then that thinking is of a book, and similarly it is necessary that if I hit a book then that hitting is a hitting of a book, this is not central to our concerns. The point to be grasped is that it is true that my thinking of a book is necessarily, or essentially, a thinking of that book; but it is false that my hitting of a book is necessarily, or essentially, a hitting of that (or any) book. Thus, mental acts are different from physical acts just in that it is essential to mental acts that they have as objects just the objects they do have as objects; but it is not essential to physical acts that they have the objects (effects) they do in fact have as objects (effects). This difference is reflected in the fact that in specifying the type of thought by specifying the object, the type constitutes a specification of the intrinsic rather than extrinsic properties of the act; on the other hand, the specification of the type to which a physical act belongs, as token, involves a specification of an extrinsic (causal) rather than an intrinsic property of the act.

Such essentialist claims are always suspect—if not as to their *sense*, then at least as to their *truth*. The best I can do in the way of rendering it plausible to make such claims in the case of events in general is by analogy to Arthur Danto's notion of a "basic action." Enormous confusion has surrounded this notion, and I favor Davidson's view that Danto (and, e.g., Alvin Goldman) mislocates the distinction: the proper distinction is between basic and non-basic descriptions. I would suggest that basic-action descriptions isolate the essential properties of (individual) actions. For example, suppose Smith kills Jones by stabbing him, and stabs him with a thrust of his left arm. Jones might have thrust his arm but missed Jones. He could have done *that*, but with different consequences—consequences which, perhaps, thwarted his intent. But if Smith does not thrust his arm, then his action has not occurred. The basic description describes the action bereft of all that is due to fortune: it describes the action in its most austere appearance. Deploying the Thomistic line demands that, in dealing with the mental, we do more than strip acts of their consequences, though we should do at least that much. Such acts do not (essentially) "pass out to external matter." Describing a mental act in terms of content is to describe it in its most basic, psychological, terms. This is why, as Chisholm says, we *must* so describe it. If we do *not* so describe it, we rely on the inessential.

This also enables us to comprehend why some Intentionalists have been inclined to emphasize that my thinking of O could have occurred even if O had not existed, and to suppose that this differentiates mental from physical acts. Suppose we have a physical event C which causes an event E and E is a change in O. We could say, then, that C has O as an object. Suppose further that we have a mental event T (e.g., my thinking of O) which has O as its object. Now while either C or T might have occurred even if O had not existed, since it is essential to T that it have O as an object, even if O did not exist, T would still be an act of the same sort (*viz.*, a thinking of O), and have O as an object. On the other hand, if O had not existed, then C could not have caused a change in O, and, hence, would not have had O as an object. In the case of mental acts, the relation to the object is such that the object might not have existed and, still, the act could have occurred and had that selfsame object as an object. The same cannot be said of physical acts.

V. *The Explanation of Representation*

If Intentionality is acceptable, or reasonable, as a distinguishing characteristic of the mental—as distinguishing the mental from the merely physical—there are at least four conditions it must satisfy. So we get:

(D1) Intentionality is a property of the mental act in virtue of which that act represents objects.

(D2) This representation must be such that the act can represent what does not exist.

(D3) The representation must be such that the act represents external objects directly.

(D4) If an act represents an object of a certain type, it necessarily represents an object of that type.

We have already seen that the relation to an object does not admit of conceptual intermediaries, though it does allow for causal intermediaries. But the causal relations to external objects cannot serve to explicate the form of representation involved.

What has been said thus far openly presupposes the notion of 'having something as an object', and cannot be construed as an explanation of this conception. It would surely be desirable to produce some explanation of this elusive notion; and the goal, in the light of the foregoing arguments, would be to provide some account consistent with the results obtained of what it is about mental acts in virtue of which they are 'directed to objects'.

As was previously remarked, there is an element in current cognitive theories that purports to be capable of accomplishing this very task. In reviewing Fodor's *The Language of Thought*, D. C. Dennett clearly isolates the element:

> . . . neo–cognitivists generally . . . [want] to be able to assign content to events or other features of systems, to treat them as information–bearers or messages. What makes it the case ultimately that something in this sense represents something within a system is that it has a function within the system . . . . Content is a function of function. [1977, p. 278]

There are, of course, a number of ways this sort of proposal might be elaborated. One of these was introduced above in discussing Armstrong's account of the Intentional objects of perception. Armstrong's proposals constitute an abridged functionalist account: the Intentional object is ascribed on the basis of the functional relations the mental state bears to stimuli and behavioral outputs. Though present (since perception, as Armstrong has it, involves the acquisition of belief), and relevant to some degree, any relations to other internal states do not play a dominant role in individuating those states or determining the Intentional objects of those states.

We are now in a position to see why such a theory will not prove acceptable by the standards developed above. The contingency of causal *relations* (not causal *explanations*) is precisely what shows that Intentionality is not to be explained causally: since Intentional attributions isolate essential properties of the mental acts, we cannot properly identify Intentional and causal relations for the simple reason that causal relations are not essential. (It may be noted that this is quite independent of whether causal laws are necessary or contingent; for even if causal laws were necessary, it would hardly follow that causal relations [or causal sequences] are as well.) Hence, even a modified causal theory such as Armstrong's is not powerful enough to deal with Intentionality.

What role *do* causal conditions have for, say, perception? A full answer would demand an account of epistemic justification. Such an account I certainly do not have, though I suspect Alvin Goldman's (1978, 1980) gestures toward a causal theory are the best going. I would wager that causal conditions become conditions for *knowledge*: my belief (or judgment) that the F is G constitutes knowledge only if caused or generated in the correct way—whatever that might be—by the F. If a is the F, then for that belief to be knowledge, it must be generated by a. If (in some other possible world) b were the F, my belief would still be a belief that the F is G even if generated by b; and that belief would even have been true were it generated by b rather than a. The Intentional 'relation' is essential to the act, and makes the act a representation of the F—or puts the subject in a 'relation to' the F—whether a or b is the F, whether or not the representation is veridical, and whether or not, indeed, there is an F at all. No causal relation could serve this role.

The disparity between causal and Intentional relations is a problem also faced by more extreme causal theorists such as McGinn. Only a conflation of Intentional and causal relations could lead McGinn to conclude that we cannot think of the non–existent. Only his good sense allows him to see and acknowledge the result; only our good sense will allow us to avoid it.

Of course, not all functionalist theories employ such a simple condition. Thus, in the comment quoted above, Dennett claims only that representational properties are to be explained in terms of "the function *within* the system" of the representational state. We may take the restriction literally: for any difference in representational properties, there is to be a difference in the functional relations of the state to other states internal to the system (cf. Fodor 1980). In Putnam's (1960) model, what a representation is a representation of is to be explained in terms of the 'machine table'. Perhaps, then, we can do without external relations, and settle for internal functional relations.

The level of difficulty which this presents us with can best be understood by turning to what has come to be known as the "analogy theory." As Peter Geach develops it in *Mental Acts*,[17] we begin by introducing an undefined non–extensional operator " §( )" which forms a relational expression when a relational expression is written inside the parentheses; the new relational expression is of the same polyadicity as the original. Geach then proceeds to introduce a technical use of the term "Idea," which he explains simply as the exercise of a concept in judgment. The resulting theory of judgment then becomes this: if we suppose S judges that ARB, then this judgment consists simply in S's Idea of A (a mental tokening of something tantamount to "A") standing in the relation §(R) to S's Idea of B (a mental tokening of something tantamount to "B"). Now, Geach's views do give us some explanation of the Aristotelian/Thomistic conception of "informing the intellect": A's informing the intellect is just the exercise of the concept of A in judgment. Furthermore, it yields a simple and elegant extension from the 'objectual' acts which we have taken as paradigmatic of Intentional acts to more full–blooded 'propositional' acts. But it will not and cannot by itself give an explanation of the Intentionality of acts save in Intentional terms: an Idea is itself a mental occurrence which has the characteristic of Intentionality. Ideas are representations. The conception of a representation, or Intentionality, remains primitive.

The other major variant of the analogy theory—that developed by Wilfrid Sellars (1963, ch. 5)—at first seems more promising. Sellars claims, in effect, that the "aboutness" or Intentionality of thoughts can be explained in terms of semantic categories: for a thought to be a thought of A is for the thought to be an inner tokening which has the same role as (or a role formally analogous) to the use of "A" in overt speech. The role of a tokening of "A"[18] is defined in terms of (*i*) the stimulus conditions in which a tokening of "A" is justified (or "language entry roles"); (*ii*) the conditions under which certain sorts of behaviors—linguistic or otherwise—are justified given a prior tokening of "A" (or "language exit roles"); and, finally, (*iii*) the conditions under which a tokening of "B" is justified given a prior tokening of "A" and *vice versa* (or "language transition [inference] rules"; see Sellars, 1963, ch. III, esp. p. 328). The playing of *these* roles is finally a causal matter: we are concerned only with the functional role in an inner tokening system (which includes 'Metalinguistic' tokenings). Now, *if* this gives us an explanation of the Intentionality of thoughts, it does so at the expense of previous results: if the act–object relation is explained in causal/functional terms, we cannot retain the notion that Intentionality, or the relation of representation between act and object, is an essential property of the acts. The fact is that it makes no difference that this functional role is given in an inner system so long as what a given state represents is a matter only of the functional relations of that state to other states. Causal relations within systems are no less contingent than causal relations of internal states to external occurrences. We cannot, therefore, hope to retain a substantive and significant conception of Intentionality if we explain representational properties in terms of functional properties.

The reason Sellars' explanation of Intentionality or any functionalist explanation of Intentionality runs aground when the attempt is made to incorporate it into the framework developed above is that Sellars' theory is designed to embody the claim that it is a *mistake* to suppose that "conceptual thinking presents itself to us in a qualitative guise" (Sellars, 1963, p. 32). If the 'having of something as an object' is to be an essential property of mental acts, it must surely be something more than the merely relational and wholly extrinsic thing Sellars takes it to be. Any functionalist analysis will in fact make content dependent on causal relations. Since any such relations are contingent, they are inadequate for the task. It makes no difference whether the functional relations are internal or external and, hence, makes no difference whether we embrace the weaker functionalism of Fodor or the stronger variant advocated by Wimsatt (see Part I above). If we adopt a functionalist analysis, Intentionality is no longer the mark of the mental.

The only direction available, thus, is one which treats Intentionality, or the 'relation' of representation, as in some way intrinsic to the act, as does, for example, Geach's. In any case, Intentionality will be explained neither in causal nor in functional terms; and if psychological explanations are functional explanations, Intentionality will not be explained by even the best-developed psychological theories. It remains an open question whether psychology is so restricted to functionalist analyses; but it is clear that the best we have got in the way of psychological theories is wedded closely to functionalist ways of thinking. We must evidently take the notion of a representation as a psychological primitive But it need not remain unexplained. If we adopt a materialist metaphysics, we could, perhaps, look to the neurophysiologist to explain the representational aspects of states of the central nervous system—perhaps as what Sperry has called "configurational properties." This sort of "solution', however, not only presupposes certain fairly specific and highly speculative developments in neurophysiology; it also presupposes the truth of reductive materialism; and *this*, of course, is no small matter.

NOTES

1. Some psychologists who would call themselves "cognitive psychologists" are actually not on this standard; this includes, in particular, many working on motivation that would, by the standards suggested, count as neo–behaviorists—behaviorists that have taken to heart Skinner's contention that the skin is not that important as a boundary.

2. Wimsatt uses "purpose" with reference to "final ends" (cf. Wimsatt 1972, pp. 22–23); that is, to ends which are not themselves means to further ends. The function of a system (e.g., pumping blood is the function of the heart) is then always relative to the *function* of a more encompassing system (e.g., replenishing oxygen supply is a function of the circulatory system) and, in the last analysis, to the *purpose* of the most encompassing system (e.g., increasing the fitness of an evolutionary unit, or serving God, or leading a good life).

3. This last element does not belong. As Wimsatt deploys it, "what *we* decide are the functions of an item or behavior, or whether or not it even *has* any functions, depends upon our causal theories" (1972, p. 29). This concerns, though, *how we tell* (or how we decide) what the function of something is and not *what* its function is. This latter issue depends, as far as I can see, only on the first four parameters.

4. In many cases—apparently, where the function is neither the (ultimate) purpose which a system has nor immediately subservient to that purpose—dependency on environment and on the function of super–systems are indistinguishable (or nearly so). For example, a flashlight (during night) aids vision and (in daylight) serves as a signal. Presumably, this is inevitable for cases where the super–system is itself responsive to environmental changes, or is opportunistic.

5. Wimsatt apparently thinks that for systems that are *teleological* the relevant (ultimate) *purpose* is the "fitness of an evolutionary unit" (1972, p. 6). This severs a potential infinite regress of functions since natural selection can fix a "purpose" independently of the "function" of higher systems. D. C. Dennett (1969) adopts a similar view in explaining *content* as a function of function.

6. The moral I draw is allied to those drawn by John Searle (1980) and Charles Taylor. (I was fortunate enough to hear these discussed at a conference on Artificial Intelligence at the Institute for the Advanced Study of the Behavioral Sciences in the spring of 1980.) For reasons I shall not develop here, I am much more skeptical about their arguments than about their conclusions.

7. Despite the voluminous literature and a clear consensus that there is no viable set of linguistic criteria, R. M. Chisholm's classic (1959) criterion in terms of failure of substitution, existential generalization, and propositional detachment survive counter–example.

8. This approach is adopted by St. Thomas, in *Summa Theologica* (Regus translation):

> A power as such is directed to an act. Therefore we must derive the nature of a power from the act to which it is directed; and consequently the nature of a power is diversified according as the nature of the act is diversifed. [I, q. 77, a. 3, 2]

Since, on Aquinas' view, the nature of an act is "diversified" according to its object, a power will ultimately be "diversified" in accordance with the objects of the acts to which the power is directed.

Plato remarks, similarly, in the *Republic* (477D): "In the case of a capacity I can look only to this: to what it is directed and what it achieves, and in this way I called it a capacity; if it is related to the same object and achieves the same result I call it the same [capacity], while that which is related to a different object and achieves a different result I call a different capacity" (Grube 1974: see also 478A–478B).

9. McGinn's error is akin to that embodied in traditional forms of the "logical connection argument." See Richardson, 1975; and the papers cited there.

10. Stitch's concern is with the ascription of belief and the conditions under which a content–ascription is justified. (See Stitch forthcoming.) Unlike Fodor and Castañeda, he does not attempt to provide an account of representation.

11. The use of "action" in such contexts tends to be misleading to most contemporaries, who are inclined to say actions are things we *do*, and which, at least, can sensibly be described as voluntary and involuntary. No such restriction is present in Aquinas. I tend to use "act" whenever there is danger of confusion; however, in conformance with tradition, I shall, in discussing Aquinas, frequently use "act" and "action" interchangeably to signify the broader notion of an act.

12. For those who find a formal regimentation more perspicuous, we can use a Davidsonian regimentation (which takes events as ephemeral particulars). The resulting transcription is this:

(1) E! (7e) T(e) & By (e,a). &. ◊ [E! (7f)(Tf) & By (f,a) . &. ~(∃ x) x = WA]
(1') E! (7e) T(e) & By (e, a). &. ◊ [(∃ f)(y)Ty ≡ f = y & By (y, a) . &. ~ (∃ x)x = WA]

The second clause in each case is *de dicto*. ("Tx" = x is a thinking of "War Admiral"), "By (e,a)" = "e is by a", "WA" = "War Admiral".)

13. Again as formalized counterparts we have, with the obvious abbreviations and indicating scope in Russell's manner:
 (3) ◊ [(7x)(P$_{39}$x)] ~ G(7x)(P$_{39}$x)
 (4) ◊ [(7x)(P$_{39}$x)] Jimmy Carter ≠ (7x)(P$_{39}$x)
 (5) [(7x)(P$_{39}$x)] ◊ ~ G (7x)(P$_{39}$x)
Eliminating in accordance with Russell we have
 (3) ◊ ~ (∃ x)(y) P$_{39}$y ≡ x=y . &. Gy
 (4) ◊ (∃ x)(y) P$_{39}$y ≡ x=y . &. y ≠ Jimmy Carter
(I assume "Jimmy Carter" occurs *de re*.)
 (5) (∃ x P$_{39}$y ≡ x=y . &. ◊ ~ Gy.

14. This is rendered, for comparison with (1) as
 (6) E! (7e)(T[e] & By (e,a) & ◊ [(∃ f) f=e & ~ (∃ x)x=WA)]
that is, as:
 (6') (∃e)(g) T g ≡ g=e & By (g,a) & ◊ [(∃ f)f=e & ~ (∃ x)x=WA].

15. The point is a logical triviality since it asserts only something of the form (∃ x)φx & ~□φx.
Causal relations, that is, are not essential relations. I henceforth leave the formalities to the reader.

16. The relation of determinate to determinable is little used in current literature. E.g., redness is a determinate relative to the determinable coloredness. Any instance of a determinate is an instance of the determinable(s) of which it is a determinate. Any instance of a determinable is an instance of some determinate form of that determinable.

17. What follows is a drastically simplified version of Geach's views. For more detail see Geach (1957), §§ 14, 15 and 22.

18. Strictly, Sellars would have us speak of a tokening being an ·A·; the dot–quoted expression is then taken as a common noun applying to anything which has the same role as "A" does in our language. (See Sellars 1968, ch. III, esp. §§ 44–53.) Also, the use of dot–quotes is normative: ·A· is defined in terms of *permissable* actions, inferences, and judgments. E.g., from an ·a is red· one may infer an ·a is colored. The

role is, Sellars would say, conveyed: it constitutes the descriptive condition needing to be approximated for functional classification. The technicalities do not affect our argument.

REFERENCES

Bealer, George. "An Inconsistency in Functionalism," *Synthese* 38, 1978.
Bergmann, Gustav. *Realism*. Madison: University of Wisconsin Press, 1967.
Brentano, Franz. *Psychology From an Empirical Standpoint*. Edited by Oskar Kraus, 1874. English edition edited by Linda L. McAlister; translated by Antos C. Rancurello, D. B. Terrell, and Linda L. McAlister. New York: Humanities Press, 1973.
Brentano, Franz. *The Origin of Our Knowledge of Right and Wrong*. Edited by Oskar Kraus, 1889. English edition edited by R. M. Chisholm; translated by R. M. Chisholm and Elizabeth H. Schneewind. London: Routledge and Kegan Paul, 1966.
Brentano, Franz. "Being in the Sense of the True." In Brentano, *The True and the Evident*. Edited by Oskar Kraus, 1905. English edition edited by R. M. Chisholm; translated by R. M. Chisholm, Ilse Politzer, and Kurt R. Fischer. New York: Humanities Press, 1930.
Chisholm, R. M. "Sentences About Believing," *Proceedings of the Aristotelian Society* 56, 1956.
Chisholm, R. M. *Perceiving*. Ithaca: Cornell University Press, 1959.
Chisholm, R. M. "Intentionality." In Paul Edwards, ed., *The Encyclopedia of Philosophy*. New York: MacMillan, 1967.
Chisholm, R. M. "Brentano on Descriptive Psychology and the Intentional." In Harold Morick, ed., *Introduction to the Philosophy of Mind*. Glenview: Scott, Foresman and Co., 1970.
Davidson, Donald. "Mental Events." In Lawrence Foster and G. W. Swanson, eds., *Experience and Theory*. Boston: University of Massachusetts Press, 1970.
Dennett, D. C. *Content and Consciousness*. London: Routledge and Kegan Paul, 1967.
Dennett, D. C. "Intentional Systems." (As in Dennett, *Brainstorms*, Bradford Books, 1978, Ch. 1). Reprinted from the *Journal of Philosophy*, 1971.
Dennett, D. C. "A Cure For the Common Code?", *Mind* 86, 1977.
Dennett, D. C.; and Haugeland, J. C.: forthcoming "Intentionality." In R. L. Gregory, ed., *Oxford Companion to the Mind*. Oxford: Oxford University Press.
Fodor, Jerry A. "Explanations in Psychology." In Max Black, ed., *Philosophy in America*. Ithaca: Cornell University Press, 1965.
Fodor, Jerry A. *Psychological Explanation*. New York: Random House, 1968.
Fodor, Jerry A. *The Language of Thought*. New York: Thomas Crowell, 1975.
Fodor, Jerry A. "Propositional Attitudes," *The Monist* 4, 1978.
Fodor, Jerry A. "Methodological Solipsism Considered as a Research Strategy in Cognitive Psychology." *The Behavioral and Brain Sciences* 3, 1980.
Fodor, Jerry A.; and Bever, T. "The Psychological Reality of Linguistic Segments." *Journal of Verbal Learning and Verbal Behavior* IV, 1965.
Garrett, M.; Bever, T.; and Fodor, J. "The Active Use of Grammar in Speech Perception." *Perception and Psychophysics* 1, 1966.
Geach, P.T. *Mental Acts*. London: Routledge and Kegan Paul, 1957.
Goldman, Alvin. "Epistemics: The Regulative Theory of Cognition." *The Journal of Philosophy*, LXXV, no. 10, 1978.
Goldman, Alvin. "The Internalist Conception of Justification." In Peter A. French, Theodore E. Uehling, and Howard K. Wettstein, eds. *Midwest Studies in Philosophy*, V. Minneapolis: University of Minnesota Press, 1980.
Gosling: J. C. "Emotion and Object." *The Philosophical Review* LXXIV, 1965.
Grube, G. M. A. *Plato's Republic*. Indianapolis: Hackett Publishing, 1974.

Hempel, C. G. *Aspects of Scientific Explanation*. New York: Random House, 1965.
Husserl, Edmund. *Cartesian Meditations*. Translated by Dorion Cairns. The Hague: Martinus Nijhoff, 1970. Originally delivered in Paris, 1929.
Kamitz, Reinhard. "Acts and Relations in Brentano: A Reply to Professor Grossman." *Analysis* 22.4, 1962.
Kenny, A. *Action, Emotion, and Will*. London: Routledge and Kegan Paul, 1963.
Kim, Jaegwon. "Perception and Reference Without Causality." *The Journal of Philosophy* LXXIV, 1977.
McGinn, Colin. "Charity, Interpretation, and Belief." *The Journal of Philosophy* LXXIV, 1977.
Mullane, Harvey. "Neurotic Action." *Dialogue* XVI, 1977.
Neisser, Ulric. *Cognitive Psychology*. New York: Appleton–Century–Crofts, 1967.
Neisser, Ulric. *Cognition and Reality*. San Francisco: W. H. Freeman, 1976.
Neisser, Ulric. "Perceiving, Anticipating, and Imagining." In C. Wade Savage, ed., *Minnesota Studies in the Philosophy of Science*, Vol. IX. Minneapolis: University of Minnesota Press, 1978.
Pegus, Anton C. *Basic Writings of St. Thomas Aquinas*. New York: Random House, 1945.
Putnam, Hilary. "Minds and Machines." As in Putnam, *Mind, Language, and Reality*. London: Cambridge University Press, 1975. Reprinted from Sidney Hook, ed., *Dimensions of Mind* (New York: Collier–MacMillan, 1960).
Putnam, Hilary. 1967 "The Nature of Mental States." As in Putnam, *Mind, Language, and Reality*. London: Cambridge University Press, 1975. Reprinted from Capitan and Merrill, Eds., *Art, Mind, and Religion* (Pittsburgh; University of Pittsburgh Press, 1967).
Reitman, Walter; Nado, Robert; and Wilcox, Bruce. "Machine Perception: What Makes It So Hard for Computers to See?" In C. Wade Savage, ed., *Minnesota Studies in the Philosophy of Science*, Vol. IX. Minneapolis: University of Minnesota Press, 1978.
Richardson, Robert C. "A Revised 'Logical Connection' Argument." *Philosophical Studies* 27, 1975.
Richardson, Robert C. "Functionalism and Reductionism." *Philosophy of Science* 46, 1979.
Richardson, Robert C. "Intentional Realism or Intentional Instrumentalism." *Cognition and Brain Theory* III, 1980.
Richardson, Robert C. "Disappearance and the Identity Theory." *The Canadian Journal of Philosophy*, forthcoming.
Searle, John. "What is an Intentional State?", *Mind* 88, 1979.
Searle, John. "Minds, Brains, and Programs." *The Behavioral and Brain Sciences* 3, 1980.
Sellars, Wilfrid. *Science, Perception and Reality*. London: Routledge and Kegan Paul, 1963.
Sellars, Wilfrid; and Chisholm, R. M. "Intentionality and the Mental." In Herbert Feigl, Michael Scriven, and Grover Maxwell, eds., *Minnesota Studies in the Philosophy of Science*, Vol. II. Minneapolis: University of Minnesota Press, 1958.
Srzednicki, Jan. *Franz Brentano's Analysis of Truth*. The Hague: Martinus Nijhoff, 1965.
Stich, Stephen P. "Beliefs and Subdoxastic States." *Philosophy of Science* 45, 1978.
Stich, Stephen P. "On the Ascription of Content." In A. Woodfield, ed., *Thought and Object*. Oxford: Oxford University Press, forthcoming.
Wimsatt, William C. "Teleology and the Logical Structure of Function Statements." *Studies in History and Philosophy of Science* 3, 1972.

Analog and Analog

JOHN HAUGELAND
University of Pittsburgh

When I began this paper (years ago) my concern was with the grand sounding claim that any analog computer can be digitally simulated to any desired degree of precision. Along the way, however, I found the definitions of 'digital' and 'analog' to be tricky and interesting in their own right and they now comprise the bulk of the paper. But the original issue returns at the end, and its resolution involves distinguishing stricter and broader senses of 'analog'—hence my curious title.

Digital

Definitions of terms like 'analog' and 'digital' are guided first by paradigm cases, and intuitions about what these cases have in common. In the final analysis, however, a definition should be more than merely adequate to the intuitive data: it should show that the cases cited are instances of a theoretically interesting general kind, and it should emphasize the fundamental basis of that theoretical interest. An ideal definition makes manifest why the term in question is worth defining. This ideal is easier to approach for 'digital' than for 'analog'.

Standard examples of digital devices include Arabic numerals, abacuses, alphabets, electrical switches, musical notation, poker chips, and (digital) computers.[1] What is important and distinctive about these cases? Several common features stand out:

(1) Flawless copying (and preservation) are quite feasible. For instance, no copy of a Rembrandt painting is aesthetically equal to the original, and the paintings themselves are slowly deteriorating; by contrast, there are millions of perfect copies of (most of) Shakespeare's sonnets, and the sonnets themselves are not deteriorating. The difference is that a sonnet is determined by a sequence of letters, and letters are easy to reproduce—because modest smudges and squiggles don't matter. The same goes for musical scores, stacks of poker chips, and so on.

(2) Interesting cases tend to be complex: composites formed in standard ways from a kit of standard components—like

molecules from atoms. Complexity can also be diachronic, in which case the standard components are actually standard steps or "moves" constituting a sequential pattern. For example, digits of only ten standard kinds suffice, with a sign and decimal point, for writing any Arabic numeral; moreover, a sequence of steps of a few standard sorts will suffice for any multiplication in this notation. Likewise, the most elaborate switching networks can be built with the simplest relays; and all classical symphonies are scored with the same handful of basic symbols.

(3) There can be exactly equivalent structures in different media. Thus, the sonnets could be printed in italics, chiselled in stone, stamped in Braille, or transmitted in Morse code—and nothing would be lost. The same computer program can run on vacuum tube or solid-state hardware; poker chips can be plastic disks, dried beans, or matchsticks.

I call these features *copyability, complexity*, and *medium independence*, respectively. The question is: What do they all presuppose? Out of what deep root do they all grow?

All digital devices involve some form of *writing* and then *reading* various *tokens* of various *types*. That is, there are procedures for producing tokens, given the types that they are supposed to be, and procedures for telling or determining the types of given tokens. For example, penciling on white paper a particular inscription of the letter 'A' is a way of writing a token of that alphabetic type, which can then be read by eye. But also, rotating a switch to a specified click-stop is a way of "writing" a token of that setting (type); and that token can then be "read" by determining which of the connected circuits will now conduct electricity. These examples emphasize that the tokens don't have to be symbols (i.e., represent or mean anything), and that writing and reading are here generalized to cover whatever it takes to produce and reidentify the relevant tokens.

But what makes the device digital is something more specific about the write and read procedures: they must be "positive" and "reliable." A *positive procedure* is one which can succeed absolutely and without qualification—that is, not merely to a high degree, with astonishing precision, or almost entirely, but perfectly, one hundred percent! Clearly, whether something is a positive procedure depends on what counts as success. Parking the car in the garage (in the normal manner) is a positive procedure, if getting it all the way in is all it takes to succeed; but if complete success requires getting it exactly centered between the walls, then no parking procedure will be positive. There is no positive procedure for cutting a six–foot board, but there are plenty for cutting boards six feet, plus or minus an inch. The *'can* succeed' means feasibly, and that will depend on the technology and resources available. But we needn't worry about the limits of feasibility, because we care only about procedures that are also *reliable*—ones which, under suitable conditions, can be counted on to succeed virtually every time. With the available technology and resources, reliable procedures are in a sense "easy," or at least established and routine.

What counts as success for write and read procedures? Evidently that the write procedure actually produce a token of the type required, and that the read procedure correctly identify the type of the token supplied. But these are not independent, since usually the procedures themselves jointly function as a working definition of the types—what counts as an inscription of the letter 'A' is determined by what writers produce as one and readers recognize as one. The important constraint is that these be the same, or rather that whatever the writers produce be correctly recognized by the readers, and nothing else be recognized by the readers at all. In other words, the requirement really applies to the composite procedures for the write–read "round–trip," plus a specification of suitable environmental conditions; and there is a kind of trade–off in how stringent the various parts need to be. Thus if the write procedures are very precise, and the suitable conditions provide a very clean "noise–free" environment, then the read procedures can get away with being fairly lax; and so on.

So we can define a *digital device* as:

(i) A set of types;
(ii) A set of feasible procedures for writing and reading tokens of those types; and
(iii) A specification of suitable operating conditions; such that
(iv) Under those conditions, the procedures for the write-read cycle are positive and reliable.

Note that the success condition, that written tokens be correctly read as written (and nothing else be read), indirectly requires that no token in fact be a token of more than one type; that is, the types are disjoint, and hence the relation are 'of–the–same–type' is an equivalence relation.

Now that the definition has been given, I want to make five follow–up points, which should explain it a little further and reveal more of the motivations behind it. First, the copyability feature of digital devices is easily accounted for; indeed, the definition itself is not far from being a fuller statement of what that feature is. The original can be read positively and reliably; and these readings (type identifications) can simply function directly as the specifications to the write procedures for a new round of tokens. The new tokens can also be read positively and reliably, and hence they are exactly the same as (type identical to) the originals—that is, a *perfect* copy.

Second, (non–degenerate) digitalness is not ubiquitous. One often hears that systems are digital only "relative to descriptions"; and too often it is inferred that any object can be construed as any digital system, relative to *some* outlandish (but true) description. Being digital, however, is no more "Relative" than being a fugue or an amplifier. True, the types and procedures (like the musical theme, or the input and output ports) must be specified before the definition applies; but whether there is such a specification according to which the definition is in fact satisfied is not at all relative or trivial or automatic.

Third, our definition differs from Nelson Goodman's (by which it was largely inspired) in two significant ways. He says, in effect, that a disjoint set of types is digital just in case:

> For any candidate token, and for *at least one of* any pair of types (in the set), it is theoretically possible to determine that the candidate is *not* a token of that type.[2]

In other words, for any candidate token, all but at most one of the types can be positively ruled out (by some theoretically possible method)—no token is ever equivocal between two distinct types.

This is most easily explained with examples. Suppose that tokens are penciled line–segments less than a foot long; let Lx be the length of segment x (in inches), and let n be an integer. Then we can specify four different systems in terms of the following four conditions on two line segments being tokens of the same type:

(a) $Lx = Ly$ (any difference in length is a difference in type);
(b) $n < Lx, Ly < n+1$ (segments are of the same type if their lengths fall between the same consecutive inch–marks);
(c) $n + \frac{1}{2} < Lx, Ly < n+1$ (as above, except that segments between any inch–mark and the next higher half–inch–mark are "ill–formed"—that is, not tokens of any type); and
(d) $Lx = Ly = n$ (as for (a), except that only segments of exactly integral lengths are acceptable—all others are ill–formed).

The first system is not digital because, no matter what (theoretically possible) method of measurement you used, there would be indefinitely many types to which any given token might belong, for all you could tell. Similarly for (b), except that the problem cases are only the segments very close to integral length, and there are only two types you can't rule out. (c) is a paradigm case of a digital device (assuming you can measure to within a quarter inch).

The last case is the trouble-maker; it is digital by Goodman's criterion, but it doesn't have the copyability feature—and that for two reasons. First, even if there were any tokens, they couldn't be recognized as such, as opposed to ill-formed "scribbles" (noise); and second, duplicate tokens could never be produced at all (except by miraculous accident). Both defects are remedied by requiring that the write–read cycle be positive (and reliable).

The second difference between our definition and Goodman's was hinted at in the remark about a stringency trade-off. It is common digital electronics practice to build pulse detectors that flip "high" on signals over about two and a half volts, flopping "low" on smaller signals. Since this is a sharp threshhold, and not even very consistent from unit to unit or moment to moment, these detectors cannot define a digital token-scheme, by Goodman's lights. What saves the day for engineers is that pulse *generators* produce only signals very close to zero and five volts respectively, and the whole apparatus can be well shielded against "static," so the detectors never actually get confused. Again focusing on the write–read cycle in the ambient conditions is the definitional remedy. But I think a broader point can be made. In making his determinations "theoretically possible," without mentioning the determination procedures, let alone the production procedures or the working conditions, Goodman betrays a mathematician's distaste for the nitty-gritty of *practical* devices. But *digital*, like *accurate, economical*, or *heavy-duty*, is a mundane engineering notion, root and branch. It only makes sense as a practical means to cope with the vagaries and vicissitudes, the noise and drift, of earthly existence. The definition should reflect this character.

My fourth follow-up point is a reply to David Lewis, and some comments on complexity. Lewis offers a counter-example to Goodman, which, if it worked at all, would work against us as well.[3] Imagine representing numerical values with a variable resistance—a setting of 137 ohms represents 137, and so on. And suppose the variable resistor is constructed with a rotary switch and a lot of discrete one-ohm resistors, such that the 137th switch position connects 137 resistors in series, for a 137-ohm total. This, says Lewis, is analog representation (hence, not digital), just as if the variable resistor were a sliding contact moving smoothly along a wire with uniform resistance per unit length. But, since the switch has click-stops, he claims it would be (mis-) classified as digital by Goodman.

I think the case is underdescribed. Assuming the representations are to be read with an ohmmeter, then we need to know how accurate the meter is, how precise and stable the one-ohm resistors are, and the total number of switch positions. If there are a thousand positions, and the meter and resistors are good only to one percent, then (whether or not it's analog) the device surely isn't digital; but it satisfies neither Goodman's conditions nor ours. On the other hand, if there are only two hundred positions, and the meter and resistors are good to one part in a thousand, then it satisfies both Goodman's conditions and ours. But I think it's clearly digital—just as digital as a stack of silver dollars, even when the croupier "counts" them by height.

Lewis, however, has another point in mind. He notes (p. 326) "the many combinations of values" that are possible when several parameters are used together. For instance, a bank of six switches, each with only ten positions, could represent any integer up to a million, even with crude equipment. This is a special case of the complexity feature; Lewis calls it 'multidigitality', and proposes it as an additional condition on digital representation. To evaluate this proposal, we should see how the multidigitality (complexity) condition relates to the other conditions, whether Goodman's or ours.

Consider two similar systems for representing wagers in a poker game. Each uses different colored tokens for different denominations, red and blue being worth ten and a hundred times more than white, respectively. But in one system the tokens are standard colored disks ("chips"), while in the other they are measured volumes of colored sand—one tablespoon corresponding to one chip, say. Though both systems are multidigital in Lewis' sense, the complexity is silly and useless in the sand case. For suppose players can measure volumes to within two percent, and imagine trying to bet 325 units. It's crazy! The expected error on the blue sand (the grains that stick to the spoon) is more valuable than the entire five spoonfuls of white sand. A stack of three blue chips, on the other hand, can be counted positively and reliably (no residual error at all); so the white chips are not overwhelmed, and remain perfectly significant.

Lewis, of course, would not deem poker sand digital, any more than we would: his multidigitality is a *further* condition, not an alternative. What the example shows is rather that multidigitality only "pays off" in systems that are already digital in our sense—the sense in which poker chips would still be digital even if they were all one color. I take the lesson to be that our definition has already captured the basic phenomenon, and that complex systems are just an important special case, which the underlying digitalness makes feasible. We see the complexity feature not as essential to being digital, but (if anything) vice versa.

In considering complex types, it is essential that not only their constituent atomic types be digital, but also their modes of combination. For instance, the power of Arabic numerals depends not only on the reliable positive procedures for (writing and reading) individual digit tokens, but just as much on the reliable positive procedures for concatenating them left to right, and so on. In effect, syntactical structures must themselves be digital types. And this point applies equally to diachronic complexity: each individual "step" (transformation, move) must be a token of a type in a set whose members' tokens can be produced and recognized reliably and positively. The types in this set might be identified with executable instructions, as in computer "languages," or with permissive rules, as in logical deductions or formal games like chess and checkers. It should be clear that complexity in digital devices goes far beyond arithmetic (or poker chip) multidigitality, and that the crucial dependence on reliable positive procedures rises dramatically with intricacy and elaborateness.

My fifth follow-up point is really just a footnote to the preceding. In digital devices, the main thing is eliminating confusion over the type of any token; and a primary motivation ("payoff") for this is the ability to keep great complexity manageable and reliable. In such cases it is generally the complexity itself—that is, the structure, form or pattern of the complex tokens and processes—which really matters; the digital atomic tokens are merely means to this larger end. Hence any digital atomic tokens which will admit of a corresponding variety of digital combinations and transformations would do as well. Since all the relevant structure is digital, the substitute will be not just similar in form but exactly isomorphic. (The sonnets can be spelled perfectly in Morse code, and so on.) The very features which make reproduction reliable and positive also make formal transubstantiation reliable and positive. Digital devices are precisely those in which complex form is reliably and positively abstractable from matter—hence the medium–independence feature.

Analog

'Analog' can be understood in broader and narrower senses; but even in the latter, analog devices comprise a motley crew. I am not at all confident that a satisfactory general definition is possible—which amounts, I suppose, to doubting whether they are a well-defined natural kind. Standard examples of analog devices include slide rules, scale models, rheostats, photographs, linear amplifiers, string models of railroad networks, loudspeakers, and electronic analog computers. As before, we can try to extract some salient common features from these varied cases; three stand out:

(1) Variations are smooth or continuous, without "gaps." There are no click–stops, or forbidden intermediate positions on a slide rule or a rheostat; photographs have (in principle) a continuous gray–scale, varying with two continuous position dimensions. This is everybody's aboriginal intuitive idea of analog systems; unlike switches, abacusses, or alphabetic inscriptions, every (relevant) setting or shape is allowed—nothing is ill–formed.

(2) Within the relevant variations, every difference makes a difference. The smallest rotation of a rheostat counts as changing the setting (a little); slight bending alters loudspeaker output; a photographic copy isn't perfect if it's slightly fuzzier, slightly darker, or slightly more contrasty. This is the complement of the previous feature: not only are all variations allowed, but they all matter (again unlike switches, abacusses and letters).

(3) Nevertheless, only certain "dimensions" of variation are relevant. Slide rules can be made indifferently of metal or bamboo, and their color and weight don't (strictly) matter. The thickness of the paper and even the chemistry of the emulsion are irrelevant to a photograph as such—assuming they don't affect the distribution of gray levels.

We call these the *smoothness, sensitivity,* and *dimensionality* features, respectively.

Though it need not (for any theoretical reason) be the best approach, we can pattern the definition of 'analog' after that of 'digital'. That is, we start with a set of types, and consider the procedures for producing and reidentifying tokens of those types.

For analog devices, the procedures for the write–read cycle are *approximation procedures*—that is, ones which can "come close" to perfect success. More specifically, there is some notion of margin of error (degree of deviation from perfect success) such that:

(i) the smaller this margin is set, the harder it is to stay within it;
(ii) available procedures can (reliably) stay within a pretty small margin;
(iii) there is no limit to how small a margin better (future, more expensive) procedures may be able to stay within;[4] but
(iv) the margin can never be zero—perfect procedures are impossible.

So all ordinary (and extraordinary) procedures for parking the car right in the center of the garage, cutting six–foot boards, measuring out three tablespoons of blue sand, and copying photographs, are approximation procedures. But there are no approximation procedures for raising the dead, writing poetry, winning at roulette, or counting small piles of poker chips. Approximation procedures are, in a clear sense, the antithesis of positive procedures; the two are exclusive, but of course not exhaustive. There is no need to write out the definition of *analog device*—it is the same as for digital, except with 'approximation' substituted for 'positive' (and a margin of error included in the specified conditions).

The follow–up points again tell the story. First, Goodman says a scheme is analog if dense—that is, if between any two types there is a third (see pp. 160 and 136). The main difficulty is that "between" is not well–defined for all cases that seem clearly analog. What, for instance, is "between" a photograph of Carter and one of Reagan? Yet it is easy to set resolution and linearity limits such that copying photographs is an approximation procedure. Similar observations apply to scale models.

Second, Lewis suggests that analog representation is representation in terms of magnitudes that are primitive or almost primitive in some good reconstruction of the language of physics (see pp. 324–25). He mentions only representations of numbers, and it isn't clear how he would generalize his criterion to non–numerical representations (e.g., portraits), or to non–representational analog devices. But more to the point, I see no reason why we could not have analog representation of numbers by, say, hue (as in multiple pH paper or various flame–tests) or even by bacterial growth rate (e.g., in a model of a resource–limited chain reaction); yet surely neither of these is "almost primitive" (whatever exactly that means).[5]

Third, it seems to me that there is an important digital–like character to all the standard analog devices—specifically in the dimensionality feature. Speaking freely for a moment, the essential point about (atomic) digital types is that there tend to be relatively few of them, and they are all clearly distinct and separated. Though the types of analog schemes are themselves not like this (they "blend smoothly" into one another), the *dimensions* along which they vary *are* relatively few and clearly distinct. Thus for photographs there are exactly three orthogonal dimensions: horizontal, vertical, and gray scale. A string model of a rail network has exactly one string piece for each rail link and exactly one knot for each junction (none of which blend together). But the best example is a regular analog computer with its electronic adders, integrators, multipliers, inverters, and the like, each as discrete and determinate in type as any mathematical symbol, and their circuit connections as well–defined as the formation of any equation. Indeed, though the state and adjustment types of an analog computer are analog, the *set–up* types are perfectly digital—the component identifications and interconnections are positive and reliable.

This "second–order" digitalness of analog devices is important in two ways. First, it is, at least roughly, a necessary condition for the write and read procedures to be approximation procedures in complex systems. In one–dimensional devices, like rheostats and slide rules, it suffices to say that between any distinct types there lies a third. But in multidimensional cases, where betweenness is not in general well defined, it is crucial to have the determinate set of independent dimensions such that a copy which is close on each dimension is ipso facto close overall—hence the intelligible importance of resolution in photocopying, of precision components in analog computers, and so on. This is what gives *approximation* its sense.

It is also what gives digital simulation its grip, and for essentially the same reason. Everybody knows that photographs can be "digitized" by dividing the area into equally spaced dots, and the gray scale into equally spaced shades; the fineness of the spacings determines the quality of the digitizing, just as the smallness of the error margins determines the closeness of the approximation. Likewise when a digital computer program simulates an analog computer, the values of all the fixed components and the initial values of all the variables are stored in specified registers, and then successive variable values are computed incrementally, using interaction equations determined by the circuit structure; and the accuracy of the simulation is controlled (primarily) by the number of bits in all those registers, and the fineness of the time increment. If the system were not second–order digital, such simulation could not get off the ground: there would be no particular set of parameters to digitize in specified registers (let alone equations for computing their interactions).

My fourth follow–up point, then, is the original sixty–four dollar question: Is *every* analog device second–order digital? Or: Is it really true that any analog device can in principle be digitally simulated to any desired degree of precision? To the extent that the suggestions in the previous three paragraphs hold up, the answers would appear to be: 'Yes'. Being second–order digital is equally the general condition for the possibility of write–read approximation procedures and of digital simulation techniques; and approximation procedures for the write–read cycle are criterial for analog devices.

They are criterial, that is, for analog devices in the *narrow* sense—that's all we've discussed so far. But the universal digital simulability claim is often made in a more sweeping tone, as if it applied to *everything*. Are there systems, perhaps "analog" in some broader sense, which are not second–order digital, and not necessarily digitally simulable (to whatever desired precision, etc.)? There are, of course, all manner of mongrel devices, analog in some respects or parts, digital in others; but these present no greater obstacle to simulation than purebred devices. If we think of digital devices as clean and resilient, and analog ones as messy and touchy (with the mongrels in between?), then the question becomes: Can there be systems even messier and touchier than pure analog—second-order messy, as it were?

I don't see why not. Consider the metabolic system of the rat, tokens of which are often used as "analogs" of our own metabolism, to predict the effects of fancy drugs, and so on. Now, some general metabolic relationships are known, and quite a few more specific local mechanisms are understood. But these by no means provide a complete description, in terms of which responses to strange chemicals can confidently be predicted. The millions of delicate hormonal balances, catalytic reactions, surface effects, and immunological responses, all interdependent in a bio–chemical frenzy of staggering proportions, can be catastrophically disrupted by the bizarrest of "side–effects." A minute occurrence on one side of a tiny membrane can have vastly different consequences from the same occurrence on the other side—and every rat contains billions of membranes.

There is essentially no way to gain detailed, quantitative control over such a mess—no hope of delineating a set of "state–variables" which fully characterize it at a time. Risky as long–term predictions are, I think it safe to announce that there will *never* be a digital simulation of human physiology reliable enough to supplant (or even challenge) biological and clinical testing of new drugs. And the reason, basically, is that metabolic systems are not second–order digital. Accordingly, there is also no specifying the "grain"or "resolution" of an approximation procedure for bio–chemical duplication of, say, healthy rats; there are no relevant dimensions along which such specification could make sense.

Fifth and final follow–up point: "But isn't physics second–order digital? What about digital simulation at the level of atoms and molecules (quarks and leptons, . . . whatever)?" I have two different replies to this question. In the first place, the idea is absolutely preposterous. Remember how impressed you were when you first heard that a computer with the capacity of the human brain would be the size of Texas and twenty stories high?[6] Well, the fastest and largest state–of–the–art computers today can be overwhelmed by the problem of digitally simulating a single large organic molecule (atom for atom); and there are more molecules in a human body than there would be pocket calculators, if the entire Earth were packed solid with them.[7] But simulating the molecules individually wouldn't scratch the surface: when their interactions are included, the required computations go up combinatorially!

But second, and more to the point, switching to the atomic level changes the subject. When the claim is made that photographs, linear amplifiers, and analog computers can be digitally simulated to any desired precision, that has nothing to do with fundamental physics; it would not matter if physicists had found swirling vortices in the plenum, or infinitely many infinitesimal monads. The digital simulability of analog devices is a claim about *macro*scopic phenomena. The range and variety of circumstances in which it holds is truly astonishing and important (the scientific revolution depended on it); but it is also important that such simulability (i.e., second–order digitalness) is *not* universal. This second important fact is completely missed and covered up by the careless shift in topic to micro–physics.

Conclusion

'Digital' and 'analog' (in the narrow or strict sense) are both best understood in terms of the kind of practical procedures employed for the writing and reading of tokens of allowed types—these being positive and approximation procedures, respectively. And, sticking to the narrow sense, it is plausibly the case that any analog device can (in principle) be digitally simulated to any desired precision. But there are other cases which, though they do not fit this strict mold, still seem to be "analog" in some broader sense; and for at least some of these, the digital simulability claim is wildly implausible.

NOTES

1. I resort to the non-committal "devices" because anything more specific seems wrong; thus (as the above list shows) not everything digital is a representation, a process, a computer, a machine, or what have you. Indeed, even the implication of plan or contrivance in 'device' should be ignored, for some biological systems might be digital.

2. See Goodman (1968) pp. 136–37 and 161. This is a paraphrase into our terminology of his definition of "syntactic finite differentiation," which is his essential condition for being a digital *scheme*. He also has a more stringent notion of a digital *system*, which has similar conditions imposed on its semantics (see pp. 152 and 161). I ignore the latter because in my view digital devices are not necessarily representational or symbolic.

3. See Lewis (1971), p. 322. He actually offers two counter-examples, but they are based on the same idea; so we consider only the simpler one.

4. Quantum-mechanical limits are almost always distracting and boring; so let's ignore them.

5. Ned Block and Jerry Fodor make essentially this point in an old (ca. 1971), manuscript which, so far as I know, has never been published.

6. I've forgotten where I heard this, or how long ago; and Lord knows how the calculation was made. But I've never forgotten the image.

7. 180 lb = 5×10^{28} hydrogen masses; the volume of the Earth is 7×10^{25} cubic inches.

REFERENCES

Goodman, Nelson. *Languages of Art* (Indianapolis: Bobbs–Merrill, 1968).

Lewis, David. "Analog and Digital," *Nous*, V (1971) 321–27.

Notes on Contributors

WILLIAM G. LYCAN is Professor of Philosophy at The Ohio State University and works primarily in the philosophy of mind and the philosophy of language. His articles have appeared in *The Journal of Philosophy, The Philosophical Review, Synthese, Mind* and elsewhere.

STEPHEN P. STICH is a member of the Philosophy Department and the Committee on the History and Philosophy of Science at the University of Maryland. His publications include *Innate Ideas, The Recombinant DNA Debate* and numerous articles on the philosophy of psychology, the philosophy of language and applied ethics.

DANIEL C. DENNETT is Professor of Philosophy and chairman of the Department of Philosophy at Tufts University and has held visiting appointments at Harvard and the University of Pittsburgh. He has been awarded Woodrow Wilson, Guggenheim, Fulbright, and NEH fellowships. His publications include *Content and Consciousness, The Philosophical Lexicon, Brainstorms* and numerous articles.

ROBERT C. CUMMINS is chairman of the Department of Philosophy, University of Wisconsin-Milwaukee. He taught at the Johns Hopkins University and has held visiting appointments at Michigan, Arizona and Northwestern. His articles have appeared in *The Journal of Philosophy, The Philosophical Review, Philosophy of Science* and elsewhere. He is currently completing the manuscript of a book, *Theory and Explanation in Psychology*.

SYDNEY SHOEMAKER is Susan Linn Sage Professor of Philosophy at Cornell University. He is the author of *Self-Knowledge and Self-Identity* and of numerous articles on the philosophy of mind and metaphysics. In 1972 he delivered the John Locke Lectures at Oxford University.

PAUL M. CHURCHLAND is Professor of Philosophy at the University of Manitoba, Canada. He received his B.A. from the University of British Columbia, and his Ph.D. from the University of Pittsburgh in 1969. His work has centered on the philosophy of science, epistemology, and the philosophy of mind, culminating in his recent *Scientific Realism and the Plasticity of Mind*. Hobbies include astronomy, stereography and flute.

PATRICIA S. CHURCHLAND is Associate Professor of Philosophy at the University of Manitoba, Canada. She received her B.A. from the University of British Columbia, her M.A. from the University of Pittsburgh and her B.Phil. from Oxford in 1969. Her work has centered on the philosophy of mind, the philosophy of language, and on the interdisciplinary study of philosophy, psychology and neurophysiology. Hobbies include ethology, 19th–century novels and piano.

KATHLEEN V. WILKES received B.A. and M.A. degrees from Oxford and M.A. and Ph.D. degrees from Princeton. She is Fellow and Tutor in Philosophy, St. Hilda's College, Oxford, and author of *Physicalism* and of articles in the philosophy of mind, the philosophy of psychology, ancient philosophy and ethics.

COLIN MCGINN is Lecturer in Philosophy at University College, London. He has been visiting professor at the University of California, Los Angeles. His interests are in the philosophy of language, the philosophy of mind and metaphysics.

ROBERT C. RICHARDSON received his Ph.D. in Philosophy at the University of Chicago, and is currently Assistant Professor of Philosophy at the University of Cincinnati. His primary interest is in topics in the philosophy of psychology and philosophy of biology.

JOHN HAUGELAND received his degree in Philosophy from Berkeley in 1976, and is currently Professor of Philosophy at the University of Pittsburgh. He spent the year 1979–80 at the Center for Advanced Study in the Behavioral Sciences, as a member of a study group on artificial intelligence and philosophy. He has written in the philosophy of mind and about Heidegger, and is the editor of *Mind Design*, a collection of essays in the philosophy of cognitive science.

INDEX

Adding machines: 85ff.
Agnosia: 158
Alexia: 158
Analog computers: 79, 220–21; see also analogue computers
Analogue computers: 79, 220–21; see also analog computers
Analytical functionalism: 104–105, 110, 117–18
Anderson, A. R.: 77
Anomalous monism (*AM*): 12–13, 15; see also monism
Aquinas, T.: 194–95, 199–201
Aristotle: 200
Armstrong, D. M.: 189–90, 204
Bealer, G.: 175
Behaviorism: 46
Belief: 17–19, 48, 58, 89
Belief–desire–perception cycle: 20, 22, 24, 28, 32
Belnap, N.: 77
Bever, T.: 175
Black boxes: 16
Block, N.: 93, 104, 112, 127, 130, 131, 133, 136
Bottom–up strategy: 143, 158
Brentano, F.: 28, 181, 184, 188, 190–92, 194–95
Buffer memory: 16
C-Fibers: 97, 100–101, 103
Causal: power, 105; potentialities, 105; laws, 106; theory of properties (*CTP*), 107–109, 116; *CTP* functionalism, 107, 109–110, 115–16; theory of representation, 185, 189–90
Chess–playing computer: 40
Chinese Turing machine: 113, 134–35, 162–63; see also Great Brain of China
Chisholm, R.: 28, 179, 190, 203
Church, A.: 43
Cognitive psychology: 46, 54, 150, 152, 154, 156, 161, 175, 179, 201
Computational equivalence: 134, 136
Computational theory: 174–75
Core realization: 97, 101
Danto, A.: 203
Davidson, D.: 10–24, 27, 29, 31–32, 179–80, 203
De dicto terms: 185
Dennett, D. C.: 24–25, 28, 31–32, 39–44, 46, 83, 85–86, 153, 165, 179–80, 204–205
Depth psychology: 112–13, 116
De re terms: 184–85, 199; attributions, 184; sentences, 199
Descartes, R.: 160
Design stance: 40, 54, 87, 90
Desire: 12
Digital computers: 213, 222
Discharged homunculi: 83, 90
Dispositional states: 182–83
Dualism: 85, 87, 124
Essence: 13, 15, 105, 111–12, 114

229

Factunorm principle: 81n.
Family resemblance: 14
Flow–chart: 16, 17, 30, 153, 155, 158
Fodor, J.: 31, 72, 127, 172, 175, 189, 192, 204, 207
Functional: essences, 14, 17, 19; types, 17; explanation, 31, 173; identity, 42, 128; states, 57–59; properties, 94, 96, 98, 101, 106; correlates, 106–107; counterparts, 109, 116; roles, 126; equivalence, 136; analysis, 174
Functionalism: 85, 87, 91, 97, 121
Garrett, M.: 175
Geach, P.: 206
Gödel's incompleteness theorem: 84
Goldman, A.: 205
Goodman, N.: 216–17, 221
Gosling, J. C.: 183
Great Brain of China: 113, 134–35, 162–63; *see also* Chinese Turing machine
Gricean communicators: 89
Gunderson, K.: 147
Hard line on intentional systems: 49–55, 73
Hardware: 157; malfunction, 30–32
Heteronomic generalization: 21
Holism: 182
Homonomic generalization: 21
Homunctional states: 18, 27
Homuncular: functionalism, 16–17, 20, 23–24, 32; model, 19; explanation, 83
Homunculi: 83, 90–91, 133, 136, 162
Husserl, E.: 181
Idealism: 85
Identity: 10, 111, 112; type, 10–12, 15, 23, 46, 122ff., 142; token, 12, 20, 128
Implicit beliefs, 18
Indeterminacy: 21, 26–27
Instrumentalism: 86, 88, 90, 91
Intentional: system, 39ff., 47, 49, 54, 83; stance, 40, 42–43, 52, 54, 63, 78, 84, 87; explanation, 51, 57
Intentionality: 21, 133, 177–81, 183, 191, 200, 206–207
Introspection: 84, 124, 131
Irrationality: 48–52, 57, 63, 65–66, 68, 75
Kant, I.: 179, 194, 201
Kaplan, D.: 198
Kenny, A.: 194
Kim, J.: 184
Kripke, S.: 104, 111, 114, 198
Lawlike statements: 12ff.
Lewis, D.: 31, 93, 99–104, 111, 217–21
Lewis–Ramsey technique: 93, 104
Lewis–type convention: 89
Machine simulation: 140
Machine table: 133, 136, 206
Madmen: 99
Marras, A.: 31
Martians: 99, 111
Materialism: 27, 44–45, 85, 98, 100, 143

McGinn, C.: 186, 205
Meinong, A.: 192
Mental: states, 13–14, 93, 95; events, 13, 179–80; properties, 106–107, 117; representations, 177–82, 186
Mentalese: 72
Methodological solipsism: 175–77
Mistakes: 64–66
Monism: 85; *see also* anomalous monism
Nado, R.: 176
Nagel, T.: 166
Natural kinds: 13–14, 20, 100, 111, 114, 123, 137
Neisser, U.: 173, 176, 188
Neo-functionalism: 83
Nominal essences: 105, 111
Non–rigid designators: 100–101, 104
Pain: 25, 96, 99–103, 121, 124–26, 165
Pegasus: 191ff.
Physical realization: 97–98, 174
Physical stance: 40, 54
Place, U. T.: 10
Possible worlds: 100, 197
Powers, L.: 74
Principle of the anomalism of the mental (*PAM*): 10, 13, 20, 22–25, 28
Privileged access: 123, 160
Pro–attitudes: 153
Propositional attitudes: 16ff., 25–26, 83, 86, 90, 130, 133, 152, 163, 184
Psychological: laws, 9, 14–17, 24, 31; explanations, 11, 24, 149; psycho–functional laws, 16, 19, 23, 27, 32; psycho–physical laws, 16, 19, 23, 27; psycho–functionalism, 104, 111, 117–18
Putnam, H.: 15, 29, 31, 98, 111, 114, 124, 173, 205
Qualia: 121, 123, 125, 128, 129, 132, 142
Quine, W. V. O.: 21, 26–27, 52, 57
Ramsey sentences: 31, 93, 96
Rationality: 21–22, 25, 50–51, 55, 57, 66, 73–74, 76
Realism: 129, 131, 179, 192
Reductionism: 85ff.
Reitman, W.: 176
Rigid designators: 104, 198
Ryle, G.: 149
Sanford, D.: 30
Searle, J.: 133, 137–41
Sellars, W.: 123, 181, 206–207
Sensation: 130, 133
SHURDLU: 92n.
Simon, H.: 75
Skinner, B. F.: 46, 175
Smart, J. J. C.: 10, 15
Soft line on intentional systems: 55–57, 73
Software: 182–83
SS–causal features: 107, 109
SS–functional states: 95, 104

Stich, S.: 64–66, 71–73, 89, 141, 143
Structural–functional theory: 147–49, 153
Sub–doxastic states: 74, 89–90, 178
Top–down strategy: 144, 155, 157–60
Translation: 85
Turing–computability: 44
Underdetermination: 26
Wilcox, B.: 176
Wimsatt, W.: 176, 207
Wittgenstein, L.: 149